I Would Find a Girl Walking

I Would Find a Girl Walking

KATHY KELLY and DIANA MONTANÉ

BERKLEY BOOKS, NEW YORK

THE BERKLEY PUBLISHING GROUP
Published by the Penguin Group
Penguin Group (USA) Inc.
375 Hudson Street, New York, New York 10014, USA
Penguin Group (Canada), 90 Eglinton Avenue East, Suite 700, Toronto, Ontario M4P 2Y3, Canada
(a division of Pearson Penguin Canada Inc.)
Penguin Book Ltd., 80 Strand, London WC2R 0RL, England
Penguin Group Ireland, 25 St. Stephen's Green, Dublin 2, Ireland (a division of Penguin Books Ltd.)
Penguin Group (Australia), 250 Camberwell Road, Camberwell, Victoria 3124, Australia
(a division of Pearson Australia Group Pty. Ltd.)
Penguin Books India Pvt. Ltd., 11 Community Centre, Panchsheel Park, New Delhi—110 017, India
Penguin Group (NZ), 67 Apollo Drive, Rosedale, Auckland 0632, New Zealand
(a division of Pearson New Zealand Ltd.)
Penguin Books (South Africa) (Pty.) Ltd., 24 Sturdee Avenue, Rosebank, Johannesburg 2196,
South Africa

Penguin Books Ltd., Registered Offices: 80 Strand, London WC2R 0RL, England

The publisher does not have any control over and does not assume any responsibility for author or third-
party websites or their content.

I WOULD FIND A GIRL WALKING

A Berkley Book / published by arrangement with the authors

PRINTING HISTORY
Berkley mass-market edition / April 2011

Copyright © 2011 by Kathy Kelly and Diana Montané.
Cover photo by Veer.
Cover design by Lesley Worrell.
Interior text design by Tiffany Estreicher.

ISBN: 978-0-425-23186-9

BERKLEY®
Berkley Books are published by The Berkley Publishing Group,
a division of Penguin Group (USA) Inc.,
375 Hudson Street, New York, New York 10014.
BERKLEY® is a registered trademark of Penguin Group (USA) Inc.
The "B" design is a trademark of Penguin Group (USA) Inc.

PRINTED IN THE UNITED STATES OF AMERICA

10 9 8 7 6 5 4 3 2 1

Most Berkley Books are available at special quantity discounts for bulk purchases for sales, promotions,
premiums, fund-raising, or educational use. Special books, or book excerpts, can also be created to fit
specific needs.

For details, write: Special Markets, The Berkley Publishing Group, 375 Hudson Street, New York, New
York 10014.

ACKNOWLEDGMENTS

For a newspaper reporter, good sources are the backbone of the job. Throughout my reporting career, I relied on a network of contacts I could depend on to tip me off to a good story or steer me away if I was on the wrong track.

Thankfully, thirty years after I first reported the heinous crimes of Gerald Stano, those sources are still here helping me out.

This book could not have been completed without the help of Paul Crow, who opened his mind and his briefcase to allow me every opportunity to make this as factual as possible.

Mel Stack, my attorney, was instrumental in making this book as complete as it could be. I am also indebted to Circuit Judge James Foxman, Circuit Judge C. McFerrin Smith, Chris Quarles, Dave Hudson, Don Slack, Francis Monaco, Ed Seltzer, Jim Tiller, Karen Duffy, and Ron Word.

I sought and got very good advice from a number of sources, including Lee Butcher, John Firestone, Amy Hill Hearth, Kathy Trocheck, Michael Connelly, and Margie Schlageter.

To family members who relived a very painful chapter of their lives—Ray Neal, Michael Basile, Ed Bickrest, Elizabeth Heard Dow, Gerry Friedman and her son, John Maher—you have my greatest admiration.

To my writing partner, Diana Montané, thank you for suggesting I chronicle the life of this aberrant soul. Your help was invaluable.

Thanks to our agent, Linda Langton, who had faith in us and our project from the very beginning. Our editor, Shannon Jamieson Vazquez, literally took us under her wing and saw the promise in our first efforts.

Friends and family supported me from day one. My nephew, Michael, was a sounding board and constant throughout the process. To all my friends who cheered me on, a warm thank-you from the heart.

—Kathy Kelly

A heartfelt "Thank you for everything" again and again to our agent, Linda Langton, who never wavered in her belief in this project and followed it through with grace and determination. And to our keen and gifted editor, Shannon Jamieson Vazquez, who managed to preserve the essence of the book while ensuring a final, precise, and polished copy.

And a very special thanks and recognition to Paul Crow, whose profiling skills put a stop to the monster that was Gerald Stano. Also, to "whoever fights monsters."

—Diana Montané

CONTENTS

INTRODUCTION   1

1. A Date for an Interview   9
2. Early Childhood: The Warning Signs   17
3. The One Who Got Away   27
4. The Pretty Star Swimmer   40
5. A Graduation Trip That Ends Tragically   46
6. "Last Dance"   55
7. Inside the Mind of the Lead Investigator   64
8. The Haunted House in New Smyrna Beach   73
9. "Tiny Dancer"   103
10. "They Told Me She Had Drowned!"   115
11. "Blackbird . . . Fly"   124
12. The Bond of Brothers   133
13. In Search of a Dream   139
14. Jane Doe—"Do It in the Dirt"   148
15. So Many Girls, So Little Time   157
16. Mary Carol Maher, the Final Murder Victim   163
17. Profile of a Serial Killer—"Here Comes That Old Red Again"   172
18. Life on Death Row, Waiting to Die   182

APPENDIX A: STANO'S LETTERS TO KATHY KELLY   193
APPENDIX B: STANO'S LETTERS TO INVESTIGATOR PAUL CROW   275
TIMELINE   291

INTRODUCTION

Kathy, as I said before, it's not easy to remember everything to a tee. I know you have copies of the confessions I wrote for Paul, and it makes me wonder why you want me to relive these homicides again? But for you, I will. Nobody else as far as I am concerned. You have my full cooperation, as you know.

—Gerald Stano to Kathy Kelly, October 21, 1985

The young woman was only too happy to catch a ride when she climbed into Gerald Stano's car. Glancing quickly at her surroundings, she found the vehicle almost obsessively neat, and the driver looked like someone right off the set of *Saturday Night Fever*—slick polyester pants and a patterned shirt, with a few buttons opened at the neck to expose his hairy chest.

When the radio began blasting out the beat of disco queen Donna Summer, she smiled. "Who listens to that stuff?" she asked. Suddenly, the face of the driver darkened, and his arm quickly left the steering wheel. Reaching beneath his seat, he grabbed a knife and began swinging it wildly, plunging the blade deeply into her chest again and again.

How dare she insult his taste in music? She would pay for that remark with her life.

From the beginning, Gerald Eugene Stano's own life seemed to be the stuff of dreary novels. When he was born, he lived in what a psychologist later called "subhuman conditions." Stano implicated himself in an estimated forty murders by the time he was twenty-eight years old. The man who lived in relative obscurity had become famous at last as one of the most prolific mass murderers in history.

The criminal mind has long been the subject of public fascination. What makes people like David Berkowitz, John Wayne Gacy, and Ted Bundy tick? More than a century later, people still are trying to find out what caused Jack the Ripper to attack British prostitutes, again and again.

Stano considered these young women as no more than prey. He would "find a girl walking," stalk her, take her, and ultimately destroy her, with complete disregard as to whether she was somebody's daughter or sister. She was just a girl walking, and that, in his mind, made her fair game. She could have been anyone.

Serial killers are the people next door, or, in my case, a fellow employee at the newspaper where I worked for many years. I don't recall ever seeing Gerald Stano at the newspaper, but it was our mutual place of employment that proved to be a touchstone at our first meeting behind the walls of the Florida State Prison.

Little did I know that the isolated murder cases I covered as the police reporter for the *Daytona Beach News-Journal* from the late 1960s until the late 1970s would ultimately be traced back to that man who grabbed newspapers fresh off the press, added advertising inserts, and bundled them together so they could be thrown on my driveway.

The young women who were strangled or stabbed and dumped like yesterday's garbage had all made a fatal mistake—falling for the low-key approach of the man who may have gained their trust with something as simple as a casual compliment.

I told their stories. I talked to their anguished families. Their photographs haunted me, pretty young women in the wrong place at the wrong time.

After Stano's arrest and death sentences for three of the slayings, I found myself drawn to this case and wanting to learn more about this man who fancied himself a lady-killer. Which he was—literally.

His attorney, Don Jacobson, was someone with whom I had worked before as a reporter. Telephoning him about my plans was easy; he quickly connected me with Stano in prison, acting as our liaison.

From that first meeting in prison, a relationship developed in which I did my best to draw Stano out. In a series of forty letters written over a ten-month period—from August 15, 1985, to June 10, 1986—Stano confessed his insecurities about women and his appearance and, yes, details of some of the slayings.

The spring break ritual in Daytona Beach hit home for me in 2009 at dinner one evening with a friend at a restaurant near the Boardwalk.

As we sat in the restaurant, the spring breakers descended upon us, like the bikers had the week before, more than the usual number, since they had been warned against going to Mexico on spring break because of the recent outbreaks of violence along its borders.

The kids, boys and girls, all good-looking and clean-cut college kids, were ordering large decanters of wine, followed by tequila shots with beer chasers, and then more wine decanters, followed by more tequila, more beer, and mixed drinks. They were growing louder and more rambunctious by the minute.

I looked at the faces of the girls, and I could visualize the faces of Gerald Stano's prey, his victims, reflected in their faces.

I wanted to say something, to warn them, to tell them that the streets were nowhere near as safe as they seemed, and that they were not as invincible as girls their age think they are. We used to think so at that age, too, my friends and I. But I didn't say anything. I knew they wouldn't listen.

At the large table next to ours, there was one girl, a pretty young woman with a tan and long, straight dark hair. She was the only one nursing a large glass of water, which she sipped slowly, through a straw.

Perhaps, I thought, it wouldn't be one of the young women drinking heavily but this girl who would wander away from the pack in disgust, and get picked up, snatched.

My friend and I finished our dinner and walked out into the nippy Central Florida March night. On the corner, we spotted an even chillier sight: a beautiful young woman, dressed somewhat provocatively, standing alone on a street corner. Not a streetwalker, though, but clearly a "good girl," another spring breaker.

"Are you all right, sweetie?" my friend asked her, to which she replied a bit defiantly, "Yeah!" I couldn't help it. This time I did speak up. "You shouldn't be standing here alone at night," I told her. Now she smiled condescendingly, as if I were a bothersome aunt to be barely tolerated, as she said, "Oh no, my ride is right over there," and she pointed to a dark street, perpendicular to the one we were on.

Although facing the electric chair, Gerald Stano had lost none of his illusions that women were attracted to him. He asked if I had a boyfriend, later telling the lead investigator on the case that our first meeting had "gone well," as if we had been on our first date.

As I probed for information that would illuminate his motivation to murder, I found myself eventually asking point-blank: Why did you do it? His answer:

As for the question, "What made me kill and kill again," I can't really answer that, except like this. I would be drinking, and lonely, and thinking about all the couples having fun together, and here I am single having no fun at all. Then I would go out riding around, and I would find a girl walking, and hopefully she would get into my car, but she would end up making some kind of remark about my weight, music or looks. That would turn me into a different person, altogether. I really don't like to talk about that person cause it gets me very upset. But for you, Kat, I will. Cause you want to know everything. Other people have tried, but to no avail.[*]

Crime stories—whether true or a sordid tale created in the imagination of an author—are a subject that fascinates millions. Early cop shows on television, like the black-and-white image of Sergeant Joe Friday in *Dragnet*, have morphed into graphic, high-definition bloodbaths like *CSI*. From years of being a crime reporter, I knew the public's saturation level for such stories was high. As I detailed a high-profile murder case years ago in which one slaying was actually videotaped, a friend, unable to wait for the next day's developments, called to ask, "What's your story going to be tomorrow?"

Psychiatrists may have described Gerald Stano as slow or below average because of his traumatic start in life, but

---

[*] Gerald Stano to Kathy Kelly, November 3, 1985

that didn't stop him from killing and killing again. He used different methods—firearms, strangulation, drowning—and left his victims' bodies in remote places. In those days, law enforcement agencies didn't communicate as they do now, and there was nobody looking at the big picture—attractive young women who disappeared off the street, never to be seen alive again.

If Gerald Stano was walking and driving the streets today and carrying out his deadly mission, a key weapon would be on the side of law enforcement agencies: DNA, microscopic genetic material that makes identification nearly foolproof. Tiny drops of blood left at the scene where a feisty young woman struck back, semen from an act of hurried sex, or even flesh under fingernails could have put Stano behind bars years earlier. That might have stopped his rides of death. He may have been caught much sooner. But the question that seems to plague friends and families of those young women murdered in the 1970s still most fervently remains: how did he talk them into getting into his car?

Gerald Stano was in rare form—killing form, that is—for seven years. In Florida alone, he killed a woman on an average of every three months. For that period, from 1973 to 1977, a total of eighteen women died at the hands, literally, of this moody man who prowled the streets in search of someone who would give him a little respect or sex if he was lucky.

From the jam-packed leather briefcase of Paul Crow, the chief investigator on the Stano cases for the police department in Daytona Beach, Florida, came a grim compilation of names. It had no header stating what it really was—a death list. But it was a summation of the lives that the former computer programmer and short-order cook had snuffed out on his nocturnal forays.

Overwhelmingly, Stano's victims were white. Only two were black. They ranged in age from twelve—Susan Basile, his former roller-skating partner—to thirty-four-year-old Bonnie Hughes, a Dundee, Florida, housewife, who appeared to be his oldest victim. She had been beaten in the face with a blunt instrument and was found slain in an orange grove February 11, 1976, in Polk County, Florida.

This coldest of lists presented its vital statistics in a phrase reminiscent of the old *Dragnet* show on television—"just the facts."

Most of Stano's victims had presented a lonely image: prostitutes walking darkened streets, glancing nervously over their shoulders; women with car trouble only too happy to see someone pull over and offer to help, especially a man driving the same model car they were; or young girls hitchhiking, ignoring the oft-repeated parental warnings about getting into cars with strangers.

Some were street-smart. They were cagey about figuring out if the would-be "john" was a cop. Accepting a ride from a lone male driver wasn't too scary, they figured. They were young, agile. They could be out of the car in a heartbeat. Or so they thought.

They didn't reckon with a radio blasting disco music that jarred their senses. And they didn't hesitate to voice their feelings. "How can you stand to listen to that stuff? Donna Summer and that disco crap are so over the hill."

They didn't anticipate stops for beer or requests for sex. By the time they began to process what was happening, it was too late.

Out of nowhere, a fist would come slamming into their faces, wildly hitting them again and again as the driver proceeded calmly. Sometimes it was a knife, the sharp blade plunging into their torsos over and over as they fought helplessly to escape. For others, the demonic turn of their captor sent a shock wave that almost immediately brought a gut response.

"If I can open the door, I can run," more than one probably thought. But even those who were alive when they left the car didn't make it more than a few feet before the dark-haired driver produced a small handgun and shot them.

ONE
A Date for an Interview

> Now, about Kathy Kelly. As you know she is the only one I
> have consented to talk too [sic]. Reason is, she is a friend of
> yours and Donald Jacobson. Is she married Paul? Let me
> know okay?
>
> —Gerald Stano to Paul Crow, September 4, 1985

As the appointment at the prison for my first interview
with Gerald Stano neared, I couldn't believe I was worried about what to wear. I was no newcomer when it came
to conducting prison interviews, having worked at the *News-
Journal* as a police reporter for about twenty-five years by
that time. But I didn't want to give any wrong ideas to the
man whose favorite song was "Just a Gigolo, I Ain't Got Nobody," sung by David Lee Roth.

In addition to the assistance of Don Jacobson, Stano's
attorney, I also had the support of Paul Crow, the police
sergeant to whom Stano looked for advice, guidance, and re-
assurance. Paul and Jerry, as Stano called himself and Paul
addressed him, had developed a good rapport thanks to Paul's
interviewing skills developed at the FBI Academy in Quantico, Virginia.

Paul and I had a long-standing friendship, having gone to
high school together. As he worked his way up the ranks, we

stayed in touch and had a good working relationship. On my beat as a police reporter in the 1970s and '80s, I depended on forming relationships with people who were going to tell me things. "You may want to check on this," someone might say, trusting that his or her name wouldn't appear in a story. News today at most law enforcement agencies is funneled through public information officers, whose job it is to keep reporters from having one-on-one contact with officers.

Early on, Paul had confided to me that a major investigation was under way, and Gerald Stano was confessing to murder, again and again. I had held off writing anything until signed confessions were in hand that Stano had admitted the slayings of at least six women.

A colleague, Rosemary Smith, and I quietly gathered all the information about six of the murders. We looked through court records, including a search warrant for Stano's car issued a day after his April 1, 1980, arrest for the attack on Donna Marie Hensley. All the basic information about the 1977 AMC Gremlin was detailed in the warrant, including the serial number and color of interior, right down to the trailer hitch on the rear.

Rosemary and I collaborated on the story that broke the news to local residents that the deaths of at least ten young women in the area over a seven-year span had been the work of one man. The front-page story ran September 3, 1981, with a headline in large type that read: "Killer Says 'Revenge' Was Motive." The final chilling detail of the affidavit filed in the charging documents was the description of the license tag on the front of Stano's car: "No riders except blondes, brunettes and redheads."

Walking into a state prison in August 1985, especially to see a death row inmate, was intimidating to say the least, and oppressive, to put it best. One door after another clanged shut, until I suddenly felt like a prisoner myself. The interior of the interview room was bare and sterile. Inside sat Gerald Stano, a slightly pudgy man handcuffed behind a small table, dressed in an orange prison jumpsuit. He didn't seem embarrassed by his restraints; quite the contrary, he appeared amiable, and even cheerful.

He immediately started asking me about people he knew at the *News-Journal*, from when he had worked in the mailroom. There, employees called inserters took the newspapers as they rolled off the press and inserted advertising sections into the finished product. For $3.50 an hour, it was mindless work, shuffling one part of the newspaper into another.

It was very conversational at first, which put me at ease. I certainly hadn't wanted to walk in and immediately start asking him about the people he had killed. So the chat about the paper was an icebreaker. He seemed confident, even flattered by the attention. It was a break in his daily routine, which he complained, time and again, was so monotonous.

He was clean shaven. Later, he told me that he shaved every day, not that prisoners had to, as some inmates even sported long beards and mustaches. But he seemed to take as much pride in his personal appearance behind bars as he did on the outside.

The initial discussions I had with Paul Crow were about the crimes to which Stano had confessed. I had only seen Stano from a distance once when I walked by Paul's office and saw him sitting inside.

I realized it would take a while to draw things out of Stano, just as it happened with him and Paul. Paul had already warned me that Stano relished playing cat and mouse to prolong the giving of information as long as possible. It was the thrill of the game for Stano, making him think he was in charge.

He didn't feel comfortable with some things that I asked him about in letters. The death of Susan Basile, one of the few—if not only—victims he had known personally, gave him bad dreams, he said. Like other serial killers, Ted Bundy for instance, Stano seemed to have preferred perfect strangers as his prey.

I went to the prison three or four times. It was always on a Thursday, since I typically had off Thursdays and Sundays, so I had to go on Thursday to comply with prison regulations on interviews. On some weeks that I didn't go, he would write that he was disappointed—although he always knew days in advance when I would be there for an interview because it involved clearance by prison officials.

We made the agreement that I would send him a series of questions that he would answer, but pretty soon the letters from him took on a different, more personal tone, commenting on the weather or a visit from his parents. I had his complete confidence and support, especially because I had the backing of Paul Crow, who had vouched for me as being trustworthy. Stano's letters were more like letters to a friend than to a reporter. He urged me to be careful, and even sent me a get-well card after I had surgery.

He knitted a scarf and hat for me for Christmas 1985, sending it through his attorney. It was bright orange and white, the style more fitting for wintry northern climates than the sunny south. I knew all along he had been gifting other inmates with many of his "creations," such as baby blankets. It was, after all, a change to the tedium of prison life. He had his radio and a small black-and-white television, his primary source of entertainment. Once he wrote me that he had watched the Junior Miss Pageant, which had been broadcast from Daytona Beach.

What intrigued me most about him was that he could have killed so many women over a seven-year period and then resumed his daily life with total normalcy. And also, the irony that I had written about so many of the crimes and had met with some of the families.

Of course, I had initially covered them as separate crimes, and not as the work of the man now sitting before me. It amazed me that he was able to pull it off for so long. The first time I went to see him, I admit I was extremely nervous—my skin felt clammy and I nervously fiddled with my pen and notebook. And when he started talking about working at the newspaper office, I think I was glad to be off the subject of why I was there.

From that first meeting in prison, I did my best to draw Stano out. In a series of forty letters over a ten-month period, he confessed his hatred for his adoptive father, devotion to his adoptive mother, and insecurities about women as well as his appearance. Stano was detail oriented to the point of fastidiousness. Today, he would probably be recognized in the psychiatric community with obsessive-compulsive disorder, that inner drive for everything to be just right.

Eventually Paul Crow would tell me, with some degree of caution and hesitation, and even a tinge of embarrassment, that he didn't know if Stano truly trusted me or if it was all part of his facade. He pointed out that where Stano had a very small social circle, I had a large network that stretched throughout several states, and even internationally. Stano craved that sort of popularity for himself. "Tell Kathy I like her very much. And I think she's beautiful too. She is the 'old fashion type.' That is what I like in a girl Paul. I would be very honored to have her as my girlfriend if I was out," Stano wrote to Paul on January 28, 1986.

"You're a pretty lady, Kathy," said my high school friend, "and I hate to say this but you probably became like a kind of Farrah Fawcett poster on his wall." Fawcett was the "it girl" back then. I cringed at the thought.

I don't know if he honestly took a liking to me or if it was all pretense, but I'm sure he welcomed any diversion from the prison routine, especially having a female visitor. I don't even want to imagine what he told other inmates about me when he got back to his cell, but I'm certain it enhanced his self-image as a macho guy. He was only too happy to comply with anything that improved his own perception of virility. Even though facing the electric chair, he had lost none of his illusions that women were somehow attracted to him, despite also claiming that "I kind of look over the girls, because of my weight problem I have. If they snicker at me, forget it. But, if they take me for what I am, that's a different story. Besides, I am not what the girls call a hunk. I am just an over-weight nobody."[*]

I don't know that I was able to penetrate his wall. He was not at all willing to talk about some of the crimes; some of the others he was only too ready to revisit in exact detail. Some, he said, were hard to remember, while others he claimed to have blocked out. Early in our discussions, he claimed inno-cence of one of the murders, saying he was in jail at the time. Prodding him for more details in some of the cases disturbed him, causing him sleepless nights on his hard prison bunk, he said.

But he also told me about the women he had killed.

He talked to me about what was believed to be his first murderous rage, in Gainesville, in 1973. He picked up two young girls who were hitchhiking. Something in the ensuing conversation convinced him they were lesbians. Comments about his manhood, his clothes, or his weight provoked him to a boiling rage, and he lashed out and killed the girls as they drove along in his car.

This was frequently his pattern. Sometimes it was his fist.

---

* Gerald Stano to Kathy Kelly, August 21, 1985

More often, it was a knife. As he drove, he would slash his victims again and again. Sometimes he shot them, usually in the temple, with a .22 caliber weapon he claimed to have borrowed from a friend.

I found it particularly unsettling because he considered these young women as no more than prey. He would "find a girl walking," stalk her, take her, and ultimately destroy her. His lack of remorse was a characteristic he shared with other serial killers such as Ted Bundy,* John Wayne Gacy, and Gary Ridgway, the Green River Killer.

Like Ted Bundy, Stano had gone from "organized" to "disorganized" in his method of operation. When a member of the Green River Killer Task Force called Paul Crow to consult with him about finding their killer, Crow told him, "Find a victim that survived the attack. You're assuming he killed everyone who got in the truck. You have to have eyes and ears in the community."

The death penalty seemed a fitting sentence or punishment for someone who had cold-bloodedly and coldheartedly taken the lives of others, but I couldn't witness Gerald Stano's final moments in the electric chair.

Initially, I had applied to be a witness to his execution, and because our newspaper had covered his crimes heavily, we were granted a spot on the list. But from the onset, Stano had told me he didn't want me there.

A week or so before it was scheduled, I knew I couldn't go, that it was not an image that I wanted saved forever in the hard drive of my brain. So I chose not to attend.

I felt a sense of sadness because a human life had been

---

* Ted Bundy was actually on death row at the same time. At some point, Stano wrote: "Yes I know, Bundy is in the next cell," but he clearly was not very interested in talking about his infamous fellow inmate. Bundy was getting all the attention.

taken and because I had developed some sort of rapport with a person who was a separate entity from the "serial killer." On the other hand, that person was truly despicable. Who was he to play God and decide that these girls shouldn't live anymore because they didn't meet his standards or he felt they had insulted him?

Unfortunately, for the families left behind, there will never be an end to their pain and suffering or that deep sense of loss.

TWO

Early Childhood: The Warning Signs

My childhood was the usual. If I wanted to buy something, I had to have a good reason. If I wanted to talk to my father, I would cringe at the sight of him. I was afraid of him, and to this day, I still am afraid of him. . . . My mother would take charge of us [Gerald and his adopted brother Arthur*] during the week, and tell him [Dad] what we did wrong on the phone. When he got home, he would march us both into the bathroom and beat us with a leather razor strap. When I cracked up the family car, he came after me with a straight edge razor opened up. When I had accidents with my cars, he would always go into a rage, and say "Why couldn't you have been killed?"

—Gerald Stano to Kathy Kelly, August 15, 1985

On September 12, 1951, in Schenectady, New York, a baby was born, the fifth child to be delivered to a most reluctant of mothers. Two of her previous attempts at motherhood failed miserably. One baby was stillborn. The other, in layman's terms, was a "blue baby."

But this child, a boy, had a normal birth, though he had no way of knowing that the sterile conditions of the hospital would be his first and last taste of cleanliness for a while, at

---

* Denotes pseudonym

least for seven months. Once at home, he was listless and cranky, often from hunger. He wasn't fed much or regularly, and his development, physical and emotional, began to suffer early on.

The baby missed the bonding that is crucial to an infant at an early age, the cuddling that's such a vital expression of a mother's love. Clearly, he was just another mouth to feed, a whiny baby to be barely tolerated at best. Dirty diapers went unchanged, and clothes remained unwashed for days.

Eventually, the New York State Welfare Department stepped in. "Extreme neglect" was the term used in the routine paperwork of the welfare system, but it did little to describe the trauma already inflicted on the infant. He met the same fate as the siblings who had survived before him. He was taken away from his mother.

Within a month, welfare authorities had found a set of prospective adoptive parents, Eugene and Norma Stano, a couple in their thirties. The Stanos had wanted a child desperately and were eager to take this pitiful little creature into their home and hearts.

The couple showered him with love, trying to overcome the neglect and harshness of his early infancy. He wasn't a warm, cuddly child, but the couple hoped that in time he would respond to their care and concern, to their caresses and affectionate words.

At the end of the first six months, as required by New York State law, the Stanos allowed the child, whom they named Gerald Eugene Stano, to be examined by a team comprised of a psychiatric social worker, a nurse, a physician, a psychologist, and a psychiatrist. It was their job to chart the child's development, to see if he was responding to his new surroundings, to find out if the nurturing of two loving parents had begun to block out the first wretched months of life. When the report came back, the Stanos were devastated. Gerald was

considered "unadoptable" in the jargon of the welfare workers. That meant he would have to be returned to the custody
of the state, probably to end up in some home for disturbed
children, sentenced yet again to a life absent of a warm, caring
family.

Norma Stano didn't take the news calmly. This woman,
herself a trained nurse, had a stake in the baby's future and
she intended to protect it. Stoically, she appealed for help
from the social worker assigned to the case and one of the
staff psychologists. She did everything she could to convince these professionals that Gerald's place was with the
Stanos, that they could give him the second chance in life he
deserved.

However, at no time did Norma Stano see the psychiatrist's report on why her adopted son shouldn't stay with
his new family. She fought back on instinct alone, not wanting to give up on this tiny little human being who seemed so
forlorn.

Finally, her wishes prevailed, and welfare workers reluctantly approved the adoption. At last, little Gerald was a permanent part of a family.

He proved a tough child to love. Aloof and withdrawn, he
never showed affection toward the couple. He continued to
exhibit some of the disturbing traits that had begun in his
infancy, such as eating his own feces. He walked early on
but was clumsy, uncoordinated. He bumped into walls, tum-
bling down the stairs several times. In early childhood, he
suffered several head injuries from his rambunctious ramblings. By the time he was three, he had suffered high fevers
of up to 105 degrees on several occasions.

As a child, Gerald was slow to talk, not really beginning
to communicate well until he was about two. But he was
extremely neat even as a toddler, despite his penchant for
eating feces, insisting his toys be a kept a certain way, a

preoccupation with having every thing in its proper place. If Norma Stano moved an end table across the room, Gerald noticed it right away. Screaming and crying, he would insist it be returned to its original position.

Gerald finally started primary school, harboring a secret from his classmates. He still wet the bed at night. Concerned, the Stanos took him to see a physician, who could find no physical cause for the bed-wetting. The child's reserved, unfriendly nature began to cause him problems in school.

As early as kindergarten and first grade, Gerald earned the reputation of being a bully, shoving smaller children around, taunting them. Principals and teachers called Gerald's parents in repeatedly for conferences, vaguely implying that something seemed to be "wrong" with the child.

If Gerald seemed sullen and withdrawn, the Stanos soon learned another dark side to their son. He was dishonest. First, it was little things like lying, but then they began to notice things missing from around the house. Their other adopted son, Arthur, claimed Gerald had stolen his toys, or money for ice cream or a movie. Once, he even stole something at school.

For Gerald, school was a constant torment. He couldn't seem to relate to his classmates and found the challenges of the academic world too much. His parents arranged for intensive tutoring, but the best Gerald could manage were Cs and Ds. The only subject he really enjoyed was music, and he would be enthralled for hours at a time listening to the radio or to records.

Years later, he would recall under hypnosis how he would murder a neighbor's chickens. A sixth or seventh grader at the time, he would pick up a fluffy little chick, then twist its neck sharply, watching and listening with glee as its tiny little chirping noises became more and more faint.

By the time he reached junior high, Gerald's childish

pranks of stealing from fellow students and his family had begun to take a more serious turn. In Westchester County, New York, he turned in false fire alarms on several occasions, enjoying the power he felt when a hurriedly spoken message to the fire department would send trucks out, sirens screaming, on some bogus calls.

His penchant for trouble became more aggressive. From a vantage point atop a highway overpass, he once tossed a large rock down on a car traveling below. Luckily, nobody was hurt, but the windshield of the auto was smashed. Gerald was caught, and Westchester County juvenile authorities told the Stanos that after the fire alarms and the rock throwing, a third brush with the law would have serious consequences for Gerald. He would be adjudicated a delinquent and sentenced to a state reformatory.

Alarmed, the Stanos decided to take immediate action. They thought taking Gerald out of the school atmosphere and getting him away from Schenectady might help, so they enrolled him in the Hargrave Military Academy, in Virginia. The structured discipline of the academy might be just what was needed to change Gerald from a youthful prankster into a purposeful young man. But it was not to be. At Hargrave, he quickly earned the reputation of a troublemaker. He borrowed large sums of money from other cadets and then refused to pay them back. The former bully became an easy target for abuse. He was the butt of jokes about his glasses and his weight. He was easily intimidated, and the other cadets sensed it and derived great pleasure from scaring him with menacing threats.

For the Stanos, this attempt at helping Gerald get straightened out was another failure. They withdrew him from the military school and sent him to Ormond Beach, Florida, where Norma Stano's parents lived. He attended junior high there for a time. Mrs. Stano's parents were clearly uneasy with their grandson being in the house. By the time the Stanos came to get Gerald to return up north, the older couple had installed locks on their bedroom doors.

The Stanos took Gerald back to Ambler, Pennsylvania, where they had moved. Perhaps a fourth change of scenery and friends would help their troubled son. But at Shady Grove School, Gerald's bad habits surfaced quickly. He was brought up before the principal for handing out money to some of the male students. It seemed Gerald had stolen money from his father's wallet and then gave it to members of the track team, bribing them to run behind him so he could finish first in competitive races. He frequently skipped school and managed to get in some kind of trouble while he was in class.

Gerald's awkward streak was having an effect on the entire family. Arthur, a popular student with good grades in school, ran away from home after Gerald came back from Florida, upset at the divisive effect the other boy's behavior was having on the family.

Gerald was home alone one day when he was sixteen. His parents were gone, but one of their cars was sitting in the driveway. Feeling adventurous, he took it and began driving around, as usual his foot heavy on the accelerator. Gerald was never hurt during these escapades, but his erratic driving habits were now a new danger for the Stanos to face.

At nineteen, Gerald went to the computer school at Maxwell Institute in Pennsylvania. At last, his parents thought, perhaps he'll settle down, try to make something of his life. Using the experience from the computer school, he got a job at the Chestnut Hill Hospital. But before long, he was in trouble there, too. He got fired for stealing money from the pocketbooks of female employees. At his next job, in the computer department of the University of Pennsylvania, he lied about his experience and training to get a job. It wasn't long before the truth was discovered. Confronted, he lied again. Again, he faced unemployment.

Gerald's life began to fall apart. He had been fired from two jobs and was languishing in a crummy hotel while he was trying to make his first attempt at independence. His frustration grew when he was thrown out of the hotel for stealing money from other guests' rooms. Desperate, he returned home to live, knowing he was giving up a lot of the freedom he had come to enjoy while he was out on his own.

He went to work for Burroughs Corporation, only to be quickly fired as "incorrigible." By then, Gerald had begun to drink heavily and dabble in drugs. At that time, at least according to Stano, he began to date a mentally disabled girl named Yvonne,* who, ignorant of the consequences of sex, soon ended up pregnant and had an abortion paid for by the Stano family.† "My relationships with women I can say was not exactly the best," Stano admitted. "It was good up north, cause you have a different type of girl. Down south, they think you got money to burn on them. Besides, I was very picky at my girlfriends. Like Yvonne up in Pennsylvania. If the young lady is a respectful type (no running around) I will take to her, and treat her with respect. But, if she is a tramp, she won't get any respect from me."‡

Eugene Stano was desperate with worry over his adopted son. He talked with his wife, and together they decided they would try yet another course of action, sending Gerald away again, this time back to Florida, where Norma was caring for

---

* Denotes pseudonym

† No other member of the Stano family corroborated this story.

‡ Gerald Stano to Kathy Kelly, August 21, 1985

her ailing mother. Maybe it would be a fresh start for Gerald, a chance to begin anew, and repair his fractured relationship with his family.

Back in Florida, Gerald met Teresa Esposito,* twenty-three, a hairdresser, and the couple decided to get married. But as the wedding day neared in June 1975, a major hurdle appeared on the horizon. Jerry was arrested on charges of forging a check from his employer. The three-month-minimum jail sentence would mean that the couple's months of planning, reserving a church and reception hall, were for naught.

On May 21, one month exactly before the day of the planned nuptials, Teresa put pen to paper to plead her fiancé's case. She told Circuit Judge J. Robert Durden that she was "looking forward to the most happy day in a girl's life— my wedding on June 21."

Because Jerry "had involved himself in a most unfortunate situation," the plans for the wedding were in jeopardy. The venues had been reserved, invitations had been sent, and Teresa had been honored at several bridal showers, she said in appealing to Durden "not only in your capacity as a judge but also to you as a parent—to beg of you to make it possible for Gerald and me to marry as planned."

His parents, Norma and Eugene Stano, got into the act as well. They recounted the couple's plans for the wedding as well as the future and implored the judge to be reasonable.

"We realize that justice must be served—and that it will. However, would it not be served as well, if not better, if you could find the compassion in your heart to mitigate the sentence and to contribute to Gerald's rehabilitation by making it possible for Gerald and Teresa to be able to follow through with their wedding plans on June 21st?" the parents wrote.

---

* Denotes pseudonym

The judge capitulated, and the Stano-Esposito wedding went on. Gerald's new father-in-law, Mario Esposito,* gave him a job at a service station as a way to keep an eye on him while he was on probation. A small announcement on the "society pages" of the *Daytona Beach News-Journal* duly recorded the marriage.

Nevertheless, within a short time, the Stano marriage was in serious trouble.

One day at the service station owned by his father-in-law, Stano said that his "ex-brother-in-law swung at me, and I came at him with my belt. . . . I took out my anger on my ex-wife's [Teresa's] dog and her. Once, in front of her aunt and uncle; and that started the divorce proceedings."†

After thirteen months, Teresa Stano had endured enough. She filed for and was granted what Florida law calls a dissolution of marriage. She received all of the items she requested, which included most of the wedding gifts. Five years later, in 1981, Stano told psychiatrist Dr. F. Carrera that his former wife had left him because of his abusive punishment.

"I'd push her around . . . hit her face . . . for sticking with her parents," the psychiatrist quoted him as saying in a report to the court. Gerald Stano admitted his spousal abuse began about six months after the couple exchanged vows. Stano criticized his mother-in-law's "smart mouth" and his wife's laziness, saying she left laundry in the washer while she watched soap operas. Stano, a self-confessed neat freak, railed at her sloppy housekeeping and insistence on always having her family members around.

Their sex life "was always bad," he told Dr. Carrera.

---

* Denotes pseudonym

† Gerald Stano to Kathy Kelly, August 15, 1985

"She never wanted to have sex except during our one-week honeymoon."

These fights over sex would lead him to storm out of the house, occasionally going "downtown looking for a woman."

He had begun to drink nonstop when he was twenty-one, and after his divorce—when he was twenty-five—he was drinking one case of beer a week and two cases on weekends. He had also been smoking marijuana and taking downers.

The tumultuous relationship with Teresa started Stano on a different path, "basically what started the change of Jerry, to the Jerry that people call a 'serial killer.'"[*]

The drinking and drug abuse, plus his incipient resentment toward women, perhaps contributed to the escalation of Stano's violent behavior.

Gerald Eugene Stano was starting to pick up a dangerous rhythm to his nights.

---

* Gerald Stano to Kathy Kelly, August 15, 1985

THREE
The One Who Got Away

> When I moved to Florida in 1974, I saw girls getting in and out of cars. After a while, they were getting in my car too. After a while, the girls said they were going to have their "old man" get me. That triggered my memory of the threat. So I would go out and get some beer and booze, and get drunk and then pick up one of the girls and kill her, knowing I wouldn't have to worry about her getting the "old man" on me.
>
> —Gerald Stano to Kathy Kelly, August 15, 1985

On March 25, 1980, Donna Marie Hensley was strolling along Daytona Beach's Ocean Avenue, which ran parallel to the Atlantic Ocean and served as the "backyard" of the tourist playground known as the Boardwalk. At night, the area turned into a darker scene, with cars driving slowly, the men inside looking for some kind of companionship to pass the lonely hours. In the shadowy arcades, drug deals were offered and financed.

The founding fathers of Daytona Beach seemed to have gotten things backward. Here, Main Street was on the peninsula, while Beach Street, the hub of downtown, was on the mainland, facing the Halifax River, part of the Intracoastal Waterway that separated the mainland and the beachside. Along the scenic ribbon of water, locals watched the smaller pleasure boats out for the day as well as sleek yachts, owned by the very rich, passing through on their way south for the winter.

For decades, Main Street capitalized on its carnival atmosphere, drawing summer visitors as well as annual invasions of black-jacketed motorcyclists. Along the Boardwalk, facing the Atlantic Ocean, crowds enjoyed the whirling rides, cotton candy, and games of chance. On a warm summer night, tourists could ride the Ferris wheel, looking out at endless miles of ocean.

By the 1980s, many of the longtime residents had moved away from their once fashionable homes. The area had become a tourist mecca, not an entirely flattering description. Tiny shops crammed side by side hawked seashells and T-shirts, mementos for the throngs of tourists to take home.

But crime was a growing problem. Teenagers ran away from homes in colder northern areas and fled to the beachside city, lured by the promise of fun by visiting nearby Walt Disney World and a magical life on the beach. Others ran from brutal family situations, failing school grades, or other circumstances that drove them as far away from home as their thumbs would take them. In town, with little or no money, the hunger pangs soon became a daily constant. They sought solace in others seeking the same paradise—life on the beach—and soon learned crime was the only way to survive. Purse snatchings and car break-ins financed their wanderings but not for long.

Spring break was a raunchy ritual with its wet T-shirt contests and even nastier sex games. Undercover cops blanket the beaches, but there isn't enough man- and womanpower to divert the hormonal herd, running amok, and drunk at that, until all hours of the night and early morning.

* * *

Donna Marie Hensley was already high on quaaludes, known in the 1980s by the street name of "Disco Biscuits," but she was alert enough to know that when you climbed into cars and later into bed with strangers, the stakes were high. Sometimes things got a little kinky, the result of a guy feeling powerful after peeling off a twenty-dollar bill for what he thought would make him feel like a real man.

A steady diet of pills had helped insulate Donna from much of her life. Most of the time she was high, and the buzz from the uppers and downers she used helped dull the pain. She had tried suicide when her dead-end life seemed too much to bear, but she wasn't even successful at that.

Her life was one long and monotonous routine, sleeping most of the day and prowling the streets at night looking for tricks. Most of the time, guys didn't notice the glazed look in her eyes. In fact, they barely noticed her at all. They just wanted sex, and they didn't care where they got it. As long as they paid up and she didn't get hurt, Donna didn't care. She was a prostitute, used to making a living off her body. By now, her memory of falling into a life of selling her body had grown fuzzy, like the shadows of passing strangers.

Time and drugs had ravaged her face and body, as well as her mind, making her look drawn and haggard. She was twenty-four and once had been a real babe. Faded signs hinted at her former beauty.

She pulled her lightweight jacket tighter around her shoulders, trying to ward off the chill of the late-night air. It was one of those cool Central Florida March nights, in the low fifties.

She spotted the small red car as it pulled up. At that hour of the morning, there were few vehicles on the street, save for bread and milk delivery trucks making their early runs to restaurants and a few cabs carting late-night drinkers home from bars.

She had seen the car before; it was a Gremlin, and the license tag on the front read, "No riders except blondes, brunettes and redheads."

The driver rolled down the window of the car, slowing to a stop right next to Donna.

"Are you working tonight?" the pudgy, bespectacled driver called over.

Donna had been around long enough to know she had to be careful about cops. They often dressed casually, wearing designer blue jeans; rode around in cars with out-of-town tags; and pretended they were tourists out for a good time. As soon as they agreed with a girl on just how much a good time would cost them, they flashed a badge, and the charade was all over.

She glanced at the man's brightly patterned polyester shirt and white belt and assumed no cop would be caught dead in disco clothing. She took her time looking him over. From his appearance, she remembered that her friend Cheryl had seen him around the night before, just cruising the Main Street area on the beachside.

"No, I'm not working, just out for a walk," she answered, biding her time until she could sense what he was after.

"In that case, how about a ride instead?" he offered, with a cockeyed smile.

Donna climbed in, quickly glancing around the inside of the car. Everything seemed worn but clean, none of the litter of beer cans or overflowing ashtrays she was used to.

They exchanged small talk for a few minutes, mostly about the weather, inane chatter. Then he asked abruptly, "How much to get laid?"

She paused momentarily, and then spewed out: "Twenty dollars."

"Sounds okay to me," the man said flatly. Instinctively, she was still wary, as she glanced sideways at the man, only half hearing the music from his car radio as she tried to scope him out.

This latest in a series of strangers who passed through her life had a pasty color to his face. He had a stale, boozy smell about him.

They pulled into the motel parking lot. The outside was painted a garish purple, and the flickering neon light on the front sign gave off an eerie glow from the vivid hue. The unlikely couple went inside room 4. It was typical of the small, cheap motels that were tucked into the narrowest strips of land. It was the kind of place where cockroaches made slithery paths up the wall when light invaded their dark haven.

For Donna, it was home. She had a few personal belongings, and the double bed with the rumpled spread was, in a sense, her office.

She peeled off her jeans and T-shirt after discarding her jacket. Turning his back to her, the stranger followed suit, stripping off his undershirt and socks.

His quiet, deliberate manner was a little disturbing to her. Some men had a forced sense of gaiety about these encounters, but not this guy. It seemed to be strictly a business proposition for him.

Predictably, the sex was quick, a meeting of thrusting hips that held little emotion for either party. Despite the chilly dampness of the room, the stranger had sprouted a mustache of perspiration. She sat on the side of the bed and began to pull on her jeans, letting out an involuntary shudder in the cool room.

She hoped he would hurry up and leave. She was starting to get a dull headache, a sign she needed something from the stash in her purse, the small supply of drugs she worked hard, on her back and on her knees, to replenish.

He gave her a twenty-dollar bill, and as she took it, her hands felt unclean, slightly greasy. She assumed he probably worked at some fast-food joint. Maybe he had had a bad day flipping burgers.

Suddenly, the quiet, sullen stranger became agitated, then enraged. "I hate hookers!" he railed. "They're the scum of the earth!"

His shouting became more intense, his breath coming in short gasps. Methodically, he began to ransack the tiny hotel room, pulling out dresser drawers and scattering clothing on the floor. That was the least of Donna's troubles. Nothing in the room was worth a damn.

Out of the corner of her eye, she noticed that now he was wearing gloves. Grunting, he moved toward her, then shoved her to the floor. "You're going to get it now," he screamed, his voice strangely high-pitched.

In his rampage through the room, he had amassed an arsenal of weapons, small things really, but sharp enough to inflict pain.

Swinging blindly, he lashed out at her with one of the objects—she couldn't tell what. Her throat seemed to freeze as she dodged his lunges. She fumbled to get out of his way.

Quickly, he found his mark. Long and angry-looking scrapes raked her arms. Her breasts bore further evidence of his murderous assault, cuts not deep enough to require stitches but enough to leave bright red rivulets of blood. He managed to stab her five or six times in the right thigh. A later report recorded the damage as having been inflicted with "a can opener and a knife."*

Finally, even he had had enough. "I'm taking my money back," he shouted. "This was a rip-off!" Still panting from the frenzied struggle, he rifled through her purse, retrieving

---

* Drs. Frank Carrera and George W. Barnard, Volusia County psychiatrists

the twenty-dollar bill he had given her and taking an extra thirty dollars she had tucked inside of the small handbag.

She thought that was getting off cheaply enough; now if only he would leave.

Donna watched as he headed to the tiny kitchenette and returned with a gallon of muriatic acid that was kept in the unit, a chemical so strong it ate away stains ground into concrete driveways from years of leaking automobile engines.

"I'm not through with you yet," he roared, advancing toward her and splashing the liquid around like some deranged arsonist.

She prayed silently as she struggled to get to her feet. She ran out the back door of the motel room, her screams attracting the attention of other tenants. She could feel blood streaming down her legs. It was nearly 5:00 a.m., less than an hour since she had climbed into the little red car. Her attacker got back into his car and drove away before the responding ambulance and police units arrived.

Donna stumbled to the hotel's main office, where the startled clerk called for an ambulance. Routinely, the ambulance dispatcher notified the police department of any call that could involve a crime, so police arrived on scene shortly thereafter.

Officer Sue Cunningham arrived, her dark hair tucked back neatly under a uniform hat in a businesslike, almost prim manner. She looked like Mary Steenburgen, attractive in a homespun sort of way, with the trim body of an athlete. Unlike most of her colleagues, she had a college degree, but her quiet demeanor underplayed the academic prowess she held over other police officers. Still, nothing in any of the books prepared her for the grim scenes of life on the street.

Officer Cunningham tried to calm Donna. "It's okay; it's okay," she told the hysterical woman. "We're going to take

you to the hospital, where they'll take care of you," she mur-
mured, trying to sound reassuring.

From the back of the ambulance in the reflection of the
flashing red lights, Donna gulped in the cool night air and
tried to tell the young officer what had happened.

"It was horrible, just horrible," she sobbed. "He went
nuts in there!"

In her heart, Donna knew she was lucky. She was still
alive.

In the small, cramped offices of the Records Bureau of
the Daytona Beach Police Department, far behind many others in terms of state-of-the-art equipment, each case was
assigned a number. It made no difference whether it was a
neighbor's dog barking all night, a stolen child's bicycle, or,
as in Donna's case, assault and battery.

She was now a victim on paper. Her name was recorded
in police jargon, as a complainant on an "A&B-knife" report,
the shortened term for assault and battery with a knife. Her
complaint became case number 80-03-10349. There it was,
in black and white, what Gerald Stano had done to her—the
puncture wounds, the lacerations. In his rage, he had used a
can opener, a nail file, a knife with a black handle, even scis-
sors. As he thrashed around, pulling out drawers from the
dresser, he grabbed a gallon of acid that was in the apartment
and started trying to splash her with that as well.

.Routinely, the serious crimes were assigned to detectives
for follow-up. The investigator on Donna Marie Hensley's
case was Detective Jim Gadberry, a serious, deeply reli-
gious man whose rapidly receding hairline belied his young
age. Later, he would leave the department to become a youth
minister, only to return to police work after becoming disen-
chanted with organized religion.

As a criminal investigator, Gadberry had to depend on
street people for information. They lived on the margins of

the criminal underworld but often had invaluable information through their contacts and savored their roles as "double
agents." Often, they gave police officers tips about crimes as
their way of staying "in" with the cops.

In major cases, like murders, palms might be crossed
with money that came from an informant fund, but the information had to be very reliable and result in an arrest that
would hold up later in court.

"I found somebody who knows where the guy lives that
drives the red car," Gadberry told a colleague.

The detective went to the apartment complex where he
had been told the owner of the car lived. "No, he doesn't live
here any more, but I can tell you who he is," the manager
told him. Indeed, that modest sedan of which Stano was so
proud would eventually trip him up because its distinctive
license plate set it apart.

Armed with Gerald Stano's name, Gadberry used a crime
computer to check the suspect's driver's license, and the cop
learned that the red Gremlin was indeed registered to him.
Stano, it seemed, was a familiar figure to prostitutes around
town, especially those on the beachside area. The detective
then proceeded to interview some of them.

"Yeah, we know him," one of the young women said.
"He's weird, kinda spooky."

The driver with the thick, dark-rimmed glasses frequently
picked up prostitutes and female hitchhikers. Several weeks
before the attack on Donna, he had picked up Sandra Washington, twenty, a young black woman with a figure as firm
as her attitude. Her story was hauntingly similar to Donna's.
Stano had engaged in sex with her, and then paid her.

"And then?" Gadberry asked, trying to establish a pattern. "Then he got mad!" she blurted, reliving the unsettling
incident. "He wanted his money back. Maybe he didn't think
he got his money's worth?"

..... she let out a disparaging laugh. "I wasn't about to give up twenty bucks that easy." She had struggled, trying to ward off a barrage of flying fists. The crazed stranger kicked her, pushing her from the car.

Gadberry wondered why she hadn't filed a police report.

"I just knew I wanted to get the hell out of there," she said. Scrambling to her feet, she had run for her life.

Pop, she heard as she quickened her pace. Glancing over her shoulder, she saw the man leaning out of the car window and aiming a gun at her. It was a sight she wouldn't soon forget.

It was now apparent to Gadberry that Stano's penchant for violence had become somewhat legendary on the Boardwalk. Another hooker, known only as Kim, remembered him well.

"Man, he was a real nut case, a wacko," she told the detective. After sex, he seemed to boil with rage, trying to grab her neck with his two hands, determined to choke her. She, too, had managed to escape.

Researching the files at the police department, Gadberry learned Stano had a previous arrest record for writing worthless checks. That meant his picture must be on file. Sure enough, it was, a round-faced man wearing glasses, with a somewhat bookish appearance.

Gadberry told Sergeant Paul Crow, "This has to be the right guy. He's got it in for hookers; they really tick him off."

For Crow, this meant a possible lead in a homicide investigation.

Gadberry set about putting together a photo lineup. Court restrictions being what they were, the seasoned cop knew he had to be careful.

"I have to get them all looking pretty close to one another," Gadberry instructed Donna. "Do any of these look like the man who cut you up?"

Donna's heart began to pound a little as she stared at the photographs. The memories of that awful night came flooding back, washing over her like the surf on the oceanfront. Without hesitation, she pointed out her attacker. *It was Gerald Stano.*

Inwardly, Gadberry heaved a sigh of relief. The positive identification would make his job a lot easier.

Gadberry drove out Orange Avenue from the police station to the office of Circuit Judge Michael Hutcheson in the Courthouse Annex overlooking the Halifax River. He signed the affidavit charging Gerald Eugene Stano with aggravated assault in the stabbing of Donna Marie Hensley.

From there, he headed back across town to the restaurant where Stano worked as a short-order cook. It was April Fools' Day 1980.

Gadberry eased his unmarked police car into the parking lot, looking for the red Gremlin to make sure Stano was working. Sure enough, there it was, the red car with black stripes on the side, chrome luggage rack, and a trailer hitch on the rear bumper.

Inside, the detective made his way into the kitchen. He was alone, but he didn't expect any trouble. His trouser leg brushed against the gun and holster he wore on the inside of his ankle just in case there was.

In the kitchen, huge pressure cookers made a sizzling noise as they steamed with frying chicken, the little family-owned eatery's specialty.

Behind the counter stood Gerald Stano, wearing a white apron to keep the chicken blood and flour coating from splattering all over his trousers. "Are you Gerald Stano?" Gadberry asked.

"Yes I am," Stano stated, trying to sound matter-of-fact as he tried to figure out the stranger's identity.

"I have a warrant for your arrest for aggravated assault,"

Gadberry said, before reciting Stano's Miranda rights, advising his suspect he had the right to remain silent and consult with an attorney.

"Man, I don't know what you're talking about," the cuffed, pudgy guy muttered, glancing around the room to meet the stares of his fellow workers as they paused from their jobs to take in what was happening. "I don't even know that broad."

"The courts will decide that," Gadberry said, motioning Stano to accompany him outside. Using his portable police radio, Gadberry summoned a marked patrol car with a cage unit, since the car he was driving had no facilities for holding prisoners. After all, Stano was charged with a felony; no sense in taking any chances.

As Stano was led outside, other employees stopped to watch, curious about what was happening with the quiet, moody cook, a relative newcomer to the staff.

Back at the police station, Sergeant Paul Crow sat in his tiny cubicle of an office with no windows, not knowing that the troubled young man he would soon meet would change his own life as much as he would alter the course of Stano's future.

For six weeks, Crow had been doggedly working a murder case. On February 17, 1980, he had been called in on his day off to view the body of a young woman found stabbed to death off Bellevue Avenue. Her killer had been brutal and exact, covering her body with branches after carefully placing the corpse on the ground.

She, too, had been stabbed in the thigh, just like Donna, the prostitute.

"He's really starting to look good for this," Crow thought to himself. The sergeant was anxious to talk to Stano, but he was careful not to appear too eager. A compulsively neat person himself, he glanced around his small quarters, absentmindedly straightening a few papers and flicking away small particles of dust.

This may very well have been Crow's first common ground with Stano, who shared the detective's fastidiousness for neatness. It would also become the killer's downfall.

FOUR
The Pretty Star Swimmer

Before being taken to the jail, I took Paul to where I put a body behind the airport. Little did I know, that was the beginning of the end of me. All during this, Paul was like a person I could talk to, and confide in. I didn't look at him like a policeman. I saw him as a real person, who cared what happened to me.

—Gerald Stano to Kathy Kelly, November 3, 1985

As Sergeant Paul Crow waited for Detective Jim Gadberry to bring Gerald Stano in, he thought back to the murder that had taken up much of his time since the body had been found, on February 17, 1980. Mary Carol Maher, twenty, had been missing since January 27, 1980. Her mother had dropped her off at the Holiday Inn Boardwalk on North Atlantic Avenue, Daytona Beach's entertainment area. The lounge at the top of the hotel was a popular gathering place for young people. Mary Carol was to get a ride with a girlfriend when she was ready to leave. If she couldn't, she would call her mom to pick her up.

She was at the bar for a while, talking with friends. She was pretty, blond, with a tanned, toned body, the figure of someone whose favorite hangouts are the gym and the swimming pool. Mary Carol had been a championship swimmer at Mainland High School and was attending Daytona Beach Community College at the time she disappeared.

Mary Carol would be capable of fighting off her attacker, agile as she was. Did she get in a car with someone she knew? Crow wondered.

Several motel employees thought they had seen her get into the elevator with a man who appeared to be Hispanic. Crow had the witnesses assist detectives in preparing a composite sketch of the man. The *Daytona Beach News-Journal* had run the sketch, but so far none of the calls that came in directly to the sergeant had yielded much information about just what had happened to Mary Carol after she left the bar.

Crow's silent musings were interrupted by a tap on the door of his office.

"We're ready when you are," Gadberry said and motioned to Stano to go in.

The three walked to a small interrogation room at the rear of the Detective Bureau office. Gadberry pointed to a chair for Stano to sit down, and then walked in behind Crow, closing the door.

"Gerald, I want you to meet Sergeant Crow," Gadberry said. Stano extended his hand and shook Crow's, then moved to a seat behind the small desk. Gadberry and Crow followed suit, sitting in the other two chairs and facing Stano behind the desk.

"Today's my birthday," Stano blurted out suddenly, prompting Gadberry to look up quickly from the police reports he had been thumbing through.

"What do you mean?" asked Gadberry, knowing Stano's date of birth on his driver's license was September 12, 1951. "Today's the day they got me," Stano explained.

"I'm not sure what you're saying," Gadberry countered.

"Today's the day my adoption was final so I kind of think of it as my birthday," Stano said.

"Oh, so you're adopted?" Crow asked.

Stano responded with a nod of his head, seeming pleased at the notion.

"What a coincidence," said the sergeant, "my son is adopted, too."

With that, Stano seemed to warm up to the burly police sergeant, whose massive shoulders and biceps were solid proof of his years of working out with weights and horseback riding. As Stano listened to Crow, he sat forward in his chair, elbows resting lightly on the desk, staring intently at the detective.

"Hey, did you know your mustache is crooked?" Stano asked Crow, pointing to the bristly row of white hair on the detective's upper lip. Self-consciously, Crow touched his face. "You should get that evened up," Stano observed.

"Gerald, Sergeant Crow and I want to talk to you about a girl who disappeared from here and see if you might know anything about her," Gadberry offered, growing a tad impatient but also being careful to leave out the fact that the girl was dead.

"Okay, fine." Stano tried to appear cooperative, almost chummy with the men.

Paul Crow knew it was time for him to establish a rhythm with the killer. "Did you know either of these girls?" asked Crow, producing pictures of Mary Carol and her sister, whose close resemblance to one another could have easily caused them to be mistaken for twins.

Crow's interviewing skills had been refined when he was among a small group of law enforcement officers invited by the FBI to attend their profiling seminar at Quantico. There, he had learned the art from the best, such as John Douglas, the coauthor of *Mind Hunter: Inside the FBI's Elite Serial*

Crime Unit, and Robert K. Ressler, who had first coined the term *serial killer* and had founded ViCAP (Violent Criminal Apprehension Program). Ressler also wrote the book *Whoever Fights Monsters: My Twenty Years Tracking Serial Killers for the FBI*. Ressler titled his book *Whoever Fights Monsters* after a quote from German philosopher Friedrich Nietzsche: "Whoever fights monsters should see to it that in the process he does not become a monster. And if you gaze long enough into an abyss, the abyss will gaze back into you."

"Sure, I know that one right there," Stano said, gesturing toward the picture of Mary Carol with an outstretched finger. "I picked her up once."

"You picked her up?" Crow said quizzically. "You mean you gave her a ride?"

"Yeah, that's right; she wanted a ride," Stano replied.

Puzzling a moment, he pinpointed the date, January 27. "She was over on Atlantic Avenue, walking, real *real* late," he emphasized, as if trying to cast a shadow over Mary Carol's habits. Crow was steaming with rage inside but made sure his facial expression relayed no emotion.

"And where did you take her?" the officer asked offhandedly, not making eye contact with Stano.

"Well, I drove across the bridge, the Seabreeze Bridge, and then out Mason Avenue," Stano replied without hesitation.

"Did you stop anywhere?" asked Gadberry.

"Yeah, I wanted to stop at Fannie Farkle's, but she didn't want to," said the cook, referring to a popular nightspot.

"Well, where did you go?" Crow was pressing on slowly.

"We went to Pantry Pride on Mason and we got a six-pack of beer. Yeah, that's right, *she* wanted a beer." Stano paused long enough to cross his leg over his knee.

"And where did you go from there?" Crow continued.

"I let her out; she wanted to get out," Stano said.

"That's not really true, is it." Crow was now purposely

rhetorical. "She didn't *really* get out, did she? You two had some kind of argument, didn't you? Did she make you mad?"

"Yeah, I guess so," Stano answered, leaning back up on the desk with his elbows.

"What happened? Did you want to, say, have sex with her and she didn't?" Crow asked quietly, also an attempt at ingratiating himself with Stano, making it seem they shared a common bond.

"Yeah, she started bitchin', bitchin' real bad," said Stano.

"So, what did you do? Did you hit her?" Crow asked casually.

"Yeah, I popped her," Stano answered offhandedly.

"Hard?" asked Crow.

"Yeah, real hard, like this." Stano balled up his fist and swung it for emphasis.

"Were you still riding along in the car?" It was now Gadberry's turn.

"Yeah, we must have been out Mason a ways by then." Stano looked straight at Gadberry.

"Then what?" said Crow. "Did you hit her again?"

"God damn, she made me mad," said Stano, his face starting to flush a bit. "Who did she think she was, better than me?"

"Then what did you do?" Crow continued.

"I reached under the seat of my car and got out my knife; then I let her have it," said Stano.

"What do you mean, 'let her have it'?" Crow was now prepared to escalate the interrogation.

"I hit her, hard. We were driving along and I hit her in the chest; then she fell over on the seat so I hit her again, this time in the back."

"Was she saying anything?" asked Crow.

"Yeah," said Stano. "She was mumbling something, gurgling a little."

"Did she try to get out of the car?" Crow asked.

"Yeah, but I wouldn't let her," Stano replied.

"No? How did you stop her?" Crow sensed he was getting close. "Now, Jerry you got a little carried away didn't you? You know, Jerry, she was a strong gal, she could be a real bitch when she wanted to be," the officer said, appearing to sympathize with the suspect.

Stano showed his anger. "You're damn right! I got my knife and stabbed her in the thigh, and then I hit that bitch in the chest."

Crow was still building his rhythm. He wanted to know about the slash in the thigh.

"That's pretty good! How did you do that?" He appeared to praise the work of the killer.

"I hooked her with the knife and pulled her back toward me," Stano answered, almost like a commentator at a wrestling match.

This was just what Crow had been waiting for, the reference to the leg injury.

It had been a closely guarded fact in the case that Mary Carol's femur bone had been broken by the force of a blow. That information had been carefully kept from the press and was known only to investigators working on the case.

Crow realized he was breathing a little more deeply, swept up in the moment by Stano's story. Small beads of perspiration were dotting his face. For the first time, he allowed himself a little cautious optimism.

Gadberry and Crow had not wanted to intimidate Stano by taping the entire interview, going to great lengths to make it seem like a casual conversation. Now the detectives knew they must follow the letter of the law, to avoid any slipups later, should Stano suddenly develop self-induced memory loss.

Gadberry left the room to get a tape recorder. Crow and Stano sat in stony silence.

FIVE

A Graduation Trip That
Ends Tragically

Then I would go out riding around, and I would find a girl walking, and hopefully she would get into my car, but she would end up making some kind of remark about my weight, music or looks. That would turn me into a different person altogether. I really don't like to talk about that person, cause it gets me very upset.

—Gerald Stano to Kathy Kelly, November 3, 1985

Cheryl Ramona Neal, 19, had come to Daytona Beach to celebrate her high school graduation, but the weekend of fun quickly turned sour.

The pretty brown-haired, brown-eyed high school senior with the open smile from Forest Park, Georgia, had gone to visit her boyfriend and childhood sweetheart, William Meadows. It was Saturday afternoon, May 29, 1976, at approximately 2:00 p.m., and Meadows was staying at the Holiday Inn Boardwalk. The door to Meadows's room was unlocked, and when Ramona walked in, she didn't like what she saw: four other young females, in full party mode. After arguing with a flustered Meadows, Ramona left in a huff and got in the hotel elevator, clad only in a blue bikini with white polka dots and wrapped in a beach blanket. She had $77 in cash on her. William Meadows had not engaged in any unusual activity with any of the four young women, who were just hanging out in his hotel room.

There were approximately fifteen students from Forest Park who'd come to Daytona Beach on May 28, members of the 1976 graduating senior class from Forest Park High School. The idea was to have a good time, marking that milestone of stepping into adulthood.

Nobody saw Ramona Neal again after midnight on Saturday, May 29.

Ramona's girlfriends grew worried when she failed to return to her hotel. They called police to make a report. An officer was dispatched to the Mayan Inn, where Ramona was staying with the two young women in room 601, at 10:30 p.m. The authorities also contacted William Meadows, who confirmed everyone's worst suspicions, that he had not seen Ramona since about 2:00 p.m., Saturday, May 29.

On Monday, May 31, a distraught Jack Neal, Ramona's father, arrived in Daytona Beach. He told police he would be staying at the Embassy Motel on North Atlantic Avenue. The next day, Neal returned to the police station inquiring if there was any further information as to the whereabouts of his daughter, one of his nine children. He also told police that he had relayed all the pertinent information to the state of Georgia and that he would be staying in Daytona Beach for one more day before returning to Forest Park. He left the family's home telephone number.

On Friday, June 4, a sergeant with the Forest Park Police Department contacted three of Ramona Neal's friends. All the girls, including Ramona, were graduates of Forest Park High School in Georgia. According to the girls, Ramona had quarreled with her boyfriend, William Meadows, when she found him with other girls in his room. She had gotten quite upset and left, they stated.

The girls added that they had seen the couple arguing heatedly in the lobby of the hotel that evening, and one of them even implied that Meadows might know more about her disappearance than he was letting on.

Ramona was one of nine children, and she had a twin brother, Ray Neal, who was stationed with the U.S. Marines in San Diego, California. Investigators ran a background check concerning Ramona's habits and associates. From all of this information, they gathered that she was a normal teenager. She did well in school and she liked to sew, and she was a lifelong friend and then childhood sweetheart of William Meadows. Mr. and Mrs. Neal said that, to their knowledge, their daughter had never dated any other boy and that Meadows had never dated any other girl. That sheltered life and having one and only one sweetheart must have added to her anger over the other women she found in Meadows's room. Ramona's personal information was verified later by interviewing numerous fellow students and acquaintances of both her and William Meadows.

For his part, William Meadows provided the police with approximately thirty-two names and telephone numbers of people who could verify his whereabouts and at least an additional ten people who could verify the time element during the day of May 28, the subsequent evening, and May 29, to the morning of May 30. To further prove his truthfulness, Meadows also said he would take a polygraph test in the state of Florida.

By all witnesses' accounts, Ramona Neal had definitely been seen heading toward the picnic area on Ocean Avenue in Daytona Beach at approximately 3:00 p.m. on May 29, 1976. She was also reported to have been seen by two other people at 6:00 p.m. and again at 8:00 p.m. The last person to be contacted supposedly saw Ramona in the elevator at the

Holiday Inn Boardwalk at midnight, on May 29. The Board-walk was a popular spot for young people, with its seaside restaurants, hot dog stands, and a Ferris wheel.

It was weeks later before there was a break in the case. On June 15, Kenneth Gordon, a student, reported finding what appeared to be a body. Investigator Deputy Sergeant Arthur Dees was called to the scene.

Gordon stated that he was traveling on Old Dixie High-way when his motorcycle ran out of gas, and he began to push it down the road until he got to a gas station.

Approximately four-tenths of a mile north on National Gardens Road and Old Dixie Highway, Gordon noticed something in a ditch on the west side of the road. He believed it to be a dead animal until he inspected it more closely and found that it appeared to be a deceased female. He then pushed his motorcycle to the Texaco station at Interstate 95 and U.S. 1 and notified the sheriff's office.

Sergeant Dees took pictures of the crime scene. The body appeared to be that of a Caucasian female, lying approxi-mately ten to fifteen feet down an embankment with her head in a southeasterly direction. An attempt had been made to cover the body with natural growth obtained from the im-mediate area.

Before the body was removed, Sheriff's Captain Howard McBride contacted Dees with the likely name of the victim. She fit the description of a young woman reported missing to Daytona Beach Police: Ramona Neal.

Meanwhile, authorities in Daytona Beach scrambled to obtain medical records. By 8:00 p.m. on June 16, 1976, the medical records as well as dental charts had arrived from Forest Park. There was no doubt the body was that of Cheryl Ramona Neal.

Ramona had been wearing a two-piece blue and white

polka-dot bikini. The halter top was secured in the back and tightly fastened. The bathing suit appeared not to have been disturbed.*

On June 19, 1976, a thorough ground search was conducted in the area where the victim was found. Members of the Halifax Fire Department assisted in combing the remote area for clues.

Shoveling the area, a slug was recovered. It was encrusted and appeared to be from a .38 or .45 caliber weapon.

One year later, in November of 1977, I covered the story of Mary Kathleen "Katie" Muldoon, a twenty-three-year-old student at Daytona Beach Community College. The young woman's lifeless body was found in a water-filled ditch along U.S. 1 at New Smyrna Beach. She had been beaten, shot in the right temple with a small caliber weapon, and drowned.

In hindsight, why hadn't the investigators taken two key pieces of evidence—spent shell casings—and begun to investigate the possibility that the two cases were related?

The problem was the location. City police investigate crimes only within their own jurisdiction, while sheriff's deputies work only in the unincorporated areas of the county. This meant there was often no immediate sharing of information, a fact that hindered the investigation and ultimately helped Stano kill again and again without being captured.

---

* Ramona Neal's polka-dot bathing suit was a key factor in identifying her remains. Because it had been exposed to the elements, however, an investigator hung it on the clothesline at home to dry it out before tagging it as evidence. Unfortunately, a dog ripped it down from the clothesline and took off with it. Luckily, however, the suit ultimately wasn't needed at a trial because Stano pleaded guilty.

And someone had gone to a lot of trouble to make sure Katie Muldoon was never seen alive again.

We published Katie's photo in the paper: a pretty young woman with long brown hair, wearing a sweater and leaning against a brick wall, her arms crossed and a haunting look in her eyes.

Ramona had been looking forward to college. Katie had worked at a restaurant-bar to pay for woodworking classes at the local college. Both Ramona and Katie liked to work with their hands. Ramona liked to sew. Katie's friends reported that she loved the feel of working with wood and had even named her golden retriever puppy Cedar. Her landlord, Ben Taylor, said that she was studious and dedicated, even "austere." Why, then, had someone wanted her dead?

These seemed more like random crimes of opportunity. The killer encountered his victims either alone or in some type of distress or some degree of intoxication, and then he struck. Young women tend to think they are invincible and that they know it all. Little do they consider the ominous presence of the friendly stranger, stalking and waiting and ready to pounce at the slightest opportunity.

Katie had been reported missing five days earlier by Taylor, from whom she had been renting a room for about a month. She had come to Florida from Pennsylvania via a series of foster homes. Her parents had died when she was fourteen, and she was placed with various families until she became of age to be out on her own. Taylor, her landlord, said she was a good tenant.

Ramona Neal had reportedly been drinking heavily after her argument with her boyfriend, William Meadows, not at all an unusual practice for the graduating seniors who flocked to Daytona Beach.

On March 12, 1981, Paul Crow interviewed Gerald Stano about the murder of Ramona Neal. First, the sergeant read him his rights, and then turned on the tape recorder.

Stano had told Crow that he had picked up a "young lady," as he invariably called his victims in his prissy and fastidious way, on the beachside in Daytona Beach.

"Can you tell on what location you found her and what she was wearing on the night in question?" asked the sergeant.

"Err . . . uh . . . the young lady was wearing a blue two piece bikini. She was picked up in front of the Holiday Inn Boardwalk, Daytona Beach, where there's a little picnic grove with a canopy." He almost seemed to be speaking in the third person as he related the events of that night.

Crow then wanted to know what the tone of their conversation had been. Stano said that he asked the girl if she wanted to get a little high. "You know, smoke a little weed, and she said, 'Fine, sure.' And she hopped in the car and I was also drinking at the time. I also had some beers in the car at the time so we were doing a little bit of both."

And then they went for a ride. For Ramona, as with the others who felt comfortable with this stranger, it would be her last.

Stano said they cruised the beach smoking pot and drinking a little bit and then they went to Granada Boulevard and on to Beach Street. Then they drove up to Bulow Ruins, a secluded and idyllic state park, all the while smoking and drinking, according to Stano, and they stopped there.

"What happened after you stopped?" Crow asked.

"Well, I believe I asked the young lady if she wanted to have sex. I say believe because we were both pretty well mellowed out or high at the time, and she started to get a sort of an edgy, pissed off side, and that got me upset and pissed off. And my hand just approached her neck and I strangled her."

With chilling, matter-of-fact delivery, Stano said that his hand "approached her neck," as if it had a will of its own separate from him. "And I also believe, say believe, that I cut her once or twice with a knife I had with me." A bullet was found at the scene where Ramona's body was recovered, although Stano never indicated using a firearm that day.

"I know this has been a long time, Gerald, but you said you cut her." Crow wanted to establish this. "Do you mean stabbed her?"

"Yes."

"Okay, what happened then?"

"I then carried her out of the car and left her up there at Bulow Ruins in a swampy area." Stano always took the victims outside for the kill. He often disabled them inside the car, with sharp blows from his fist, then dragged them to a secluded spot.

"Is there anything specific you did with the body when you laid it down? Think hard, Gerald. It's been, I know, since 1976, but what did you do with the body once you laid her out by the swampy area? Describe that scene to me, if you can." Crow wanted to know about the method of concealment of the body.

"We got out there and, as I said before, I got her out of the car, and put thickets, or weeds, whatever you want to call them, over the girl's body to conceal her from sight from anyone who might happen to pass by."

Crow asked if it had been nighttime. Stano again nodded and said yes.

"Was your car running or was it off?" To the investigator, every piece of the puzzle held a special significance.

"Car was always running and facing the same direction I come in at."

Crow wondered why.

"Just in case there happened to have been anybody left behind me to, eh, find out what I was doing so I could easily leave the scene as fast as I could."

Crow asked if Stano used the same method of conceal-ment with most of his victims.

"Yes, sir!" Stano asserted emphatically, almost with a hint of pride.

Crow then proceeded to show Stano a series of photo-graphs taken at the location where the body was found.

"These photographs that you are looking at are all the bones and the description. Do all those match?"

"Yes, sir, they do," he stated, staring at the photos.

Crow was thinking that the Bulow Ruins were a very long stretch, and he wanted to know if Stano recalled seeing any landmarks.

"What can you recall that could give me a marker, that I could use to help me focus on where this girl was at?"

"I believe I might be able to help you with that," he of-fered, which was his way of using "forced teaming" with the officer by pretending to be on his side. "There was . . . uh . . . two little bridges that . . . uh . . . cross below the ruins. I believe she was . . . uh . . . placed by one of those two little bridges in 1976." Again, "placed," as if he had nothing at all to do with it.

SIX

"Last Dance"

Music I like all types, esp: the oldies, dance music (disco) and todays music of the 80's. I use to like to dance, go for rides, play the organ (which my mother still has), roller skate.

—Gerald Stano to Kathy Kelly, August 15, 1985

When The Pointer Sisters play the following: "Neutron Dance," "Jump" and "Automatic," think of me skating around the rink and dancing too.

—Gerald Stano to Kathy Kelly, April 2, 1986

A *News-Journal* story about the death of a local teenager—Cathy Lee Scharf, whose body was discovered, partly covered by palm fronds, in a drainage ditch near Titusville on January 19, 1974—ultimately led investigators to Gerald Stano.

Cathy Scharf was a pretty seventeen-year-old with long, straight blond hair and big blue eyes. She liked to party, as did most teens her age, and this visit to the Anchor Bar would be her last dance on earth.

Years later, after Stano's arrest, Paul Crow sought me out.

"Can you look and see if there are any other murders around here where the bodies were covered up?"

In the library at the newspaper, darkly dubbed "the morgue" by veteran newspaper reporters, I went through files of clippings. Newspaper librarians laboriously cut and pasted almost every story that appeared in the paper. This, of course, was long before computers meant stories could be found with a few keystrokes.

Flipping back, I found the story we had published on Cathy Scharf, a young woman from Port Orange whose body had been found in the neighboring county, Brevard. Her body, according to the newspaper story, bore several stab wounds to the front and back and had been taken to a remote area, where the killer had placed small branches over it in order to conceal it.

The local police department hadn't handled the Brevard County case, so Crow wrote a letter to the state attorney's office, which in turn sent in a county investigator.

Sergeant Johnny Manis, of the sheriff's office, traveled to Daytona Beach to interview Gerald Stano. Stano had been taken from Florida State Prison and placed in the Daytona Beach Police Department Jail under court order at the request of Crow so that he could be questioned.

Crow told investigators in Brevard that Stano had written him two letters, requesting to talk with him and "clear up some homicides." Stano was then serving three life sentences for the murders of Nancy Heard, Toni Van Haddocks, and Mary Carol Maher, to which he had pleaded guilty. But Daytona Beach was out of Brevard's jurisdiction, and the interview was now conducted by Manis.

After he arrived at the Daytona Beach Police Department on August 11, 1982, Sergeant Manis contacted Crow to set up the meeting with Stano. Several people were present when Stano was read his rights, and then waived them.

Just before the interview, investigators had uncovered

the physical evidence tying Stano directly to Cathy Scharf's murder.

On June 9, 1982, Lieutenant J. Bolick, also of the Brevard County Sheriff Department's Homicide Unit, traveled to Union Correctional Institute in Raiford, Florida, for the sole purpose of getting an article of clothing belonging to Stano.

On July 22, 1982, the clothing taken from Stano was used in an attempt to place his scent at the scene of the homicide of Cathy Lee Scharf. The dog used in this track was Harrass II, owned by John Preston, of Preston Kennels, Galeton, Pennsylvania.

Preston scented Harrass II on items of Stano's clothing by having the dog sniff it closely. Harrass II pricked up his ears and immediately went to check the precise area where everyone was standing. Then the dog sauntered east on a small trail through the underbrush, where the suspected killer had probably walked. Harrass II kept walking, haltingly panting and sniffing, east on the trail for approximately one-half mile to a spot where the body was found, approximately eight years prior, on the opposite side of the canal. He attempted to cross the canal, but became frustrated by the heavy underbrush on the other side, and could not advance any further.

The posse decided to terminate the track until the north bank of the canal could be cleared. On July 24, 1982, agents returned to the site with the large dog.

Harrass II was scented on the clothing of Stano again, and he immediately waded across the canal to the north side. The dog checked the cleared area, and on three different occasions it returned to a spot on the canal bank where Cathy Scharf's body had been found on January 19, 1974.

Mr. Preston, the dog's handler, pointed the spot out, and

confirmed that Stano's scent was most predominant in that area. He was then told that he'd indicated the exact spot where the body had been found.

There were several other law enforcement officers present as Sergeant Johnny Manis began his tape-recorded interview with Gerald Stano.

"Okay, the particular case we want to talk about today was one that occurred in 1978. It had to do with a girl who was picked up on Cocoa Beach. If you uh . . . would kind of start where you came from, what you did, and so forth . . ."

Stano seemed oblivious to the presence of the others in the room and started what he appeared to treat as a "day in the life," another day that would end yet another life.

"Well, in '78 I was living in the Derbyshire Apartments in Daytona Beach, and I was driving a 1973 Plymouth Satellite." He cleared his throat. Stano always took great pride in the cars he drove, which he described in great detail. "I was proceeding to pull out of the apartments. I heard the nicest place would be the Anchor Bar on Merritt Island." He mentioned that he had dressed up for the outing because he didn't "want to look like the average run of the mill bum." So he had put on a light blue leisure suit with a blue multi-colored silk shirt.

"I am no slouch when it comes to clothes," he later bragged.*

"I used to fold the sleeves back over the sleeves of the jacket," he told investigators in 1982. Those were the days of the popular television show *Miami Vice*, and Stano entertained many fantasies about his fashionable appearance.

"I always used to wear a gold chain around my neck, a

_____
* Gerald Stano to Kathy Kelly, January 19, 1986

gold ring on my right hand, and also a gold Timex digital watch with a gold ID bracelet," he said. "And after I had done all that, I proceeded to go south and went out to U.S. 1. The reason I go down U.S. 1 is because uh . . . being an alcoholic, which I'm using a word, a true word for myself, I used to uh . . . go down that way because there were more stops, more . . ."

"Beer stops?" Manis deduced.

"Yeah, beer stops on the way down; 95 is kinda dry. And I went down U.S. 1 to State Road 520, which is I believe uh . . . Cocoa Beach, Merritt Island and Titusville exit. Then uh . . . I went towards the beach, went towards Merritt Island." He cleared his throat again. "Excuse me, and I went down 520 all the way down to the Anchor Bar."

He said he arrived at the Anchor Bar after dark, because he got there just before the musical show started, at around 9:00 p.m. or so.

"Okay, do you remember what you were drinking at the bar?" Manis asked over Stano's whistling, perhaps a tune he had heard at the bar on the night in question.

"Uh . . . probably uh . . . probably Jack Daniel's and Coke, or a beer, one of the two because that's all I drink."

"Okay, you are sitting at the bar. Tell me what happened from there."

"Okay, the show started and this young lady got up to dance, and I watched her dance. She looked pretty, you know pretty cute in my eyes. She kinda struck a fancy to me, and after she got done dancing, she mingled with the crowd. After she'd go back, she'd change." Stano did not explain what he meant by "change," and Manis didn't ask.

The sergeant now inquired whether the young woman appeared to be inebriated.

"Oh yeah! She was tipping the glasses or whatever, I guess." Stano let out a laugh.

When prompted by the officer as to the kind of clothing the girl was wearing, her abductor described her attire with a critical tone in his voice.

"She had a uh . . . nice pair of pants on, nice blouse; she wasn't dressed shabbily. She was not your, uh, highly sophisticated way the girls wear." He added that she was wearing some jewelry that looked like "Indian jewelry."

"Do you remember what age she may have been?"

"Roughly between 19 and 23."

"Did she ever indicate that she might be a hooker, that would go out for money or anything like that?"

He coughed. "Excuse me. Something, part of her wanted to, it looked to me. Part of her looked, you know, like she might be like that. The other part didn't, you know, her personality, the way she handled herself." That was the usual fantasy dichotomy he projected with his potential victims.

"She never approached you for any favors for money or anything?"

"No, nothing like that. For a little drink, though."

"She wanted a drink?"

"Oh man!" He whistled for emphasis, then laughed, unaware as to where the interview was headed and just reveling in the moment. "I remember I was pretty well gone by then, and I just told the bartender that was there to go ahead and give the young lady a drink."

"Okay, all right, after you struck up a conversation with her, did you dance with her?"

"I believe we did, I believe we did. Because I like, I like music, I like to get out there and dance a little bit when I'm loaded and I know I gotta drive. That helps, you know, sober me up a little bit."

"Then what did you do?"

"I said, 'Hey let's go for a little ride,' and she said yeah, and we left the bar together. We get in the car, we went west to U.S. 1. Well, before I got to U.S. 1, my car had a uh . . . tendency to pull into ABCs by itself, with a little help from me." He chuckled again, a self-deprecating laugh; and the account of the trip to the liquor store was told with utter detachment, as if his actions had nothing to do with him. "And I pull in there and got a . . . another six-pack."

"After you bought the six-pack, did you continue west of 520?"

"We come to the intersection of U.S. 1 and . . . By that time she was talking pretty good and I was too, and I just made a right-hand turn and went on my merry way on U.S. 1 going north, but it was a little way up, and the heated argument started."

"What was that about?"

"Oh slightest drop of a pin I guess, at that time." The interview was finally leading up to the juncture where, as Manis by now realized, there would be that trigger, the one that made Gerald Stano snap and turn into what he called "Jerry the serial-killer." "Because we're both dipping into the six-pack, and uh, I pulled over the side of the road; I just lost my senses and I killed the young lady."

Stano said he had a gun in the car but that it wasn't his, that he had borrowed it from a friend. He said it was a .22, a six-shot revolver.

"I pulled off, you know, like I had a little car trouble. We just pulled off and I had the gun out of the glove box. It was loaded, all six chambers were loaded, and I uh . . . I pulled the gun out and I said, 'This is the end of the line.'" His face became distorted. Cathy Lee Scharf must have been paralyzed with fear.

"Is she out of the car, the girl?"

"Uh . . . she's getting ready to get out of the car. I said, 'Let's go.' By then I reached over and unlocked the door, and both of us got out on her side."

"After you both got outside, did you walk to the back, or the front, or . . ."

"Well, the passenger side was left open, and I took her down at gunpoint a little way, so that the car traffic couldn't see us. And from there I uh . . . proceeded to pull the trigger, I believe several times." And again, a different method of murder from most of the other victims, who met their fate by being drowned, strangled, or stabbed.

"Did she ever say anything that you remember? After you shot her the first time, for instance?"

"Not really. I don't know. No she didn't say anything."

Manis breathed in and out slowly as he mused about what Stano would recall. *Oh, she must have said something. She had to have said something. What had she said to him?*

"All right, afterwards, what did you do with her? Did you just leave her on the side of the road, or did you shove her off to the side?"

"She was laying down on her side, ways off the road, and I uh . . . proceeded to go due north again."

"You remember how much you had to drink by this time?"

"Whoa!" He whistled. "A good amount, a good amount because, I don't know. Too much!" He laughed. "Too, too much, because I know I was sick on the way home; I had to stop a couple of times, because I was sick on the way home."

At some point, he must also have thrown her purse in a trash can, where it was later recovered.

"Okay, then you went, found your way to U.S. 1 back to the Derbyshire Apartments. Do you remember having sex with this girl?"

"Some, some of them. Some of the girls I did, and some of them I didn't." He shrugged.

Although Stano had confessed to forty murders and was serving three life sentences at the Florida State Prison after pleading guilty to three of the murders in Volusia County, it was this homicide, that of seventeen-year-old Cathy Lee Scharf, in Brevard County, that would bring him to trial for first-degree murder and eventually send him to the death chamber. After two trials, he was convicted of first-degree murder on December 2, 1983, and sentenced to death. In the case of the forty murder confessions, there was a conspicuous lack of physical evidence, making it impossible for jurisdictions in Florida to prosecute.

Sergeant Manis was ready to conclude his interview with Gerald Eugene Stano.

"Can you think of anything else that may have happened in this particular case that I haven't asked you, that you can remember that kind of stands out about this particular girl, anything at all?"

Again, Stano's remorseless detachment came through.

"Not really, except she was a heck of a dancer."

SEVEN

Inside the Mind of the
Lead Investigator

Meeting one of Satan's children is a feeling I can't put into words.

—Sergeant Paul Crow

Paul, your [sic] right about you and I having the inside track of the real me. But, I am covering it with Kathy too. People would fall over if they knew what type of real relationship we have.

—Gerald Stano to Paul Crow, September 4, 1985

In 1984 there were several serial killers that hit the FBI's radar screen at the same time: John Wayne Gacy, Wayne Williams, Ted Bundy, Gerald Stano, and Gary Ridgway, later to be identified as the Green River Killer.

After Stano was arrested and subsequently indicted for murder, Paul Crow, the Florida detective sergeant, received an urgent call from the Green River Killer Task Force in Washington State, asking him how he had managed to "get" Stano.

They had one suspect in mind, who turned out to be Gary Ridgway, except by the time they caught up with the "real" Green River Killer, the department had spent more than $1 million and shrunk to one man: Sheriff Dave Reichert, who later became a congressman. The capture of the Green River Killer took twenty years.

Law enforcement officers were ill-prepared then to track down serial killers who were constantly on the move and used different methods to kill their prey. Establishment of DNA testing—a critical tool to link cases—was years down the road. There was Wayne Williams, the child murderer in Atlanta; Ted Bundy in the Pacific Northwest, the West, and Florida; and Gerald Stano. John Wayne Gacy, who killed and tortured young men and posed as a pillar of his community near Chicago, also surfaced at the time. So it was Williams, Bundy, Gacy, the Green River Killer, and Stano converging. "It was like five aircraft crashing overhead at once."

A few years earlier, in 1979, then sergeant Crow had been selected by the FBI to attend its profiling school in Quantico, Virginia, headed by John Douglas. Agent Robert K. Ressler was also a lead instructor. The Central Florida investigator compared the experience to being invited to study at Harvard.

He had the opportunity to gain different and new skills, such as handling the interview process, which he had previously gathered by sheer instinct. "I have always tried to befriend the person," he said, referring to his relationship with the suspects. "I try to find some common ground with them, and try not to show any emotion about what they did. That way, they relax and feel comfortable." This made it much easier to extract a confession.

At the bureau's profiling school, the sergeant studied with John Douglas, the pioneer investigator who would eventually cowrite *Mind Hunter*. Crow remembered that Douglas "liked to play mind games" and that he was a "very dapper dresser."

Another instructor, Robert K. Ressler, who coined the term *serial killer* and later founded and headed ViCAP (Violent Criminal Apprehension Program), was different. "He looked like he had just gotten off the midnight shift, which was odd because his mind was sharp and he did not miss a beat." The older investigator reminded the sergeant of TV's Columbo, played by Peter Falk, who was always dressed in an old trench coat and going back to ask more and more questions until he completely wore out his suspect. "He always appeared to be confused," Crow said about Ressler, "but he had his radar on all the time." Whereas Douglas had more of a pit bull style, the Florida investigator recalled, Ressler was more laid-back, and the two worked best as a team. In retrospect, Paul Crow looked upon the "nightmare," as he put it, that was Gerald Stano, and how casually he talked to him about crimes that brought such pain to so many.

The seasoned detective knew that he had to tread into that territory very carefully.

"Meeting one of Satan's children is a feeling I can't put into words," Crow would later say, referring to Stano. "One side of me gets mad as hell remembering how casual he was about the murders, like they were no big deal at all."

No one ever wins was his conclusion. The parents don't win, the relatives don't win, and obviously, the victims never did.

Paul Crow did enjoy a Pyrrhic victory of sorts with Gerald Stano's admission of guilt. And although he would wait patiently for his answers, engaging in small talk with his subject until he was willing to be forthcoming with the information at hand, at times the investigator would also reach the end of his rope, as in the case of two unidentified victims. He and Stano had already established a rapport, and at some point during the course of that particular interview, the detective said, point-blank:

"I'm getting tired of talking to you, Jerry. Just where are we with this thing?"

Stano replied, flatly: "About 90 percent."

And then, after Crow prodded him with, "Where else should I look?" Stano answered, succinctly, "Gainesville. It was in Gainesville. There was two of them, two girls. One had a pair of boots on, so I could run her down. The other one had a gypsy outfit on and she didn't have a chance." And then the two men just silently stared at each other.

From Stano's savage attack on Donna Marie Hensley, the prostitute who escaped from his grasp and led Detective Jim Gadberry to the short-order cook, Sergeant Crow was able to determine that the killer had become, as he put it in the profiling lingo, "disorganized" once he "went inside." By his own admission, he forced some of his victims out of his car so they wouldn't leave any traces of evidence; others met death right in the front seat, by a severe pummeling or stabbing. Completing the murder inside the car or apartment or whatever the case might be was what tripped up Ted Bundy, finally, when he went from "organized" to "disorganized" serial killer. Bundy had gone "inside," to the Sigma Chi Sorority house in Tallahassee. Stano had taken Donna Marie Hensley back to the seedy motel room she called home in Daytona Beach.

What Crow did know was that, like Bundy, Stano was also, in his own way, a "charmer." Even though he was not good-looking like the suave, smooth-talking law student from Seattle, Stano dressed well, wore cologne, and his approach was friendly; he talked a good talk. The detective also recognized that these killers killed quickly, within fifteen minutes of having a victim in their cars.

Crow believed that Stano, like Gary Ridgway—who would eventually admit that he thought of killing women as his "career"—was not a part-time serial killer but had probably been at his "job" for quite a long time. It was the only job that he would ever truly hold.

Just like with the women he couldn't keep unless he snatched them and killed them, Stano had never been able to stay at one job for very long. That may have been one of many reasons for his sense of restlessness, and the rage that festered and grew inside him.

Looking at Stano's patterns of behavior earlier on, Paul Crow instantly detected what he had in common with other serial killers: a penchant for being cruel to animals, setting fires, and pulling malicious pranks, such as throwing rocks from an overpass to cars driving below. He also was teased by his fellow classmates. Another part of the pattern was the lying, the cheating, and the stealing.

A major factor was his sense of abandonment, first by his biological mother, then by his adoptive parents when they were no longer able to cope with his shenanigans at home and shipped him off to his grandparents.

And the adoptive father was violent toward him, Stano would complain. He admitted that he was deathly afraid of the elder Stano.

Crow wanted to be sure he had given Stano every chance to be truthful during the hours of interrogation. It seemed highly unlikely Stano wasn't the killer, given the amount of detailed information he had provided, but the detective sergeant wanted to give him one last chance.

Bluntly, he said, "Jerry, after this is sealed we'll never be able to speak again, so I'll work as hard as I can with you to get out of this thing. If you didn't do any of these things, tell me that."

He said, "No, we'll leave it alone."

Gerald Stano had killed about fifteen young women on the west coast of Florida alone, but those police departments did not cooperate with the news ban proposed by the Daytona Beach Police Department and released all pertinent information to the *St. Petersburg Times* prematurely. The true total number of victims, some unidentified, some never found, may never be known.

There was also the issue of multiple crimes and case overload. At the same time that Crow was working the first murder Stano was linked to after his arrest—Mary Carol Maher—he was also investigating a serial rapist case, at the Derbyshire Apartments complex. Coincidentally, Stano had once lived there and later encountered one of his victims, Susan Bickrest, in the parking lot.

The only rape victim who could identify her assailant was a topless dancer who was also bisexual. Crow didn't care who or what the women were or what they did. The bottom line, he felt, was that "the S.O.B.," meaning the rapist, "had done seven others in the area." Those issues alone, however, the ones casting a shadow over the character of a victim, could become an uphill challenge for any prosecutor. Unfair, but sadly true.

In this case, the victim who escaped the serial rapist had been approached by the suspect at the bottom of the stairs of the apartment complex. He was posing as a security guard and began by telling her to be careful. This was a ruse very similar to one that Ted Bundy used, sometimes pretending to be a police officer, like he did with one young woman at a mall, whom he approached telling her someone had broken into her car.

The would-be rapist attempted to assault the victim, but she was a physically strong woman who turned the tables on her attacker, beating him until he fled. Crow identified two different approaches and styles in the attacks: the anger rapist, who came on strong and got angry and violent, or the con approach of the "security guard," who pretended to "protect" the victim.

Paul took the case of the serial rapist to the press, releasing a composite sketch of the man terrorizing women. Ironically, he turned out to be the night-shift security guard at my newspaper. This would be at least the second person who worked there—Stano was the first—who showed a proclivity for violence against women. How often had he urged my fellow workers to "be careful" as they walked to their cars on a dark night?

Gerald Stano had used both styles in each of his attacks. First he would befriend or "rescue," as it were, a prospective victim, and then he would strike, relentlessly, with the stealth and fury of a shark.

This was similar to the strategy that Stano had used on Mary Carol Maher, the champion swimmer who was in top physical shape, and also during his attack on Donna Marie Hensley, the prostitute. Full force, and then, the overkill. Except that Hensley was able to get away.

Paul Crow believed that Stano suppressed a dangerously high level of anger and frustration toward women. As with most serial killers, his attacks were not about sex, but about power and control. Although he also had a highly developed sex drive, most of the time he could not perform, since he was a long-term alcoholic and used drugs for a period of time. His ex-wife rarely wanted to engage in sex with him, Stano would tell the psychiatrists who evaluated him. Did he use the knife, as he did with Hensley and Maher, as a phallic symbol of penetration?

During the interview that he conducted with Jerry Stano after his arrest for the attack on Hensley, Paul Crow let Detective Jim Gadberry do most of the talking because he wanted to watch how Stano phrased his answers, and also his body language. He noticed that when Stano was telling the truth, he would lean his body forward and place his elbows on the table. When he was not telling the truth or leaving something out on purpose, he would push away, fold his arms, and lean back in his chair, appearing to seem confused.

For the case of Mary Carol Maher, Crow had a two-hour sit-down with his detainee before he was able to extract a full confession. Finally, the killer's take on how he had inflicted the stab wound to the girl's leg unfolded as follows: she tried to get out of the car, and he hooked her in the thigh and pulled her back inside the car. She then fell forward, and he stabbed her a couple of times in the back. Then, he said, "The bitch started bleeding all over my car floor, so I took her out behind the airport and dumped her; then I went home and cleaned my car out."

For Mary Carol, hers was clearly the typical case of being in the wrong place at the wrong time. She was at a beachside hotel at the dance floor upstairs. She was a regular at the popular spot for young people. She had won several gold medals for swimming in her high school. She was a perfectly normal teenager, exemplary even: Daytona Beach's golden girl. And then she was murdered for no reason at all.

Like some of the other notorious serial killers, Stano took trophies. He would take the young women's purses, ankle bracelets, or driver's licenses. Crow was certain that he kept them all in a particular place. Stano even told him, on one occasion, "Some day, we will go there."

In the cases of all of the girls who had fallen prey to Gerald Stano, the investigator from Daytona Beach had kept in mind a sound piece of advice once offered to him by a friend, well-known criminal defense attorney F. Lee Bailey: "When you ask a question, know the answer."

Paul Crow already knew all the answers with Gerald Stano.

The only time Crow saw Stano shed a tear was when he took detectives to the location where he had left Mary Carol Maher. "It still smelled, but he walked us to the place and stopped, and then he turned, like he did so many times with other victims, and pointed to the exact spot. I really feel that was the moment he knew it was over."

Sometimes, a person is said to "blink" when caught in the act, and when they know there is no turning back.

To Paul Crow, that was the only time that Gerald Stano "blinked."

EIGHT

The Haunted House in New Smyrna Beach

Well, I had just been fired from the Burroughs' Corporation in Paoli, Penn., and I wanted to be alone for a while. So, I got into my 1973 Plymouth Duster: (green over green with avenger 60's and slotted disk mags, 3 speed on the column, and a beautiful stereo system. It was also jacked up in the back with air shocks). I made it as far as Holly Hill Plaza, where I wanted to buy a few tapes for my car. While in the parking lot, I saw a Duster's hood up, and thought I would help. It turned out to be a young lady with a Duster like mine, but only an automatic. Hers was blue on the bottom with a white vinyl top. She had a dead battery, so I took my jumper cables and gave her a jump start.

—Gerald Stano to Kathy Kelly, October 21, 1985

When it comes to ghost hauntings and paranormal activity, New Smyrna Beach is the place to go! This laid-back beach town is located on Florida's east coast, nestled between Daytona Beach and Cape Canaveral. Originally inhabited by Timacuan Indians for more than 2,000 years, many of the legends and hauntings in New Smyrna Beach are connected to this tribe.

One of the most notorious places for close encounters with the other side is Flagler Avenue. The best way to get up close and personal with these entities is to participate

*in the New Smyrna Beach Historical Ghost Tour. This
90-minute guided tour is led by Susan Thompson, re-
nowned psychic medium and spiritual guide. It begins at
twilight and is filled with mystery and intrigue.*

*The tour consists of numerous places along Flagler
and the surrounding area which are believed to be
haunted. Breakers Restaurant is one of those locations.
According to Thompson, the female spirit who frequently
visits this popular beachside restaurant was burned to
death in a hotel fire across the street. Many Breakers
patrons report seeing her image in the restaurant's upstairs window.*

*Continuing west on Flagler, the next stop on the ghost
tour is a tiny abandoned restaurant, which had previously been a home. This location is believed to be haunted
by the spirit of the man who used to live in the house. Just
walking by the location in broad daylight sends shivers
up my spine. At twilight, it's the freakiest stop on the tour.*

*There is a negative energy that surrounds this build-
ing that feels as if it is pushing you away. I attempted to
walk up to the broken out windows and take a peek inside, but became so freaked out by the energy that I practically ran away from the building. Creepy!*

*The next stop on the tour is known as Bauer's House.
Although this house is in extremely poor condition, you
can tell that at one point in time it was quite a magnifi-
cent home. It's a huge two-story house with French doors
and a large porch. According to Susan Thompson, the
Bauer family resided in this home during the 70s. The
family consisted of the mother, father, and their son and
daughter, who were twins.*[*]

---

[*] February 26, 2008, by Kathy Browning, Associated Content. Reprinted courtesy of Kathy Browning.

In 1973, Barbara and Burt Bauer were the seventeen-year-old twins who called this once grand residence their home.

Barbara Anne Bauer was a cheerleader, popular in school, and on the honor roll. She was vivacious and outgoing. She and her twin brother were inseparable, except for one sunny September afternoon when Barbara drove to Daytona Beach to pick out fabric to make her cheerleading outfit.

The pretty teenager with long sun-bleached brown hair had driven her Plymouth Duster out of the garage of the family's sprawling two-story house on the afternoon of September 6, 1973. She was dressed casually for her shopping trip in cutoff blue jeans, sandals, and a T-shirt bearing the logo "OHIO STATE."

Hours passed and Barbara did not return home, never to be seen again by her family and setting off a months-long search.

Her mother, Audrey, became frantic and phoned all of Barbara's friends, who confirmed that Barbara had told them that she was planning to drive to Holly Hill Plaza in Daytona Beach, at Nova Road and Mason Avenue, to a fabric shop there.

Her mother then called the New Smyrna Beach Police Department and was told to consider the possibility that her daughter had run away. Like so many other parents, Audrey Bauer assured the responding officer unequivocally that her daughter wouldn't leave of her own free will without telling her parents.

Mrs. Bauer waited the required forty-eight hours, then filed a missing person report at the Volusia County Sheriff's Office on Flagler Street at New Smyrna Beach on September 9. The teenager's name was officially entered into a police report as missing, whereabouts still unknown three days after she had left on a simple shopping trip. Audrey Bauer described the clothing that Barbara had been wearing when she left home and reported that her daughter was last seen on September 6 at 3:30 p.m. at the Hancock's Fabric Shop in the Holly Hill Plaza, a busy shopping center at a major intersection on Daytona Beach's mainland. She was driving a 1973 powder blue Plymouth Duster, and the front tag had the name "BURT" in black with silver letters.

Mrs. Bauer further stated, "My daughter is not a runaway. She went to Hancock's to purchase fabric for her cheerleader's uniform, which she definitely did, and she hasn't been seen since."

For his part, Albert Bauer, a prominent local veterinarian known to everyone as simply "Doc," asked that investigators talk to a few persons he considered to be of interest.

Despite widespread news coverage in Barbara's hometown, a full seven months passed before the first break in the case came from Starke, a town about a two-hour drive from Daytona Beach, northwest of Gainesville. At 12:28 p.m. on April 10, 1974, Jimmy Green, jailer and dispatcher on duty at the Bradford County Jail, received a telephone call from Lillie Browning, fifty-nine, who lived just east of South Road 100. Mrs. Browning stated that her husband, Clifford Browning, had found what appeared to be a human skull near their home, in a wooded area. Green then notified Chief Deputy Robert Green, who in turn notified Sheriff Dolph Reddish. At 2:21 p.m., Mrs. Browning left her home with the officers to show them the skull.

The first thing officers did was examine the scene for further clues. During the preliminary search, they discovered that the area surrounding the skull contained the remains of a human skeleton. The investigators took photographs and then removed the remains: two leg bones, a skull, and then the rest of the skeleton. They placed the parts in bags, and then inside a cardboard box.

The skeleton had been located under a dead branch, broken from a crape myrtle bush about twenty feet away. The bones were partially covered with only pine needles from last winter's shedding. A small nylon string appeared to be tied around the rib area. The team also found the lower part of the jaw, teeth, finger bones, hip joint, vertebrae, and ribs. In addition, officers recovered one sandal, three rings, one locket and chain, one gold earring for a pierced ear, one pair of shorts, and a shirt.

After completing their investigation at 5:55 p.m., the officers returned to the Browning residence. The officers asked the Brownings if they could recall anything suspicious or unusual that had happened over the past few months.

Mrs. Browning was the one who spoke. "Well, before they closed the dump road, me and my husband would [often] hear yelling, screaming and carrying on in the vicinity of where he found the skeleton," she began. "You see, some hippie type young people go to the area at night to party."

Mrs. Browning also recalled that during the season of winter collard green planting, she and her husband had heard what sounded like screaming between 6:00 and 8:00 p.m. "I heard the person scream, 'Don't hit me no more!'" she said. Her husband came to the house from the field and also heard the person scream, "Don't do it anymore!" Mr. Browning was going to get his rifle to see what was going on, but Mrs. Browning dissuaded him.

On April 11, 1974, about 2:45 p.m., a Florida Department of Law Enforcement agent noticed the picture of a missing person on the bulletin board of the Bradford County Sheriff's Office, in Starke, Florida. Studying the picture, he realized the white female, age seventeen, from New Smyrna Beach, was a girl he had read about, Barbara Bauer. The flyer indicated that she had pierced ears and had been wearing a shirt with "OHIO STATE" printed on it, and cutoff blue jean shorts.

The agent placed a call to the New Smyrna Beach Police Department.

Barbara Bauer wore a locket engraved with the letter *B* around her neck, along with leather sandals with the big toe in a loop, a class ring in yellow gold with an *S* on the top and sides, and a turquoise ring. She had perfect teeth and a deformed toe on her left foot that was turned inward.

Lieutenant Chuck Nelson tried to contact Audrey Bauer but was unable to reach her. Later, he placed another call to the Bauer residence, and Mrs. Bauer's niece said that her aunt was not at home at the moment but that she would have her contact Deputy Don Denton in Bradford County.

Mrs. Bauer called back a short time later, and Deputy Denton requested she come to Starke to identify other personal effects he believed belonged to her daughter.

At this point, Mrs. Bauer seemed to remain unfazed by the exchange, apparently still stunned in disbelief. After all, her daughter Barbara had only driven across town to a shopping mall in the middle of the afternoon. How did she get so far away, and what happened to her?

Audrey Bauer, however, agreed to be at Starke early the following morning, on April 13, 1974.

When Mrs. Bauer arrived at the Bradford County Sheriff's Office, she was shown several items recovered from the crime scene for purposes of identification. But from the outset, investigators realized she was not going to believe for one minute the items could have belonged to her daughter.

When Deputy Denton showed her the first item, an earring, she simply blinked, and then replied, stoically, "It could be, but I don't think it is Barbara's. She had several pairs."

Then, upon glancing quickly at a chain-link ring: "She

had about a thousand rings and I can't remember all of them but I have never seen that one." That simply meant, to the detectives, that the mother's denial ran as deep as to imply that she had mentally cataloged all the many rings in her daughter's jewelry box.

Audrey Bauer responded in much the same manner about the rest of the rings, and then Denton showed her a locket with the *B*. "That definitely is not Barbara's." She shook her head emphatically. "She had on a gold-colored necklace with the zodiac sign of Leo on it. The only locket she ever wore is a heart-shaped one of mine that I gave her."

The mother was even more vehement about the one shoe found at the scene. "No, that is not hers. She had a pair of sandals similar to these but they had been at the house and became mildewed and I threw them out a couple of weeks ago."

Mrs. Bauer did admit that the cutoff shorts could have belonged to her daughter, but not the pocketbook. "No, she wouldn't carry anything like that," she stated. "She was carrying a brown leather shoulder bag."

Looking at the recovered T-shirt forced the first few cracks in Audrey Bauer's stoic demeanor.

At first she tried to fend off the inevitable. "It is like the one she had on, but since you can only determine that it says 'STATE,' it could have been any state name." Real doubt had begun to set in. Deputy Denton then opened up a section of the shirt that revealed the word "OHIO." Audrey Bauer left the room in tears.

Five months later, on September 30, 1974, Patrolman Harmon Weldon of the Valdosta Police Department in Georgia called the Daytona Beach Police Department to report finding Barbara Anne Bauer's vehicle abandoned behind the Azalea Motel at Interstate 75 and U.S. 84.

Six years later, in Daytona Beach, Sergeant Paul Crow remembered that when he had first questioned Gerald Stano about the assault on Donna Marie Hensley, and the murder of Mary Carol Maher, he had also mentioned helping a girl with a vehicle like the one he drove, a Plymouth Duster, when it broke down at Nova and Mason Avenue in Holly Hill.

Within two weeks, Deputy Don Denton, from the Bradford County Sheriff's Office, came to Daytona Beach to interview Stano on August 23, 1982, about the Bauer case. Denton turned on his tape recorder after identifying himself.

"I'm at the Daytona Beach Police Department in Daytona Beach. Present in the room with me is Gerald Eugene Stano. Is that how you pronounce it?"

"Yes."

"And the occasion is to take a statement from Mr. Stano in reference to the disappearance and the death of a white female by the name of Barbara Anne Bauer, who is age 17 at the time of her disappearance. She lived at 214 Flagler Avenue in New Smyrna Beach, Florida. Barbara Bauer was missing from the Daytona Beach area on September 6, 1973. Mr. Stano, do you realize there is a tape recorder player recording our conversation?"

"Yes."

Denton then proceeded to read Stano all of his Miranda rights, with full explanations as to evidence given during an interview and its admissibility in a court of law; his right to an attorney; and, in the case of insufficient funds, the availability of a court-appointed attorney at no cost to the defendant. Stano replied that he understood.

Denton then wanted to make certain that Stano had not been threatened or coerced or promised anything in exchange for a confession. To all of it, Stano, again, said no.

"Do you still wish to talk to me at this time?"

"Yes," Stano replied, flatly. It was a routine he knew too well by then.

"Gerald, I want to ask you first of all to just go back to the best that you can recall of September of 1973 and tell me in your words what you can remember about an incident that took place where Barbara Bauer disappeared in the Daytona Beach area."

Stano went on with great attention to detail, as usual, to recount his vacation at the Imperial Beach Motel, which was owned by the parents of a teenage friend, Sammy Henderson.* Sammy was your typical Florida teenager who loved to hang out at the beach. He was totally unaware of Stano's darker side.

This would be the first—and only—time in which agents heard Stano claim to have had an accomplice. They also would learn that Barbara Bauer knew she was going to die much sooner than she should have.

He and Henderson, Stano continued, were driving through Holly Hill, on the mainland side of Daytona Beach, looking for some parts for Stano's car. They ended up at the Holly Hill Plaza, where, Stano stated, they "noticed a young lady standing there with the hood of her car open."

"And Sammy and I, the young man I was staying with, proceeded to ask her what the problem was and she said that her car wouldn't start. So I climbed in to see if it would turn over and it wouldn't turn over. It was a dead battery. So I brought the cables out of Sammy's car and we jumped the car off and then it started. So I told the young lady, I said, 'Let me drive the car for a while with you in the car and charge up your battery and I will reimburse you for the gas that we use during the process.' So, so as it stands, Sammy

---

* Denotes pseudonym

followed in his car, proceeding out of the parking lot and over Nova Road making a left on Mason Avenue going eastbound towards U.S. 1. Reaching the intersection of Mason and U.S. 1, we made a left hand turn and following behind each other, proceeded north on U.S. 1. Getting to the intersection of somewhere around 95, Sammy took over, but I motioned that we needed gas, so I stopped for some gas. We also picked up some beer on the way along with something to kill the hunger pains that was being driven at that time also. So he said, 'Follow me, follow me for a while.' So . . ."

Barbara Bauer must have felt comforted by the view, in the rearview mirror of her car, of the vehicle right behind them driven by a clean-cut teenager.

Stano related the entire ordeal to which he had subjected Barbara with his usual detachment, a narration that would later be gone over in depth by Assistant State Attorney for Bradford County Tom Elwell, at the Bradford County Court House in Starke, Florida, later that day.

It was 4 in the afternoon when Assistant State Attorney Elwell began to question the defendant. Present were also Deputy Don Denton and Mack S. Futch, another assistant state attorney.

Once again, Elwell advised Stano of all of his rights, explaining every single one. He also asked Stano if he was now under the influence of alcohol or any drugs. Stano said no. He verified Stano's age, thirty, and confirmed his education, which Stano said was comprised of high school, some computer training, and several other courses he never completed.

Elwell then wanted to be sure that Stano could read, write, and speak the English language clearly and that he had not been intimidated or harassed in any way, or promised anything in exchange for his testimony. Stano said no.

And then the attorney made a dramatic statement.

"I believe that you are aware that when Deputy Denton spoke to you the only understanding that you two had was that you could get additional time consecutive to what you are now already serving."

A tired nod from Stano. "Yes."

"But you are now serving three twenty-five year mandatory consecutive sentences." The investigator was referring to the three life sentences Stano received when he pleaded guilty to three of the murders. Serving at least twenty-five years in prison was mandatory with that sentence.

Stano, with his penchant for remembering dates and times and numbers, knew this only too well.

"Which would make your tentative release date somewhere around the age of 105?"

"Yes."

"So the extent of your understanding with Deputy Denton you had was that they would not seek the death penalty but that you could do consecutive time in addition to the time you are serving?" Consecutive sentences, rather than concurrent ones, meant Stano would die in jail, as the stacked jail time would outlive him.

"Yes."

Before proceeding any further, Elwell explained the provision in the agreement of Stano with the state.

"The part that you are required of the agreement and are still required of the agreement is that you truthfully and accurately tell all that you know regarding the death of Barbara Anne Bauer, seventeen years old, white female. Gerald, I am going to ask you to raise your right hand, please."

Stano complied.

"Do you swear and affirm that the testimony and statement that you are about to give is the truth, the whole truth and nothing but the truth so help you God?"

"Yes."

Stano put his hand down.

Stano confirmed details such as the spelling of his name, present and former addresses, and a time in 1973 when he came to Florida on vacation. That was before the family moved there permanently, in November 1973. The attorney then had Stano spell his full name—Gerald Eugene Stano—and give both his present and former addresses. For six years, Stano had moved back and forth from Pennsylvania, staying with his grandparents in Ormond Beach, Florida, for a time while he attended Seabreeze Junior High School, then returned to his home state. Finally, in December of 1973, he came back to Florida and took a job as a stockman at a Jefferson Ward store, where he was fired after six weeks for suspected theft.

But Elwell determined Stano had been in Daytona Beach on September 6, 1973.

"How do you come to be down in this area and away from your residence in Pennsylvania?" asked the attorney.

Stano answered casually. "I took a week's vacation by myself back in 1973 to come down and stay with a friend of mine, who at that time lived at Henderson's Imperial Beach Motel on South Atlantic Avenue in Daytona Beach."

"Who was your friend that either lived there or owned that establishment?"

"It was Sammy Henderson."

Elwell inquired how old this Sammy Henderson was at that time, and Stano stated he was in his late teens. Henderson was about a year and a half younger than Stano, having been born in 1953. Stano proceeded to explain that he had originally met the teen when he had lived in the Daytona Beach area while he attended seventh and eighth grades at Seabreeze Junior High School and lived with his grandparents. "I would spend a weekend at his parents' motel and then he would come over the following weekend and spend the weekend with my grandparents and I at 46 Country Club Drive."

"On September 6, were you with him during the course of that day?" The attorney meant Henderson.

"Yes, I was."

"Do you recall if you were [also] staying at Henderson's Imperial Motel?"

Stano stated that he had, and that Sammy's parents, June and Chuck Henderson,* were the owners of the motel.

When the attorney asked Stano about the sequence of events that took place on the day in question, the defendant relayed that he and Sammy were just "moping around" and doing some chores for the Hendersons during the first part of the day.

"Then we decided that we were going out that evening, just have a night out on the town."

"Did you drive down, did you have a car available?" the attorney wanted to know.

"Yes I did, a 1973 Plymouth Duster with a 6 cylinder engine, with an AM-FM stereo player in it, with Craig or slider disk mags and Rickey Thompson's gator hijack."

"All right," Elwell cut in. It was more information than he had solicited, as if the car were now the crux of the deposition.

Stano stated, however, that he and Henderson went out riding in Sammy's car, which was a 1973 Pontiac convertible. They went to the Holly Hill Shopping Plaza to look for a pair of matching chrome mirrors for Stano's car, and not finding anything he liked, they decided to return later and check out a couple of other places.

"Did you make any purchases while you were in the Holly Hill Shopping Center?" Elwell asked.

---

* Denotes pseudonym

"Only at the Pantry Pride there and that was for a six-pack of beer."

It was 4:30 in the afternoon, both the attorney and his subject concurred. And when Elwell asked Stano where the two went from the shopping center, he answered:

"We started to drive out and encountered a young lady who had car troubles."

Stano added that he believed she was at the Hancock Fabric Shop in the Holly Hill Plaza. He also remembered that the girl's car was a blue 1973 Plymouth Duster.

"How did you remember or know that?" Elwell inquired.

"Because it was similar to mine. Because I had a blue Duster with a white vinyl roof before I got my green one in Pennsylvania."

"Do you know a lot about cars?" asked the attorney, who had been advised that Stano did know his vehicles. He often remembered those details better than any other kind.[*]

"Yes."

"Can you describe what [the girl] looked like?" Elwell asked.

"Oh, I say about 5' 5" or 5' 8" or somewhere between there. Shoulder length hair."

"About that time you were about twenty-two," Elwell pointed out. "Did she look older or younger than you?"

"Uh, I'm not too hot on girls' ages, so give or take a couple of years. I would say younger than I was. I would say late teens or early twenties."

"What appeared to be wrong with her car and what was

---

[*] "I had . . . a light green 1973 Plymouth Duster. It was a small about six engine with a 3 speed on the column, with Avenger 60's with chrome slotted mags and high-jack air shocks, am/fm stereo eight-track, anti-theft door locks, and always in immaculate condition. It even had two chrome mirrors I put on. I was really proud of that car. I got it brand new from Cheltenham Chrysler in Penn."— Gerald Stano to Kathy Kelly, August 29, 1985

she appearing to be doing about it?" asked Elwell, wanting to get the entire picture of when the girl first got in trouble.

"She had the hood of the car up and we pulled over. We had the top down, and we asked her, I leaned up and said, 'What's wrong?' She said, 'My car won't start.' I said, 'Let me give it a try.' She was happy because two guys were going to give her a hand to try to start her car. I immediately got in her car and turned the key and found out it was a dead battery. So Sammy pulled his car around front, broke out his cables out of his trunk and we charged or whatever fast-jumped his car to her car. And we got it started. And I told her, 'Let's charge your battery up a little bit and I drive it a little bit and you ride with me so you won't think I want to steal your car,'" Stano said.

"Her motor had a slight knock coming from it, which didn't sound right to me. So, I locked up my car, and we drove off in her car. It seemed to me she liked the way mine looked. But hers was a mess though."*

Had Barbara Bauer been more street-smart, she would have realized that the helpful stranger was overstepping the mere act of helping a stranded driver. He continued to reassure her, "We will drive it just a little ways. I will make sure your battery is going to hold for you."

"What was on your mind at that time?" Elwell began to direct.

"Hoping to have a little sex with the young lady," Stano said. During the course of the interview, he used the eerie juxtaposition of "sex" and "young lady," as if he were escorting a girl to a picnic.

"Had you and Henderson had any conversations with one another before you came up to the car where this young girl was disabled?"

---

* Gerald Stano to Kathy Kelly, October 21, 1985

Stano nodded. "Yes, we were hoping to find a couple of young ladies that night for a good evening." He then added that he had noticed the girl first and that Sammy hadn't said anything about her until he, Stano, started jumping her car battery.

"He said that she looked pretty cute and he wouldn't mind having a piece of that."

"After her car was started, did she agree to let you drive her car?" The attorney wanted to know if the victim had been forced or coerced in any way.

Stano smiled. "No, as a matter of fact she was very happy because she didn't know much about after you jump-start a car whether it was going to start again after you turn it off or not."

"Is there anything you noticed particularly about her car other than the make and model? Anything about the contents of the car, anything special in the car?"

"There was some red fabric in the back. I'm nuts for red and that caught my eye."

The school colors of New Smyrna Beach High School are red and black. Their mascot is a barracuda.

"Can you tell us more about that red fabric?" Elwell did not want to leave any loose ends.

"It was like a smooth on one side and like a crushed velvet on the other side, something like that."

"How much fabric did there appear to be?"

"Enough to make a blouse or a skirt."

"Where was it located in the car?"

"It was located in the backseat in her car in a bag." Stano motioned as if to place it there.

"Can you tell us more about the bag?"

"It has a Hancock Fabric Shop label on it." Barbara was obviously headed home to sew her cheerleading outfit when her car malfunctioned.

Elwell continued.

"So you got into the car and began driving. Did you say anything to Sammy about going?"

Stano nodded again. "I said, 'Sammy, just follow us a ways while I charge up the battery,' because I noticed that her alternator gauge is running all the way over the C which seems to me that her alternator is bad. And then after a while he came to the normal position after an hour's worth of driving."

"Where did you begin driving in the car with her?" The attorney now wanted to know the exact route.

"We went out Mason Avenue and approached U.S. 1 and went up U.S. 1 and went towards 95," Stano recalled.

"How far from the shopping center and Holly Hill had you gotten?" Elwell now asked.

"Approximately twenty to twenty-five minutes or somewhere around there."

Since most serial killers never wanted to know the names of their victims nor establish any contact with them, the attorney asked Stano: "Did this girl tell you who she was or what her name was?"

"No, she didn't mention any names at all."

It seemed to Elwell that Stano and Barbara had been driving for some time now.

"How long had you been driving before she said something about where you were going?"

"About half an hour. About half an hour later she started saying 'Isn't this . . . don't you think it has been charged up enough? The alternator gauge is reading straight up and down,' and I just said, 'Shut up for a while and let me handle the situation because that could mean your alternator gauge could be off, you know, and we don't want to take any chances.'"

"Where were you when this conversation took place?" Elwell asked.

"We were up around the . . . U.S. 1, up underneath 95. I believe at that time, I believe we went under 95, somewhere around that area at that time."

And again, as the attorney would determine, at no point had there been any personal discussion between Stano and the young woman.

"Did she tell you anything about herself or where she lived?"

The answer was, of course, "No."

"Where was Sammy while you were driving this car?" Elwell asked, since Stano had not mentioned the teenager for quite some time.

"He was following in his car."

Barbara Bauer must have grown suspicious by this time, the attorney surmised.

"Was there any point in time when this young lady no longer wanted to travel in the car with you and wanted you to stop?"

"Yes, when we stopped for gas, because I told her I would put some gas in her car for her so that she wouldn't be left without any gas. We stopped, I stopped at a gas station, and put some gas in it."

"Do you remember where that was?" Elwell was now mapping the entire route.

"Offhand, somewhere up by U.S. 1."

"Did you pay cash for it?"

"Yes," Stano assented.

"What happened there at the gas station?"

"She started getting a little belligerent," Stano remarked, setting the stage for the trigger, the confrontational attitude coming from a young woman that would cause him to snap. Later, he would elaborate. "We talked for a while, then she started to act a little strange. Like she was nervous, and then asked, 'When were we going back for my car?' I believe at that time I hit her with my right hand, and said something like, 'If you do what I say, you won't get hurt.' By that time, I was in a place I wasn't familiar with. She was also complaining a lot at that time, and was getting on my nerves."*

Stano told Elwell, "She looked like she was going to take over driving and she looked like she knew where she was at, and I just reached over and hit her. And I said, 'Just shut up and get in the passenger's seat.'"

"How did you hit her?"

"I hit her with the back of my right hand," he said as he motioned to illustrate the blow.

"Where did you hit her?"

"In the face."

"What did she do?" Elwell asked offhandedly.

"She cringed and started crying a little bit and just went over to her side of the car, crouched by the door, sort of shaking and scared. She didn't know what was going on."

For Gerald Stano, describing Barbara Bauer's last seconds of life meant reliving the moment when he took complete control over another one of his victims.

"Was the car moving at the time you hit her?" The attorney wanted to know how Stano had managed this.

"Yes. We were moving again, just pulling out of the gas station," Stano recited in a monotone.

"Was she saying anything about wanting to get out of the car?"

"Not at that time."

"Was she asking you where you were going?"

"No."

"What was the next thing that happened?"

"Then Sammy said, 'Follow me.'"

Elwell wondered about the accuracy of the statement.

---

* Gerald Stano to Kathy Kelly, October 21, 1985

"Sammy said that?"

"Yes."

"How did he come about to tell you that?"

Stano did not hesitate in his explanation. "He thought that if we got up far enough he would probably get a little sex from her and send her on her way."

Now the sequence of events was becoming problematic for the attorney.

"Did he tell you that?"

"No, I am just assuming that."

Elwell now wanted to make certain. "How did he physically tell you this?"

"He told me, 'Well, look, just follow me a ways. I think we can get to a spot where we can get the young lady to do what we want.'" Again, "young lady" was an expression favored by Stano. Wouldn't it be unlikely that a teen would employ the same expression in referring to a girl? Elwell was a bit puzzled by this.

"When did he tell you this?" he narrowed in.

"When we were getting back into the car," Stano answered.

"Was she present when he was saying that?" Elwell wanted to know if Barbara could hear the lurid exchange.

"Yes," Stano stated.

"Did he say it loud enough so she could hear it?" the attorney now pinpointed.

"I don't think she heard it."

"What is the next thing that happens?" Elwell proceeded with his initial line of questioning.

"Then we went down, we drove, me being green to the state of Florida, around this part of town. It is called the National Gardens. I hadn't been there in a while, around the National Gardens area. I was just following Sammy to where he was driving. And we just drove and drove." There was no mention of what Barbara Bauer was doing during the long drive, so the attorney now wanted to know: "How long did you drive before you eventually stopped?"

"Roughly about an hour or an hour and a half," Stano replied.

Elwell now had to ask: "What was the girl doing at this time?"

"Crying and shaking like a leaf," Stano said, casually minimizing the terror Barbara Bauer must have felt as she waited her fate at the hands of the angry stranger.

"Were you saying anything to her?"

"Just telling her to shut up," he answered in the same tone.

"Did she tell you anything about herself, or where she lived or plead with you to let her out?" Investigators and criminal lawyers strongly believe that the more contact a victim establishes with her killer, the better her chance of survival. But this would not serve Barbara Bauer during her final hours.

"She did ask a couple of times," Stano said, impervious. "She said, 'Look, just let me out of the car and I will hitch-hike back or something or I will walk back, you know just please don't hurt me. Let me out.'"

"Was there ever a time that she could have gotten out of the car while you were driving it?"

"Yes," Stano nodded.

"Without injury to herself?"

He now shook his head. "No, not without injury."

"How fast were you traveling from the time she got into the car?"

"Roughly about 55 to 65." Barbara Bauer undoubtedly was weighing the risks of trying to jump from a fast-moving vehicle or taking her chances and staying put.

"Did you eventually go to a spot or a place?" Elwell said, pushing to resolve how the drive ended.

"We ended up at a dump site. I call it a dump site, where you see a couple of people with pick-up trucks back their trucks with their trash and everything and just start sweeping and pushing it out."

"Did you stop anywhere before you got to this dump to tie her up or to do anything with her?" Elwell realized that the girl had been in this dire predicament for quite some time.

"Before we got there, we stopped, and I hit her again," Stano replied with perfect ease.

"Where did you stop?"

"Some road, I don't know which road it was."

"How did you hit her?"

"The back of my hand but a little harder this time." Stano did not explain why he did this and Elwell did not ask. The attorney was more interested in the girl's reactions and if they would ever elicit any human emotions from her tormentor.

"And what did that do to her?" he asked.

"That kinda brought more tears to her eyes, she kinda froze in her tracks, she didn't know what to expect. Then Sammy came up with some rope."

"Where did he get the rope?"

"Out of his trunk. It looked like some nylon, like you use for Venetian blinds, something to that effect."

"Was it thick rope or thin rope?"

"Mediocre." By that Stano meant that the rope was of medium thickness.

"What color?"

"White."

"What did he say to you when he came up with the rope?" Elwell was still unclear about Henderson's participation in the crime.

"He said, 'Do you want to use this?' I said, 'Yes, that will do good.'"

"Had he seen you hit her?"

"Yes."

"How did he do that?"

"It was when he was coming back that I hit her. He saw it."

"Whose decision was it to stop this time?"

"Mine."

"I stopped the car, and then tied her hands and feet together with either rope or something like that," Stano later said. "I think I choked her till she passed out I thought, and I carried her from the car. I'm not sure if I had sex with her before this happened. Maybe, maybe not."*

Elwell opened his tape recorder, took out the tape that was now full, inserted another tape, and pressed "record." The other assistant state attorney followed suit.

"Mr. Stano, while we were changing the tape, did anybody ask you any questions about this homicide?"

"No."

"Is it not correct that all we did was change the tapes on both tape recorders?"

"Yes."

Elwell now proceeded. "I believe that my question, my last question, was about the type of rope that was used to tie up the young lady. You were telling me that it was white, similar to a Venetian blinds cord."

"Yes, something like a Venetian blinds cord. Something you use to bore a bolt with. Not that thick consistency, a thinner type of rope."

"How long was the piece of rope you used?"

"They were about four feet in length."

"Where was she when you tied her up?" Elwell was still more concerned with Barbara.

"She was in the Duster at that time, in her car."

---

* Gerald Stano to Kathy Kelly, October 21, 1985

"How did you tie her up?"

"I put her hands together and tied her feet together."

"Did you tie her hands in front of her or in back of her?"

"In front of her."

"And her feet, did you bind her legs together or her feet?"

"Yes, around the ankles."

"Was she doing or saying anything at this time?"

"She was struggling at this time."

"Tell me what you mean by struggling." Elwell wanted to get a mental picture of the abuse, as well as Barbara Bauer's mental state at the time.

"She was trying to kick at that time and hit with the hands that were tied together. But Sammy held her hands while I was tying up her feet."

"Did you use a single piece of rope or did you use more than one?"

"Two pieces. One for the feet and one for the hands."

"And Sammy was helping you with this?"

"He was holding her hands because at that time she was trying to beat me on the back, trying to hit with both hands coming down like this," he said, mimicking the girl's motions to illustrate his point.

"When you were hitting her and when you were tying her up, what was on your mind?" Elwell wanted to know.

"Just shake her up a little bit," Stano replied casually. "Just have some sex with her and just turn her loose and send her in her car, and Sammy and I would get in his car and go. But it didn't end up like that."

"Did Sammy talk with you while you were tying the girl up?"

"No."

"Was she screaming?"

"Yes."

"Did you in any way try to prevent her from screaming?"

"Yes I did. I believe I knocked her out. I hit her hard enough to knock her out."

"Where was she seated or lying when you struck her?"

"She was in her Duster at that time when she was knocked out. She was put in the back seat of Sammy's convertible and he put the top up." Stano was using the passive tense again, as if he was not responsible for his own actions.

"Was she tied, hands and feet, when you struck her and knocked her out?"

"Yes."

"How did you strike her? Which hand did you use?"

"With my right hand." Stano lifted his arm to show. "It's got a class ring on the ring finger."

"Was it a full blow? Where did you strike her?"

"In the temple."

Elwell now wanted to get back to the presumed accomplice.

"When you struck her, was Sammy present?" he asked.

"Yes," Stano replied.

"And was he doing anything while you were striking her?"

"He was busy bringing his windows up on his car."

"Did he pull her behind you, in front of you, or to your side?" The attorney wanted to know the position of the second car.

"In front of me at that time."

"About what time was it?"

"It was dark, somewhere around eight or nine o'clock. Between the hours of seven and nine."

Now Elwell wanted to zero in on how many times, and how, Stano had hit Barbara Bauer, knocking her into unconsciousness.

Stano replied, casually again, that he had hit her "a couple of times," recalling he was wearing the same ring he had on now, a gold-plated class ring. Stano added that he and Sammy carried the unconscious Bauer to the back of Sammy's car, and the attorney then asked how the girl was dressed.

"She had on a pair of shorts," Stano described, again, in detail. "Cutoff shorts with a dungaree cut-off, jeans cut off, and a shirt with some writing in front, like one of these colleges, like a Ohio State shirt."

When Elwell asked if there was a number on the shirt, Stano said yes. It had already been established that the number was twenty-one.

The two then drove on for some time again, with Barbara Bauer in the backseat of Sammy's car, Stano said, until they reached the dump site.

"And I reached into the car and she was screaming at this time. I was reaching for her with both hands, but I strangled her in the backseat of the car," he stated.

"Why did you reach in there and strangle her?" Elwell tried to establish motive. With Stano, there usually was none. It was just a matter of silencing and controlling a prey.

"I was reaching up to pick her up and she started to scream and I didn't want anything to be heard so . . . I reached in and just choked her."

"Show us how you did that," prodded the attorney.

"Like that." Stano put his hands together around the width of an imaginary human neck.

"You put both hands on her neck."

"Right."

"And . . ."

"Come round your Adam's apple."

"And she stopped breathing at the time."

Another young life snuffed out by Gerald Stano, just like that.

Then Stano and his presumed accomplice took the body out of the car and disposed of it. "On the road, on the side in the grass area," he explained.

Elwell then inquired about the manner of placement of the body on the ground, to determine if it was like that of his previous victims.

"She was laid on her side," Stano answered, again in the passive tense. "It was like that in all the cases I have here. Their heads are like facing north for some reason."

"Did you do that intentionally?" Elwell asked.

"No, it just seems that the first victim, the way I lay the body down, the body just faces the north direction," Stano said, as if the bodies were still there, where he had dumped them.

The attorney then wanted to know in which direction Stano and Henderson traveled after they disposed of Barbara Bauer and drove off.

"We backtracked out and got on the Interstate 75."

Stano later described it: "When I left her, I believe I covered her like the others were, I'm not sure though. I then thought, I have to leave Florida, and get back to Pennsylvania. My car had slipped my mind till I got to Georgia. I got as far as Valdosta, Georgia, and left her car in a motel parking lot. I went back to the interstate and thumbed a ride back to Florida, and got in my car and left for Pennsylvania."*

Stano had disposed of Barbara's handbag, he said, without even peeking inside. He had enough cash with him at the time. What he did take was the red fabric that was in the back of her car.

_____

* Gerald Stano to Kathy Kelly, October 21, 1985

"I was going to have my girlfriend try to match the material that I had up north," he explained.

"For what?" Elwell asked.

"To see if she could make matching vests because vests were big back then up north."

No matter that this was fabric just bought by a teenage cheerleader whose life abruptly ended after having the misfortune of developing car trouble. Just like that, it became a trophy—an article of clothing for himself, taken from a dead girl.

Elwell then asked Stano where he and Henderson were planning to go.

"Well, what having consumed a good amount of beer I was fixing to go north."

When asked, he said he had had about three-quarters of a case of beer.

Stano added that the two were headed for Georgia. And when Elwell asked if he was working at the time, he answered: "Yes, I was working—I wasn't working. In 1973 I was . . . I had been fired from the Burroughs Corporation and was getting ready to go into the service."

Something about this did not compute with the attorney, who then asked, "Did Sammy have a job?"

"With his parents," said Stano, meaning at the motel.

He added that they then stopped at another motel along the way to get rid of Barbara's car. This was around Valdosta, Georgia, Stano said. The motel's name started with an *A*, "either Aladdin or Alaskan," he added. By then, the investigators knew it was actually the Azalea Motel in Valdosta.

There, he said, they parked both cars, Stano leaving the Duster that Barbara Bauer had been driving when she was abducted, and Sammy his Pontiac, in which he had been following Stano.

From Valdosta, Stano said, he had driven Sammy's car to

the Henderson family motel the following day. The day after, Stano, by his own admission, returned to Pennsylvania.*

"When was the last time you spoke to Sammy or saw Sammy after you left to go home to Pennsylvania?" asked Elwell.

"The last time I spoke to him, was when I was in my car, it was all filled up with gas. I was pulling out of the parking lot, I kissed his mother good-bye and shook his dad's hand good-bye, acknowledged with a wave to Sammy and headed up A-1 North."

"Since that time, when was the next time you saw him?"

"I haven't seen him since."

The attorney began to close the deposition by reminding Stano of his rights and asking him if he had been aware of them during the full length of the interview, to which the defendant replied that yes, he was and he had been.

Then Elwell concluded by asking him, "Is what you have said in this course of this one hour fifteen minutes a complete and accurate recall from your memory of the events that occurred on September 6, 1973, when you and a friend, Sammy Henderson, took the life of a young girl whom you had abducted from the Holly Hill shopping center?"

"Yes."

Stano's buddy, Sammy Henderson, was later arrested in connection with the Bauer murder. Gerald Stano finally exonerated Sammy Henderson of any complicity in the kidnapping and murder of Barbara Bauer, and the charges were dropped.

"I had stated first that Sammy Henderson was with me

---

* This version of events was somewhat contradicted in a letter Stano later wrote to Kathy Kelly dated October 21, 1985, where he indicated that he left Bauer's car in the motel parking lot, then hitchhiked back to Daytona Beach, retrieved his car, then drove back to Pennsylvania.

during this ordeal. Well, he wasn't at all. It was all fabricated about him," Stano later admitted. "You see, we went to Junior High School together here in 1965. We were friends at one time but his parents would treat me very nasty. They bought him everything he cried for, no matter the cost. That really rubbed me the wrong way from the start."[*]

Paul Crow believed that Gerald Stano *did* have an accomplice in the Barbara Bauer case, but not Henderson. Crow was friends with Dr. Albert Bauer, a veterinarian in New Smyrna Beach, and the two often talked of the case, which had taken a grave toll on both Bauer and his wife.

But whoever the true accomplice might have been, Gerald Stano took that piece of information with him to his grave.

---

* Gerald Stano to Kathy Kelly, October 21, 1985

NINE

"Tiny Dancer"

And now she's in me, always with me, tiny dancer in my hand.

—Elton John

On about June 1975 in the afternoon . . . I approached a young girl walking down the side of the road. She was wearing jean type pants and a blouse, and was carrying schoolbooks with a purse of some sort.

She got into my car with no force of any sort from me. She recognized me from Starlite Skate Centers. . . . I was a very good skater along with her. I believe we used to skate together during "couples" and "all-skate."

—Gerald Stano to Daytona Beach Police Department, October 1, 1982

About a month after his deposition for the murder of Barbara Anne Bauer, on the last week of September of 1982, Gerald Eugene Stano confessed to Detective Sergeant Paul Crow that he had also killed twelve-year-old Susan Basile.

It was more than just a break in a dramatic case. For Paul Crow, it was affirmation of his long-held suspicion. For Marjorie and Sal Basile, Susan's parents, it was the words they had dreaded to hear. After seven years of waiting and hoping to learn what had become of their youngest child in 1975, they still weren't convinced this was the final chapter.

"I think there's a little part of my mother that believes she is still alive," said Mike Basile, Susan's older and only brother. She was his youngest sister. Susan was twelve years old when she disappeared, the same age her brother Mike had been when she was born, a surprise—but a welcome one— for the Basile family.

After her birth, the Basile infant was "everybody's baby," he recalled. "It was a blessing and it meant a lot to my parents even though it wasn't planned." News that his mom, a pediatric nurse, was expecting a baby had come as a "total shock," he recalled.

"She retired to take care of Susan; she didn't have that option when [my other sister] Sharon and I were growing up."

Stano had showed absolutely no remorse for any of the victims, but taking the life of this beautiful child—the light of her parents' eyes—was abhorrent even to him.

After all, he knew her. He had probably clasped her small hand as the two glided around the rink at the Starlite Skate Center on Nova Road in Daytona Beach.

At first, Stano only admitted to having picked Susan up when she got off the school bus in Port Orange that Tuesday, June 10, 1975, but he insisted he just "took her for a ride" and let her out. And that he never saw her again.

The sergeant had been certain for months, however, that Stano had killed Basile, whose highly publicized disappearance had remained a mystery until then.

Stano finally confessed that he had killed her. According to Crow, Stano said he enticed Susan Basile into his car by offering to take her to the skating rink. She objected when he turned the wrong way on Nova Road and demanded to be let out, but Stano said he drove into the woods and strangled her. He said he left the body there in the woods, partly covered by small tree branches, his signature method of covering his tracks, literally.

Susan's disappearance had been a puzzle from the start, to her family as well as to investigators.

"We're using standard police procedure in this case, but believe me, if someone comes to us with something they've seen on a Ouija board, we'll check it out," Port Orange Police Chief Ed McQuaid had said, leaning back in his chair and glancing over at a growing file of reports on the disappearance of Susan Basile.

Twelve-year-old Susan had vanished less than a quarter-mile from her home about 3:30 p.m. on June 10, 1975. She had gotten off a school bus and was last seen walking down the winding, tree-shaded lane.

"Sometimes she went with her friend, Joy Bothwell, to a convenience store for a soft drink, but this particular day her friend hadn't ridden the bus so she started home alone," recalled Lieutenant Randy Milholen, a young police officer who headed the search for the missing child.

When some two hours later Susan still wasn't home, her parents went to the Port Orange Police Department to report her missing. They had spent two hours searching on their own and checking with all of Susan's friends before deciding to seek help from law enforcement authorities.

Police broadcast an alert with the girl's description to the city's patrol officers on duty as well as surrounding law enforcement agencies.

Mike Basile had returned to his hometown after graduating from college. After nasal surgery, he recuperated at his parents' Nixon Lane home. He went to his apartment that afternoon, then returned to find his mother frantic that Susan hadn't come home after the school bus had dropped her off.

"I asked, 'What's wrong?' and she said, 'Susan's not home yet.' That wasn't like her, and it just went downhill from there. And the police came, and their theory was that she ran away. I knew that couldn't possibly have happened."

Meanwhile, neighbors of the Basile family had organized a search and were hunting through the wooded area near their home.

A close friend of the family, Joy Bothwell's mother, learned that another neighborhood resident, a young boy, had seen Susan as she walked toward her house. The witness was taken to the police station and questioned.

At first, he told police he had seen Susan as she walked toward a 1975 dark blue Chevy van parked on the side of the road. He gave a description of the vehicle and occupants.

Investigators then assumed that the dark-haired girl was abducted by the occupants of the van, although they conceded that there was no other evidence that the girl had been forced into the vehicle.

An exhaustive search of the area by volunteers failed to turn up any clues as to the girl's disappearance. The description of the van was publicized nationwide, and a $5,000 reward was posted for information leading to her whereabouts.

Despite numerous "sightings" throughout the state, nothing definite turned up.

If the van was owned locally, why hadn't some neighbor called the police department to report seeing it, the lieutenant wondered.

After checking out several possible leads, police conceded that they were "grasping at straws."

To help determine what happened that fateful day when

Susan walked away from the bus, Lieutenant Milholen and
Detective Dick Vineyard assembled as many members of the
original cast as possible nearly a month later. Although most
of Susan's schoolmates were away on summer vacation by
then, about six showed up at the Port Orange Police Department on Wednesday morning for the "instant replay" of the
day when the youngster disappeared.

They were taken in separate cars to Mainland Junior
High, the start of the bus ride. Detectives synchronized their
watches and kept track on the charts of all the time spent
from the time the bus left the school until it stopped at Herbert and Jackson, Susan's stop.

As the bus slowed to a stop Wednesday morning, Vineyard was waiting as Joy Bothwell stepped from the bus. Joy,
Susan's longtime friend, played Susan's role. From inside
the bus, the driver and the remaining youngsters peered out.

The blond-haired child walked down Jackson as Vineyard
kept track on a stopwatch of just how long it took her to reach
a small bend in the road where a blue van was parked.

A similar blue 1975 Chevy van was the only clue investigators had as to what happened to Susan Basile. The neighborhood boy who knew Susan was the last person to see her
that day as she was walking toward the blue van.

The fifteen-year-old boy was there on Wednesday, too,
doing the same things he had done that day. He had arrived
on an earlier bus and had stopped to get his bicycle from the
house on the corner, where he always left it. That day, as
he had done in the past, he helped the woman who lived in
the house with some odd jobs.

As she had twenty-nine days earlier, the woman pointed
out to the boy several piles of grass clippings she wanted
picked up and had her back turned as "Susan," played by
Joy, walked down the road.

The young witness, whose name was withheld by police

for protective reasons, pedaled off on his bike to a nearby convenience store, then rode south toward the van.

Vineyard, who was at the wheel of the van, borrowed from a local auto firm, drove away as the youngster approached, just as the young witness said it happened nearly a month ago.

A short time later, Susan's father, Sal Basile, drove down Jackson toward Herbert as he had done the day his daughter vanished.

The drama, played out against a background of police radios blaring as detectives posted at different spots talked back and forth and an occasional bellow from a cow grazing along the side of the road, lasted less than thirty minutes.

It took Joy two minutes and ten seconds to walk down the road and reach the spot where the van was parked. At least twelve minutes passed from the time the young witness first saw her walk down the road to the time he saw her near the van. It was about eighteen minutes from the time she stepped from the bus until her father came along.

For Joy, Susan's young friend, it was a walk she had made many times, but not that particular day. She usually walked home with Susan, but that day she had stayed after school for a softball game.

"I want to do anything I can to help," Joy said.

For a haggard-looking Sal Basile, it was another try to piece together the mystifying puzzle of what had happened to his youngest child.

What clinched Susan Basile's case for Paul Crow was that Stano constantly talked about the skating rink. "He put himself there long before we got to discuss Susan Basile," Crow said. Always seeking some degree of authority, Stano was a skating guard, and he was at the rink to help the skaters who fell.

Susan Basile loved to skate. Small and lithe as she was, she could turn and pirouette with ease, like a little dancer.

And she loved the sense of freedom that it gave her. Years later, her brother, Mike, described how full of life Susan always was, and how in turn she filled everyone else's lives with sheer joy.

Gerald Stano frequented a skating rink in Ormond Beach and another one on South Nova Road, in Daytona Beach.

During several interviews and a series of letters, Stano remained most reticent to talk about the Basile case. Despite his having killed and killed again, details of the hours and minutes leading to the death of his tiniest victim had been locked away a long time, perhaps for good.

Crow gave Stano a yellow pad, and told him to write about it. "Then I'll come back and talk to you," the sergeant said as he closed the door behind him.

Finally, Stano recalled the chilling scenario.

He was just on his way to the skating rink on South Nova when Susan Basile got off her school bus at her usual stop, just a few miles away from her home.

Stano and Basile knew each other. They had skated together. He wrote that when he offered the child a ride home, she got in his car without hesitation. He was her friend, she thought.

He drove his car along Nova Road, and instead of turning north towards Susan's house, he turned south. Just before he reached the railroad crossing, which was along a densely wooded area, he choked the child to death.

This was what Gerald Stano wrote about Susan's final day, which Crow then asked him to copy on an affidavit and which the sergeant himself notarized. The statement was taken at the Daytona Beach Police Department on October 1, 1982, at 9:00 a.m.:

I, Gerald Eugene Stano, age 31, date 10-1-82, do hereby make this statement upon my own will and accord.

On about June 1975 in the afternoon [I] was driving down Herbert Street in a 1973 Plymouth Satellite Custom—4 Dr. Green over Green. When I approached a young girl walking down the side of the road. She was wearing jean type pants and a blouse, and was carrying schoolbooks with a purse of some sort.

She got into my car with no force of any sort from me. She recognized me from Starlite Skate Centers on Nova Road, South Daytona, because I used to assist the floor guards there. The young lady broke her arm once I remember, cause I think I helped her to the office where Glenn, (owner's son-in-law) took over the situation. I was a very good skater along with her. I believe we used to skate together during "couples" and "all-skate."

In the car, the conversation was about skating. The young lady thought we were going to the Skating Rink. But I turned south on Nova Road going towards Port Orange.

At one time just after turning on Nova Road, she started to try and get out of the car. I reached over and hit her at that time with the back of my right hand which carries my class ring.

At that point I was just before the railroad tracks on Nova where I turned off on a dirt road to the right. Then I reached over to her and pulled her to me by the hair. With both hands around her neck I strangled her at that time. After that, I got out of the driver's seat of the car and went around to the passenger's side and opened the door. Reaching with one hand to hold her head I pulled her out of the car and put her by some trees and covered her over with some twigs and branches.

I can't remember to this day where the body is or what happened after I covered her over. All I remember

is leaving and going back to my trailer on Hull Road
(now called Timbercreek Road.)

I was working for Mario Esposito [who later became
Stano's father-in-law] at the time on US 1 and Granada
Boulevard, Ormond Beach, Florida, and that day I was
drinking very heavily (Miller Beer) due to an argument
we (the family) had at the station.

—Gerald Eugene Stano, October 1, 1982

Stano later retracted his statement, though, and by 1985
had decided against accepting responsibility in the Basile
case:

This letter I am writing to you is in reference to your let-
ter about Susan Basile.

I have written to Paul about it and showed him where
[Florida Department of Law Enforcement] messed up
on their part. They were interested in clearing their
books, than taking time to verify where I was, what I was
doing, etc. . . . I was in the Old County Facility (before
the new one) til 6/3/75. Then, I was put on probation for
1 year, with my father-in-law being in charge of me. I
even had to have permission to leave the county for my
honeymoon which was for two weeks.*

In the years following Susan Basile's disappearance, a police reporter for the *Daytona Beach Morning Journal*, Bob
Ford, did several follow-ups on the exhaustive search for the
young girl. Bob also talked to the family repeatedly.

"We try to keep our minds on something else," said Mar-

---

* Gerald Stano to Kathy Kelly, October 27, 1985

jorie Basile, Susan's mother. Susan's father, Sal, kept looking out from his driveway in the direction of the spot where Susan had supposedly vanished. "It's bad enough if one of your children dies and you know about it," he said. "At least you can give them a decent burial. But this way, I just don't know." The father added that the family kept on checking drainage ditches. "At night, we check the beaches," he said. The Basiles combed all of the remote and wooded areas from south of New Smyrna Beach to Flagler County and westward to DeLand.

One piece of circumstantial evidence that had somewhat deflected the investigation was the sighting by a sign painter who told Sal Basile of a van with "Aries" written on the side. The fifteen-year-old boy, who had participated in the re-creation of the sequence of events leading up to the crime, also said that he, too, had seen a dark blue Chevrolet with the white letters "Aries" painted on the side driving on Jackson Street, close to where Susan had disappeared.

Sal Basile, a letter carrier, had added $3,500 to the $1,500 reward money collected by colleagues at his postal service branch. "What we need is a break," he said. "There is so little to go on—just the van."

For his part, Detective Vineyard, who had been assigned to the Basile case, stated, "We spent more time, manpower, money, and used more elaborate investigative techniques on the Basile case" than any other investigation the department had ever handled.

Hundreds of volunteers searched for miles around the area where the little girl had disappeared. The State Department of Transportation offered the use of an airplane especially equipped with stereoscopic cameras and a three-man crew. The photo plane used infrared stereo film and took between two hundred and three hundred frames of film in the area. Film processing was done by NASA at Cape Kennedy and was analyzed the next day in Tallahassee. It was all to no avail. By then, it had already been a year since Susan Basile vanished after she got off her school bus.

After Susan disappeared, Mike left home. The stress of Susan's disappearance and the mounting anxiety as the weeks and months went by made him flee his familiar surroundings. He watched his mother's health deteriorate to the point that "it didn't appear as if Mom was going to make it through it."

"It turned out to be such an awful ending," said Mike Basile. "[Susan] was so beautiful, you know, just beautiful."

Sal Basile bore his grief stoically and privately.

"My father suffered silently and that's his personality," recalled Mike. "I saw him break down, and I'd never seen him cry before, even when he lost his parents." As for Marjorie Basile, "I know that my mom, even when they told her that [Gerald Stano] had confessed, she didn't believe Crow," said Mike years later, by then a ponytailed city worker who indulged his passion for music by playing in a band. "She almost had some animosity for Crow," he recalled, often wondering if Crow had been taken in by Stano or if he was being untruthful about the confession.

For those years following Susan's disappearance, the topic of what had happened to her became taboo, her brother recalled. Family pictures of her disappeared from the walls, and she was a subject best not discussed.

Mike Basile handled his loss resolutely. He contemplated attending Stano's execution at Florida State Prison in 1998 but changed his mind. He watched television coverage of Stano's death instead, then went to see his parents.

"My dad almost died that day," he recalled. Sal Basile suffered panic and anxiety attacks after the execution was carried out. "I thought, well this guy is doing it again," said Mike. "He killed my sister, and now he's going to kill my dad." Sal, who had internalized much of his grief over his daughter's death, was finally able to calm down, averting a call for an ambulance.

Stano's guilt or innocence and whether he deserved to die in the electric chair was not a question Mike Basile spent much time pondering.

"Even in the event that he was not my sister's murderer, he deserved the death penalty," Basile felt, likening the serial killer to a rabid dog. "You have a rabid dog running down the street, you put him down. And that's what he is to me."

TEN

"They Told Me She Had Drowned!"

I asked her if she wanted to go for a ride and she climbed in you know and just talked for a little bit and ahh we got back out there on the road and . . . she started to get a little on the . . . on the crabby side and ahh I just went ahead and hit hit [*sic*] her in the face with my right hand it carries a school ring . . . ahh I hit her and that shut her up for a little while.

—Gerald Stano to Paul Crow, August 15, 1982

"**T**hey told me she had drowned!" Emma Bickrest recalled the police telling her of her daughter, Susan.

Mrs. Bickrest then proceeded to explain how Susan had come to move to Florida from Ohio during the fall of 1975.

"My mother was living with us and she had to stay with Susan," she said. "Susan wasn't comfortable with this arrangement so we bought a larger house. And just as we moved there in 1975, she decided to go to Daytona Beach."

This was in November 1975. "And I told her, 'Susan, at least wait until after Christmas.'" This was a concerned mother's apparent last-ditch effort to dissuade her daughter from such a far move away from family and friends. "But she told me, 'I have to find a job.'" Susan was a cosmetologist, but the only job she could find when she moved to Daytona Beach was a waitress job. However, it suited her temporarily.

She had been in the Daytona Beach area for only five weeks when the unthinkable happened.

Two fishermen, Pete Rosen and Larry Gump, reported finding a body floating in Spruce Creek, in Port Orange, just south of Daytona Beach, on December 20, 1975, at approximately 4:45 p.m. The men had been fishing underneath the East Bridge on Spruce Creek on I-95, and they observed what appeared to be a human body floating face down in the water. The two called the local police and told the officers that the individual was wearing blue jeans, a maroon jacket, and platform shoes and had long blond hair.

Deputies recovered the woman's body from the river and transported it to the Halifax Hospital Morgue for autopsy. Medical examiner Dr. Arthur Schwartz noted that the victim had lacerations to the bridge of her nose, the tip of her nose, and around her nostrils. He also noted a laceration to her lower lip and a minor laceration to the chin. She also had a small abrasion beneath her left eye.

From his pathological findings, Dr. Schwartz determined the cause of death as manual strangulation with extensive abrasions and bruises. The medical examiner's report indicated that the victim had been in the water for six to eight hours prior to recovery. According to forensic science, it takes about four minutes for a person to die from strangulation, to stop the blood flowing to the brain, and Schwartz also determined that she might not have been dead when her body was placed in the water. He later identified the body as Susan Bickrest, age twenty-four.

"And next thing I know is, the sheriff calls me and tells me my daughter drowned. I screamed and yelled and hollered for my husband. I thought I was going crazy!" Emma Bickrest recalled.

At the time investigators notified the Bickrests of their daughter's death, it appeared she had drowned, given that she was found dead in the water. An autopsy later determined she had been strangled as well.

On December 31, 1975, Special Investigator Ernest Gibbs, of the Office of the State Attorney in the Courthouse Annex of Daytona Beach, Florida, brought Sandra Linda Gutaucks, Susan Bickrest's roommate, to his office for an interview. Gutaucks, twenty-one, was also originally from Ohio, like Susan, and she informed Gibbs that the two girls had planned their move down to Daytona Beach together.

When questioned by the investigator, Sandy Gutaucks said that Susan drove a 1970 Chevy Camaro. "She just kept her tape player in there, and you know, Kleenex and all kinds of stuff in there, usually her glasses," she said.

Gutaucks added that Susan's glasses were missing one of the arms, so she hardly ever wore them, and that although Susan had contact lenses, she claimed that they bothered her, so she never wore them either. Both young women worked as waitresses at P. J.'s Lounge.

Gibbs asked Gutaucks when she had first noticed that Susan was missing. The roommate stated that when she had returned home on the evening of Saturday, December 19, at around 6:30, she had noticed Susan's car in the parking lot out in front of the building.

"And then I figured, oh well, Susan is home," Gutaucks said. "Good, I wanted to talk to her. I ran for the stairs, I went in, [but] there were no lights on, so I figured she was asleep like she normally is when I get home. So I put the stereo on, it was rather loud so, the lights were still off and it was dark. I walked to her bedroom and closed the bedroom door [still] thinking she was asleep, put the lights on in my bedroom and went into the kitchen to make me something to eat. I noticed there were no dirty dishes or anything so I figured she hadn't eaten yet. So I walked to her bedroom, opened the door and yelled, 'Susan! Do you want to eat?'"

Sandy Gutaucks went back to P. J.'s Lounge to wait for Susan to show up for work, but her roommate never showed. Gutaucks pointed out that Susan had never notified P. J.'s Lounge that she would not be reporting to work that night.

"And that's where . . . they knew . . . it wasn't like Susan, not to call, you know, she was really conscious of work and everything, her job," the roommate said.

Special Investigator Gibbs then prompted her. "She liked her job, then. How did she like life?"

Gutaucks replied, without hesitation, "A lot."

"She enjoyed it?" asked the investigator.

"Yeah. Everything is, was, just like she always wanted to do, move to Florida, you know, live down here."

More than six and a half years later, on August 18, 1982, Investigator Dave Hudson, of the Volusia County Sheriff's Office, received a call from Sergeant Paul Crow, of the Daytona Beach Police Department, regarding the Bickrest murder.

Crow revealed to Hudson that on August 15, 1982, at 12:25 p.m., he had interviewed Gerald Stano in regards to the December 20, 1975, murder of Susan Lynn Bickrest, and Stano had confessed to the sergeant that he had murdered her.

After reading Stano his rights and asking him the required questions about his name, age, and current residence, which was the Florida State Prison in Raiford, Florida, Paul Crow began his interview with Gerald Stano.

"Mr. Stano, let me take you back to December 19, 1975. . . . Could you tell me in your own words what you did that night and what contact you had and what was the result of it?"

Stano paused for a moment and proceeded with his account of the night in question.

"Alright . . . ahh . . . she ahh . . . she come out of P. J.'s where I was," Stano said, referring to the lounge where Susan Bickrest worked as a waitress.

"I went down to P. J.'s to check it out; I'd never been down there. I'd heard a coupla good things about it. I decided to go down and check it out. I went down, I had a '73 Plymouth Satellite at that time, green over green and I had to park it on the street. So . . . I went in you know and I had a coupla drinks. They were two for one. I like that, and then I decided well, you know, it's closing hour so I'm gonna go ride around for a little bit. Coming out of there was this sandy brown-haired girl that got into a white Camaro with a black top and she ahh . . . she took off one way and I took off the other way. And I got to thinking after a while, you know, 'cause . . . I got myself a six-pack in one of these stores when I got to thinking about her and I figured well, I'm gonna see if I can find her. So I was going back up to . . . I forget which road it is . . . I was going back up . . . what pulls out of one of the side streets but the white Camaro with the black top? So I said, what the heck, I'll follow her you know, just try to talk to her before she went into her house and she pulls in this Derbyshire Apartments on Derbyshire Avenue."

Crow wanted to know the approximate time of the encounter.

"I'd say somewhere around . . . between the hours of three and four." Stano meant the early morning hours.

Crow wanted Stano to clarify whether he had been out purposely looking for the girl, and if he had followed her to her apartment complex at the Derbyshire Apartments. Stano replied that he had.

"Okay," Crow went on. "Then tell me again, in your own

words, what happened when she entered the complex at Derbyshire Apartments."

Stano looked up, trying to remember with his usual fastidious exactness.

"Well . . . she went over to ahh . . . she drove in and parked her car in one of the parking spaces by the complex. I just drove up and just stopped behind her car and started talking to her for a little bit and you know . . . she climbed in, you know." Stano implied that Susan Bickrest had willingly entered his car, but later, during his trial for her murder, he confessed that he had actually forced his victim into his vehicle at gunpoint.

"I asked her if she wanted to go for a ride and she climbed in you know and just talked for a little bit," Stano told Crow during the initial interview, seeming to relish this version of the story, "and ahh we got back out there on the road and . . . she started to get a little on the . . . on the crabby side and ahh I just went ahead and hit hit her in the face with my right hand it carries a school ring . . . ahh I hit her and that shut her up for a little while but I got out on 95 and she started bitching and raising hell and I just pulled over and I just strangled her right there and then and put her out on the side."

"What was she wearing that night, Gerald?" Crow asked, in an effort to further ascertain that the victim was indeed Susan Bickrest.

"Blue jeans and . . . like a brown leather type jacket and some type of sandals but with an inclined heel on them."

Crow then asked Stano where he had taken Susan Bickrest after he strangled her.

"To a little marsh area, where ahh . . . the cat-of-nine-tails grow, something like that, where there was a little bit of water. And I laid her down there."

The sergeant inquired if Stano had deposited the limp body in the water.

"Not exactly in the water. There was like a little bit of ahh . . . what you call it? A sandy area, a beach area like a little miniature beach. I put her down."

"Gerald, I'm confused about this," Crow said. "You didn't put her on the beach and put her in the water?"

"Somewhere around the water's edge," was Stano's reply.

Crow then decided to backtrack a bit and confirmed the route that Stano took to the water, then he asked, "And at what point in time was the first violent act that took place between you two?" Crow wanted to know where Stano was driving when he first punched Susan Bickrest in the face.

It did not come as a surprise to the detective that Stano remembered where he was and what he did vividly.

"Out around Mason and Clyde Morris. I hit her in the face and then she started to get a little bitchy."

"Was that because she wanted to know where you were going?"

"She wondered what was going on, she ahh . . . had a funny feeling I guess that something was not ahh . . . kosher, you know that it wasn't mixing right and that something was gonna happen."

The sergeant then asked Stano what the victim's condition was at this point.

"She's a little on the stunned side, I believe she was from . . . when I hit her. I might have dazed her a little bit because she didn't say anything, she hadn't said anything for a long period of time. I may have stunned her a little bit."

"Did she make any effort to get out of the car?" Crow asked.

"She tried to at one point when I . . . I had to stop for a rest stop right quick and she tried to get out of the car once, but I pushed . . . I pushed her back in the car and pushed the door locks down. I had door locks that if you got your hands a little sweaty or something you couldn't get them to anti-theft lock."

"So after you left from your rest stop, where did you go then?" asked the sergeant.

"Went to ah . . . the Taylor Road Area."

"You pulled off the road somewhere in that area?"

"Somewhere in that vicinity I had pulled off the road and . . . there is a little body of water around there."

Crow wanted to zero in on the exact area. "Is it real dark around that area? There are no lights, is that correct?"

"Yeah. No lights around there."

"And again you strangled her, you say?"

"Yes."

"And you picked her up from the car and dragged her? Or did you carry her?"

"No, I carried her, she wasn't that heavy, I just picked her up and carried her."

"And you laid her either by some water or in some water as you said before, or close to a pond or something?"

"Yeah, it looked like a pond. I thought it looked like a pond. I put her down at the water's edge."

On March 11, 1983, Gerald Stano entered a plea of guilty to the first-degree murder of Susan Bickrest and proceeded to the penalty phase, where he personally waived an advisory jury.

"On June 13, 1983, this court entered the written findings of fact in support of the sentence of death. Four aggravating circumstances exist: the defendant had previously been convicted of six counts of first degree murder.

"The murder was committed while the defendant was engaged in kidnapping. The murder was especially heinous, atrocious or cruel. The murder was committed in a manner that was cold, calculated, or premeditated. The kidnapping was established by Stano's admissions that she tried to escape and he pushed her back in and pushed down the special car locks that sweaty hands could not open. The court found that the confinement was not merely incidental to the murder. The state established that Stano abducted the victim and transported her over seventeen miles.

"Strangulation and pre-death blows, as well as Miss Bickrest's knowledge of her impending death support the heinousness and cruelty of the murder. The location of the murder and lack of moral or legal justification indicated to the judge that murder was cold, calculated and premeditated."

The medical examiner, Dr. Arthur Schwartz, described Susan's death as "prolonged," and the court sentenced Stano to death for the murder of Susan Bickrest.

ELEVEN

"Blackbird . . . Fly"

It ended up with me killing the young lady.

—Gerald Stano, police interview, May 9, 1980

Paul McCartney wrote the song "Blackbird" as an homage to black women ("bird" being British slang for *girl*), in light of the mounting racial and social unrest of the late 1960s. The song could well describe—posthumously and tragically—Toni Van Haddocks.

On February 20, 1980, Detective Larry Lewis of the Daytona Beach Police Department phoned me at work to tell me about his ongoing investigation of a missing person. He asked me if we would publish a story and the missing girl's photo in the *Evening News* as quickly as possible.

The detective told me that he was giving me all the necessary information on the missing victim, Toni Van Haddocks, including one thing that would make her highly identifiable. She wore a cast on her left arm. I obtained a booking mug shot of her at the police department from a prior arrest for solicitation.

Detective Lewis informed me that a man named Bobby Jackson had come into the police station on February 18,

1980, to report that he had dropped off his twenty-eight-year-old girlfriend of six years at the 7-Eleven store at North Ridgewood Avenue at approximately 9:00 p.m. on February 15, 1980, and had not heard from her since.

Meanwhile, the victim's mother, Jackie Haddocks, a city employee, called to inform me that her daughter had returned home. Investigators had told her they had furnished information about her missing daughter to the *Daytona Beach News-Journal* and requested a story be done, so she tried to circumvent them by calling me.

On the morning of February 21, 1980, Detective Lewis contacted me at work again, wanting to know why the story had not appeared in the paper. I told him about the phone call I had received from the victim's mother, who requested that I cancel the story in light of her daughter's return.

Detective Lewis persisted. He phoned Mrs.Haddocks and inquired as to the whereabouts of her daughter Toni. Mrs. Haddocks replied that she actually had not seen the young woman, but one of her friends had. The detective then inquired as to the identity of the friend who had supposedly seen Toni, but Mrs. Haddocks refused to give him a name.

Lewis told Mrs. Haddocks that he was conducting an official investigation and needed to know the name of the person who'd reported seeing the victim. Mrs. Haddocks still refused to give out the name and further stated that she wished to have all reports involving her daughter canceled. Lewis told her that no reports would be canceled until he spoke to the victim in person.

The detective also informed me that Toni's boyfriend, Bobby Jackson, had told him that Toni would occasionally take johns to the area of Hazel Street and the railroad tracks. I began to wonder if perhaps her daughter's prostitution was the reason why Jackie Haddocks wanted all the reports surrounding Toni's disappearance canceled.*

A few weeks later, on April 15, 1980, a little boy named Brian Wolff was walking on the grounds close to his home in Holly Hill, a suburb of Daytona Beach, and found a decomposed cranium in a wooded area. The area was covered with pine trees and palmetto bushes. The child, curious as kids tend to be, took his find home in a bag, and his parents immediately notified the sheriff's office. From April 16 through April 22, personnel from the sheriff's office and the Florida Department of Law Enforcement, including Catherine Bisset, of the Sanford Regional Laboratory; Paul Brackman, of the Florida Department of Law Enforcement; and investigator Steve Lehman, of the Volusia County Sheriff's Office, conducted a search of about nine acres. Bones, clothing, and other materials were recovered.

Many of the bones were completely skeletonized, although those protected by clothing—such as a pair of woman's pants and underpants that were also recovered from the scene—were still in the process of decomposition. These were mainly the pelvis, including the sacrum, both femora, and the articulated thoracic and lumbar vertebrae with many ribs. Ligaments and other soft tissue were present, and there was a foul odor.

The examiners identified the victim as a black female, age twenty-six, about five feet five. The skull showed extensive damage, perpetrated with extreme savagery:

- There were numerous cuts and punctures on the frontal, parietals, occipital, and left temporal bones, most concentrated in the left frontal area.

---

* Even decades later, Toni's mother, Jackie Haddocks, never responded to repeated contact attempts. Perhaps she wanted to forget. Perhaps she remembered too much.

- On the left side of the cranium, there were approximately nineteen longitudinal cuts.

- On the left parietal area, there were at least eight cuts.

The examiners reported their findings to the Volusia County Sheriff's Office, which in turn notified the Daytona Beach Police Department. After the first few weeks, the murder disappeared from the headlines, and investigators found the trail to Toni Van Haddocks's killer very cold.

In 1980, Detective Sergeant Paul Crow went to interview Gerald Stano at the Volusia County Jail, where Stano was being held without bond after his savage attack on Donna Marie Hensley, the prostitute whom he'd picked up on the Boardwalk, taken to her motel room, relentlessly attacked with sharp household instruments, then attempted to douse with muriatic acid.

Given how the repeated wounds, puncture marks, and lacerations on Toni Van Haddocks's remains resembled the attack on Hensley, Crow had a suspicion that Stano might also have committed Haddocks's murder. After reading Stano his rights, and obtaining his assurance, on tape and later in a written statement, that he had not been subjected to any threats or duress during the course of the interview, nor had he received any promises of reward or immunity, the sergeant then turned on his tape recorder.

"Gerald, what I'm here to talk to you about is a homicide case involving a black female by the name of Toni Van Haddocks." Stano nodded. "I have reason to believe that on February the 15th, 1980, that you did come in contact with this girl. Is that correct?"

"Yes."

"When you saw the girl, did you stop and pick her up?"

Another nod. "Yes, sir."

Crow wanted to know the time and the location when Stano first saw the young woman. Stano stated it was a weekend night, around 10:00 or 11:00 p.m., in an area between the 7-Eleven and the Shingle Shack, a local bar.

"When you saw this girl, Gerald, what did you think she was doing for a living?" asked the sergeant. At this point, Crow was wondering if it was the victim's occupation as a prostitute that set Stano off, the same way Donna Marie Hensley had set him off, so he went after the trigger that made Stano snap.

"I thought she was a prostitute." Stano could not help a slight sneer.

"What was your intention when you saw this girl?"

Stano shrugged his shoulders. "Oh, fixing to get myself a little, a little action on the side, piece of tail, as you'd call it."

"Gerald, when you saw the girl, did you stop and pick her up?"

"Yes, I did."

"Did she get in your car?"

"Yes, she got in the car."

"Describe this girl to me."

"She was about 5' 7", 5' 8", about 115 pounds, no more. Dark, dark complexion . . . uh . . . black, of course. Short dark hair, pushed-in nose. She had a cast on her left arm, was wearing slacks at the time with a blouse and a jacket or something covering her shoulders."

"Okay. You're telling me that she got in the car for the purpose of prostitution, that you were letting her believe that you would pay her, is that correct, for whichever sex acts she wished to prescribe. Did she quote you a price?"

"No, she was waiting for me to say a price."

"Did you?"

"Yes. I said thirty dollars for it."

"What did she say?"

"She said, 'Fine, let's go baby.'"

"Where did you go at this time?"

Stano proceeded to give Crow a step-by-step, detailed account of the route he took, while the sergeant concealed his bewilderment at Stano's photographic memory for streets and names and twists and turns, on the road and inside his own mind.

Then, Stano said, he "proceeded to have sex with the young lady at that time."

Crow could almost anticipate, from Stano's violent reactions after he had sex with Donna Marie Hensley, how his behavior might have escalated with Toni Van Haddocks.

"After the sex was completed, when did the price come up for the act?" Crow asked.

"It come up after I had gotten my clothes on at that time, and I was reaching underneath my seat and she asked for her thirty dollars at that time."

"Why were you reaching under your seat?"

"I was reaching under the seat to bring out a concealed knife I had underneath the seat."

"Was your wallet underneath the seat also?" Crow asked, knowing full well that Stano would have never reached for the wallet to make good on his offer.

"Yes, my wallet was there which was, uh, empty at the time."

"You had no intentions to really pay her, did you," the sergeant said more as a statement than a question.

Stano agreed and said no, not really. He had a payment in mind all right, but it wasn't cash.

"Gerald, when you reached down underneath the seat, was your intention to get your wallet to pay her, or was the intention getting the knife?" Crow confirmed.

"Getting the knife," Stano stated matter-of-factly.

"Once you got the knife in your hand, Gerald, what did you do?"

"I reached over and stabbed her once with my left hand, which it was in, and retracted the knife from her body with my right hand and repeatedly stabbed her and then got out of my car and took her out and stabbed her a couple more times outside the car and put her down on the ground and covered her with some branches and twigs." Again, he showed no emotion; only the detached account of the hunt.

"Gerald, when you got her outside of the car and you say you stabbed her a few more times, did you take her away from the car, or did you just cover her right there in the road?"

"No, I took her away from the car and covered her with branches off the side of the road."

Stano told the sergeant that after he dumped the body he got back in his car and on the road and drove down Wildrose Avenue. He said he thought of stopping at the home of his brother, who lived on the same street, so he could spend the night there because he had been drinking heavily before the attack on Van Haddocks. But he decided against it because there were no lights on in the house, so he headed back to the hotel where he was staying, the Riviera Hotel on U.S. 1 in Ormond Beach.

"After getting to the hotel, I had a T-shirt on that was covered with a little bit of the young lady's blood," he said as casually as if he was referring to mustard from a hot dog. "I wiped off the blood on the seat, and left the knife and the shirt in the car at that time. I remember locking the car when I got out."

Crow wanted to go back and pinpoint the moment right before Stano stabbed Toni Van Haddocks, wondering what made him explode at that particular time.

"Well, she was starting to get a little edgy, and I don't like being forced, or pushed, really, by verbal statements. And she had said something to the effect of 'Well, let's get on with it or let's not get on with it,' and I just saw red. And that was it."

"Do you like black girls?" Crow asked, already surmising what the answer would be.

"No."

"Did the fact that she was black tend to heighten your anger a little bit?"

"A little bit."*

Crow inquired if there was any specific reason why the suspect had taken the young woman to that particular location.

"Yeah, yeah there was. My brother and I don't seem to see eye to eye and I was trying to get back at him. By what means I couldn't tell you, but I figured I could get back at him by doing it over there."

Crow wondered aloud how Stano had anticipated the evening going when he first picked up Toni in Ridgewood. "Did you think about, well, I'll just go have sex with this girl? Or, will I just go out and take her and kill her?"

"Well, my thoughts at that time when I picked her up were having sex with her and bringing her back, but it didn't work out that way."

A lot of things had a way of "not working out" with Gerald Stano.

Nothing seemed to ever work out right for Toni Van Haddocks. She was street-smart, but on February 15, 1980, the

---

* In later years, Stano never discussed Toni Van Haddocks's murder. Maybe he felt his macho image would be tarnished if he discussed buying sexual favors. This was probably made even worse by the fact that Van Haddocks was black, since misogyny and racism ranked right up there, along with murder, in Stano's long list of deplorable qualities.

night following Valentine's Day, she was a wounded bird, with her left arm in a cast. Against the enraged Gerald Stano, she didn't stand a chance.

"It ended up with me killing the young lady," Stano stated at the end of the interview.

TWELVE
The Bond of Brothers

> I got the worst of everything growing up. What I mean is, my brother could do no wrong. If he did, I would pay the penalty. But, I loved him like a brother, even though we were both adopted. Sure, we had our differences, but that's normal though.
>
> —Gerald Stano to Kathy Kelly, August 27, 1985

> For some reason, [my brother] doesn't want to see me anymore. Why, I don't know. It could have been from an article a reporter wrote from Sanford. She said I hate my brother. That is not true, Kathy. I love my brother very much. Sure we had our differences growing up, but that is only normal. Especially for two boys.
>
> —Gerald Stano to Kathy Kelly, December 16, 1985

With each murder, Gerald Stano severed a most important bond. Linked by blood and love, the young women whose fate rested in his hands left grieving families to ponder their loss. In two cases, the young women had twin brothers: Ramona and Ray Neal and Barbara and Burt Bauer. Their connection and relationship began in the womb. The girls' brothers were their protectors, their confidants, their heroes. Their brothers felt the burden of their sisters' murder all the more significantly because of the unique relationship they shared.

The first time Ray Neal ever saw his twin sister Ramona's killer, Gerald Stano was just minutes from death. Ray and his brothers, Keith and Ronnie, had front-row seats at the Florida State Prison, at Starke, Florida, for the execution.

"We got there early so we sat on the front row," Ray Neal, a sheriff's deputy in Texas, recalled. Ramona Neal, one of Stano's victims, was not only Ray's sister, but his twin. Ramona had been born first, on October 3, 1957, and had tipped the scales at a few ounces more than the six pounds her brother weighed. The Neal twins were babies number seven and eight for their parents, Juanita and Jack, and they grew up in a large, loving Christian family. The nine Neal children crowded into a three-bedroom home. Their dad worked, while their mom stayed home to look after her brood.

Their brother Keith was older by fifteen months and recalled that it was his never-ending delight to chase the younger toddlers around trying to steal their baby bottles.

"Me and Ray and Ramona did a lot together," recalled Keith. "We were real close."

She and her twin brother did everything together, attending many of the same classes together. They first walked to school, then rode the school bus together. "She was very bubbly and had a wonderful personality," said Ray Neal.

Often, they would fall asleep talking about their hopes and dreams for the future. "We would talk about what we wanted to do together as adults once we were both grown." The sister who shared his love for jarred pickles endured kidding from her brother when she sucked her thumb until she was nearly thirteen.

"She would always try to hide it," said Ray.

Ray had been stationed at Camp Pendleton, California, when he learned that his twin sister had gone missing while on a senior trip to Daytona Beach, Florida. Although they were precisely the same age, Ray hadn't walked across the stage with Ramona for their graduation from Forest Park High School because he had gone to summer school so that he could finish school early and enlist in the Marine Corps.

"I knew she was going [on the trip]," Ray Neal recalled. It was the highlight of the year for the graduating class in that Georgia town. When he got a telephone call at Camp Pendleton, he knew instinctively that "something was wrong."

The Neals faithfully attended services at a Southern Baptist church where they lived, and Ramona's funeral was held in the church her father helped found. Her trip to Daytona Beach for graduation had caused her to miss Sunday school for the first time in ten years. Back home in Forest Park, she proudly owned pins signifying ten years' continuous Sunday service attendances.

Ramona's death affected the entire Neal family. "We have never been the same since," said Ray. His older brother, Keith, became more like a surrogate twin once Ramona was gone. "We talk on the phone every day," said Ray. Although his dark-haired sister died more than three decades ago—her body was found June 15, 1976—the years have not dulled the pain.

Keith was right there with Ray and their brother Ronnie when Stano was put to death. The three Neal brothers were approved by the state to witness Stano's death. "We all promised our mother before she died that we would not rest until Stano was tried and executed," said Ray Neal. Most of the rest of the family was also on hand, waiting in a nearby room.

"I was in the witness room," said Ray Neal. "It was dead silence."

Gerald Stano, the man who somehow talked Ramona Neal into getting into his car, entered the room, never looking out toward the seated witnesses. "He focused completely on his attorney," said Neal.

But even years later, haunting questions remained. How did Stano persuade Ramona to get into his car? Why did she let her guard down?

"Guys like that are very slick," said Ray Neal. "They know what to do. Trust me, I don't know what happened; all I can say is she would not have just jumped in a car with him."

The final moments of his older sister's life were a mystery to Ed Bickrest as well. His sister, Susan, had just pulled into the parking lot of her apartment complex in Daytona Beach after leaving her waitress job when she met her killer, according to statements Gerald Stano later gave to detectives about how he had followed her from the restaurant.

"I can't see her getting in the car with someone," said Bickrest, from his home in Cumberland, Rhode Island. "She was a little stubborn," he said. "She wasn't going to have someone push her around; she wouldn't take that kind of crap."

Susan and Ed were the only children of Ed and Emma Bickrest. Two years separated the siblings, who grew up near Cleveland, Ohio, in a close-knit suburb, the kind of place where folks didn't lock their doors and neighbors often dropped in on each other.

It was just five days before Christmas in 1975 that the Bickrests learned their twenty-four-year-old daughter's dream of moving to Florida to start a new life had ended tragically.

The initial call to the Bickrest home indicated Susan had drowned. It wasn't until the next day, after hours of tearful worrying, that the couple learned she had actually been murdered. Alive when Stano threw her unconscious body into

Spruce Creek, the battered cocktail waitress hadn't been able to summon enough strength to get out of the water.

Emma Bickrest was consumed by her daughter's death, calling investigators periodically to check on the progress of the hunt for the killer. It would be more than four years before Gerald Stano was arrested and ultimately confessed to the crime.

"My parents always said: 'If it was an accident, [we could understand], but for someone to murder your child for no other reason for being in the wrong place at the wrong time' . . ." said Bickrest, his voice trailing off as he repeated his parents' rhetorical statement.

When Emma Bickrest learned Gerald Stano was to be executed, she was determined to come to Florida and face the man who had taken her daughter's life, but a week before the date of the execution, she was hospitalized and wasn't able to go.

"It was a message from God that he didn't want her to go," said Ed Bickrest. Susan's younger brother had no interest in seeing such a horrific sight as someone being electrocuted. "I never considered it; it was just taken care of."

The Neal and Bickrest families endured one of the saddest rituals of death, the funeral, but Susan Basile's family was robbed of that kind of psychological closure to her death. Twelve-year-old Susan, who may have been the only one of Gerald Stano's victims whom he actually knew beforehand, had skated with him at the neighborhood roller rink. She was the picture of innocence, her brother, Mike, said. Why didn't anyone notice an older man paying such attention to a child?

Looking back, he said he doesn't think his parents were any more protective of his younger sister than they were of him and his sister, Sharon. But those were times when people weren't as aware of child predators as they are now.

"It was an era when girls weren't sexually aware like they are now," said Mike Basile. "They weren't on the Internet or Twitter or looking at role models like Britney Spears," he continued.

When police suggested that Susan might have run away, the family knew better. Though it would be nearly seven long years before they would learn her fate, Marjorie Basile knew the minute her daughter failed to arrive home at her usual time after school that her child was in danger.

The Basiles, now in their eighties, dealt with their grief in their own private way. Pictures of Susan were put away, but nothing could stop the daily reminders in their hearts and minds that their youngest never had a chance.

Echoing his mother's doubts as to whether Stano was actually the killer, Mike Basile was philosophical.

"Even in the event that he was not my sister's murderer, he deserved the death penalty."

Killers like Stano could never be rehabilitated, he believed.

"It's ingrained and it's never coming out," said Basile. "They'll tell you anything you want to hear just to get out and have the chance to do it again."

THIRTEEN

In Search of a Dream

Young women should go out in 2–4 girl groups. Never go out alone, cause that is asking for trouble. I don't care where it is, that is trouble for one girl.

—Gerald Stano to Kathy Kelly, January 28, 1986

Some of Gerald Stano's victims came to Daytona Beach to chase a dream, though happiness could be elusive at the "World's Most Famous Beach," like catching that perfect wave. To some, it was the last frontier, where they came to escape from the cold, or a restrictive family structure, or to simply start a new life. Others, like graduating senior Ramona Neal, came down to celebrate a new beginning. For Ohio native Susan Bickrest, it was a combination of getting away and the postcard-perfect vision of sunny Florida, while Katie Muldoon hoped to finance her goal of becoming a wood sculptor by working as a server at a restaurant while studying at Daytona Beach Community College.

For another of Stano's victims, Nancy Heard, moving to the "Sunshine State" in late 1974 was part of the process of figuring out the path she would take, whether to stay married or strike out on her own. She came to the Daytona Beach area

from South Carolina. She had been married to Tom Heard
for about a year, since November 1, 1973. Before she moved
to Florida, Nancy worked at a credit union office in Myrtle
Beach and spent her spare time with Tom and three other
couples.

Tom was one of Elizabeth Heard Dow's three sons and
the first to get married. After their marriage, Tom found himself immersed in work as a radar technician, covering holidays and weekends for others on leave. Tom had dropped out
of Clemson University to enlist in the U.S. Air Force, but
according to his mother, he was having second thoughts
about a military career. "It was pretty stressful," recalled
Mrs. Dow, now a resident of Greenville, South Carolina.
When Tom decided he wanted to return to Clemson, the family asked then senator Strom Thurmond and other elected
representatives to intervene on his behalf for an early release
from the U.S. Air Force. After some inquiries, Nancy learned
that she probably could get a job at the university, too, if she
brushed up on her computer skills.

The couple decided on a trial separation. Nancy would go
to Florida, where her mother lived, while Tom pursued his
college dream of studying entomology.

The perky-looking twenty-four-year-old with the long,
wavy blond hair took a job as a maid at the Mandarin Motel
in Ormond Beach while she set up a plan of studies. She
wrote to her mother-in-law that she had purchased a bicycle
for transportation to work. She had loved the shores of Myrtle Beach and looked forward to being in a beach atmosphere again.

Leaving her bike at home so that she could ride to work
with her sister proved a fatal plan. As Nancy took a break
from work January 2, 1975, she walked down the motel's
steps to the beach and encountered Gerald Stano. She fit his

perfect profile of a victim—alone, and with an outgoing, friendly nature that allowed him to begin to spin his web of deceit, offering a ride in a friendly manner.

Nancy Heard officially became a crime statistic when Charles Austin Hill IV reported finding the body of a white female to the Volusia County Sheriff's Office on January 3, 1975. Hill and a friend had been hunting by the dirt extension of Old Dixie Highway north of Bulow Creek Road near Tomoka State Park when they found the body of a young woman lying beneath a power line.

Volusia County Sheriff's Office deputies who examined the woman's body found it lying on its back with her clothes in disarray. Her knees were spread and her feet were together. The body was cold. The deputies described the young woman as having light brown to blondish hair and wearing glasses, a blue denim jacket with red lining, a light blue long-sleeved sweater, a bra, blue denim pants, light blue panties, dark blue canvas shoes with red soles, and gray socks. To the southeast of her body was a blue denim bag with red straps, approximately eighteen inches away from her head.

The deputies notified the medical examiner, Dr. Arthur Schwartz, who went to the scene with Investigator Mike Cook of the state attorney's office.

After Dr. Schwartz viewed the body, he and Cook obtained, among other items, a book of matches imprinted with the name of the Mandarin Motel on South Atlantic Avenue in Ormond Beach, Florida. Following a preliminary investigation by Dr. Schwartz, the body was removed to Halifax District Hospital via Beacon Ambulance for an autopsy. Reporting Deputy Sergeant Arthur Dees and Investigator Cook proceeded to the Mandarin Motel with Polaroid pictures of the victim, whom the manager of the motel and two fellow maids identified as Nancy Heard.

* * *

In a written statement dated March 6, 1981, Gerald Stano wrote:

"I remember taking a girl up there with me (Bulow Creek) with a blue purse trimmed in brown and light colored clothes. During our travel we got into an argument and I hit her in the head with the back of my hand. . . . She said she wanted to go back to the beach and I said shut up bitch and I hit her again."

Stano's account of the slaying continued:

"We then stopped along some little path and I began to move towards her and she was nervous. Then I put my hands up to her and I strangled her."

Armed with Stano's written statement, Sergeant Paul Crow interviewed the suspect at the Daytona Beach Police Department on March 12, 1981.

Once more, Sergeant Crow advised Stano of his rights and ascertained that his current address was the Volusia County Jail. Crow then said the name "Nancy Heard" into his tape recorder, spelling it out, "H-E-A-R-D," and opened his line of questioning.

"And you're willing to talk to me at this time about a case in 1975, a white female who has been identified as Nancy Heard in reference to a homicide investigation?"

"Yes, sir." Stano knew the drill by then.

"Mr. Stano, in January of 1975, do you recall ever picking up a white female in the Ormond Beach area?"

"Yes, I do."

Then, as usual, Crow asked Stano about the approximate location where he had picked up his victim, as well as a physical description of the girl, if only to determine with final certainty that she was indeed Nancy Heard. Stano was as precise as he was detached in his answers.

"In regards to the first part of the question, I picked her up around the Mandarin Motel on the beachside. She was walking down the beach, down the beach stairs from the Mandarin Motel. It was towards afternoon. She was wearing a blue pair of pants, or excuse me, strike that, jeans, uh, a light shirt, uh, uh a blue Wrangler jacket with red trim and a blue pocketbook with red trim, or reddish brown trim."

The sergeant wanted to know if Stano and the young woman had any type of conversation that would have personalized the victim to her attacker. At this point, the investigator had no idea that the attack had been all too personal.

"Uh, the conversation was just, just a little. She said she worked at the Mandarin Motel as a maid and, um, asked me what I did and I told her I worked for Publix Supermarket." Stano did not, of course, but it was his way of ingratiating himself to a potential prey.

Crow wanted to broach the subject of favorite hunting grounds.

"Are you very familiar with the motels along Daytona Beach and Ormond Beach, the names of the motels?"

"Yes, sir. I could name at least half the motels down the beachside."

"And you're positive of the name of the motel you've mentioned that you picked her up behind, or whatever?"

"Yes, sir, the Mandarin Motel. Yes."

Crow wanted to know what time of day it was, and Stano replied that it was early afternoon. Nancy Heard had apparently decided to take a walk on the beach behind the motel where she worked, an impulse for some fresh air, perhaps, or a break from the monotony of making beds and cleaning toilets. It was a decision that would seal her fate.

Then the sergeant asked where the two went after Stano picked her up.

Stano mapped out a route taking several twists and turns

until the pair reached an area near Old Dixie Highway called Cobb's Corner.

That's when Crow interjected:

"Are you very familiar with the area up there?"

"Uh, so-so. But I could find my way around there pretty, pretty good."

"We're talking about the Tomoka State Park area, are we not?"

"Yes. Yes. Somewhere around there."

"What, or where, did you take this young lady to?"

"Uh, there is a, uh, power line, uh road, there is a dirt road that runs, um . . ."

Crow was growing impatient. He already knew about the power line and about the hunters on the stretch of dirt near the highway.

"Gerald, where about on Old Dixie Highway are you talking about? Is it a specific area that you know or was it a dirt road or a hunter's trail? What are we talking about here that you got off the road?"

Stano sensed some irritation on the part of Crow but continued his vagaries as if to purposely raise the sergeant's level of exacerbation. It was his game, and he was very good at it.

"Uh, up around Old Dixie Highway there's a little, um, you could call it a hunter's trail going down there. It's big enough for a tractor-trailer, you know, and 4 by 4's, what have you, you know. And I took my car down that way, which was my green Satellite at that time, 1973. I took, I went down that road to some power lines which was about a quarter of a mile to half a mile, if not a little more, and I disposed of the body."

After providing Crow with so much extraneous detail, now Stano had jumped ahead and left out the most important part of his account.

"You disposed of the body," Crow stated slowly. "What do you mean you disposed of the body?"

The sergeant tried to stay within the exasperatingly meandering rhythm of the interrogation. "Did you kill her in the car? Give me some details. What was she wearing when she was in the car? Give me some details."

"I choked the young lady to death, and finding out that she was dead, I dragged her out of the car leaving her in some thickets on the side of the road, and then turning around and then just leaving," Stano said. Again, though, Stano had skipped a critical part of his confession.

Crow just looked at him, and after a beat, asked point-blank: "Gerald, why did you kill her?"

Stano, though never at a loss for words, sat silently. No answer, only the slightest hint of contrition.

"Gerald, let me ask you again, why did you have to kill her, son?"

"Well, I was engaged at the time to a young lady, and this young girl, Nancy . . ."

Crow looked up. "Is that the name she used?"

"Yes. Yes. Nancy. And, uh, she started to sound like my future wife, bitching, bitching, bitching, and I wasn't about to take it from anybody. . . . I just, I just went ahead and, uh, put my arms around her and just strangled her. I put my arms around her neck and strangled her."

Crow was somewhat taken aback by Stano's association of this victim with his then fiancée, and now he wanted to recap.

"Gerald, what you've told me is simply that you picked her up on the beach at the Mandarin Motel, took her up to the Tomoka State Park area . . . [and then] something from her attitude or conversation irritated you to the point that you felt there was a need to kill her, choke her. Was it your intention to kill her when you started choking her or did you . . . What was on your mind then?"

"Not exactly. I didn't intend to choke her. I was just meaning to, uh, keep her mouth shut because she was trying to run her mouth so goddamn much she sounded like my future wife that I was gonna marry."

The sergeant had nothing left to say except to ask Stano if he recalled anything else, about Nancy or the conversation with her. He did not. All he remembered was that after he killed her and left her body by the side of the road, he had driven down Old Dixie Highway to U.S. 1 and then back home.

More than thirty years later, memories of learning of her daughter-in-law's murder were still as fresh to Elizabeth Heard Dow as they were then.

An uncle of Nancy's called the Heard home to let them know what happened. "I've got some sad news," she recalls being informed.

The family was shocked. "I loved my Nancy, and I can't believe what we went through," said Mrs. Dow in her genteel southern accent.

She waited for her son Tom, Nancy's husband, to get home. He walked in "happy as can be," she recalled. He had just learned he had gotten permission to be discharged from the U.S. Air Force and allowed to return to college. Later, he would say that day "turned from the happiest day of his life to the saddest day of his life."

The Heard family gathered later in Georgetown, South Carolina, for Nancy's funeral, some of them no doubt remembering that happy day less than two years earlier, in 1973, when they'd attended Tom and Nancy's wedding at St. James Episcopal Church in Greenville.

Years would go by before they would learn through a

newspaper article read by a friend that Nancy had been the victim of a man who had killed and killed again. Was she too trusting of the friendly stranger that day?

Mrs. Dow remembered warning Nancy of the dangers of going anywhere by herself.

"People treat you like you treat them," Nancy had reassured her mother-in-law. "I know my way around."

FOURTEEN

Jane Doe

"DO IT IN THE DIRT"

It's what a girl wears and carry's [*sic*] herself, that "makes a girl an easy victim." If she wears clothes that are tight, revealing, etc., and the way she carries herself—like, the way she talks, walks, etc.

—Gerald Stano to Kathy Kelly, January 28, 1986

Gerald Eugene Stano left several "Jane Does"—the female counterpoint to a "John Doe," a term used mostly in police jargon to refer to an unidentified corpse—in the wake of his murderous rampage, young women who wouldn't be missed, nor mourned, by anyone. Unlike the champion swimmer, the cheerleader, the preteen, the wife, or the churchgoing high school graduate, he chose mostly lost girls, those who were aimless and wandering. In other words, the most vulnerable. Not that any of his victims were safer than the others, really, given that Stano's were crimes of opportunity. But the executioner of the nameless girls would never have to answer for their deaths to some higher court, except to some investigators.

The Jane Doe known simply as "I-95," and only identified by the eerily prophetic slogan on her T-shirt ("Do It In
The Dirt"), was one of these nameless girls, and her memory
serves as a reminder of all the others now resting in unmarked graves.

She could have been any one of the girls who disappeared
off the streets of Daytona Beach in the late 1970s. Nobody
reported them missing, because no friends or family knew
where they had ended up, and possibly nobody cared. These
girls became mere statistics, each one an unsolved "Signal 5"
in the parlance of the police dispatcher.

The dead girl had been found wearing shorts and a logo
T-shirt. Identifying her was problematic for a team that en-
compassed the Florida State Highway Patrol Division, the
Tallahassee Crime Lab, the Port Orange Police Department,
the Volusia County Sheriff's Office, and the Daytona Beach
Police Department, among others.

The body was first reported on the afternoon of November 5, 1980, by Edward Glenn Hayden to Corporal Donald
Wolf of the Volusia County Sheriff's Office Patrol Division.
Wolf notified Investigator Dave Hudson, who arrived at the
death scene shortly after. As traffic whizzed by on busy Interstate 95, investigators gathered in the median to search for
clues. Soon, the Florida Department of Law Enforcement
Crime Lab also responded to the scene for processing.

Bob Kropp, an investigator with the Medical Examiner's
Office, examined the bones found at the scene and stated that
they appeared to him to be female, although the examiner
could not determine how long the body had been there. Volusia County deputies Loren Smith and Bruce Morrow also
responded to the scene to ensure that the area was kept se-
cure overnight.

On November 6, 1980, when Investigator Dave Hudson

returned to the area, he learned that Deputy Smith had obtained some information overnight: Dennis Andrew Ellis, of Port Orange, had reported that approximately one year earlier, a woman's purse had been found in the woods on the west side of the southbound lane of I-95 along with a man's wallet. All of the property was first turned over to the Port Orange Police Department, then to Sheriff's Investigator Bernard Buscher for follow-up. This would prove only the first in a series of frustrating detours for law enforcement officials.

Shortly after the discovery of the remains, the Florida Department of Law Enforcement Crime Scene Unit arrived and took photographs. Upon doing a complete scene search, Mike Rafferty, who was in charge of the crime-scene team made up of Pam Fowler and Leroy Norris Parker Jr., found an almost complete set of human bones. Some skin remained on the skeleton near the areas of the shoulder, back, and leg bones. Found approximately ten feet away were a green pair of slip-on clog type of shoes. Later found in the same general vicinity were red shorts with blue trim, possibly jogging type shorts, with a stretch waistband, and a red T-shirt with an iron-on patch on the front featuring a picture of a matador, a bull, and the inscription "Do It In The Dirt." On the bottom left-hand corner of the T-shirt were the words "Rat's Hole Copyright 1974."

Investigator Hudson followed up on the slim lead, calling the Rat's Hole in St. Petersburg, Florida, in an attempt to run down any possible lead in reference to the slogan. But the employee he reached stated that the T-shirt in question could have been sold anywhere in the United States by any T-shirt shop. The investigators had hit the proverbial wall.

Hudson also learned from Kropp, of the Medical Examiner's Office, that he estimated the body to have been that of a white female, approximately five feet seven, twenty-five to

thirty years of age. Investigator Dave Hudson started a card
file with the names of all people reported involved in any
suspicious activity in the area. The data was obtained by
Corporal Wolf, who learned that a 1969 Plymouth Wagon
had been seen in the area approximately three to four months
earlier. This would prove another in a series of frustrating
detours for law enforcement officials.

On November 7, 1980, Kropp reported to Investigator
Hudson that the bones that had been found at the scene had
been examined at the University of Florida Anthropology
Lab and her age determined to be no more than nineteen
years of age, as opposed to the original range of twenty-five
to thirty estimated by the medical examiner investigator.

Several names were initially linked to the Jane Doe, a
puzzle with a trail that led to more and more missing girls as
the investigation progressed. Among the tips that Investigator Dave Hudson received on November 11 and 12, 1980,
were the following:

- A dispatcher with the Port Orange Police Department
  reported that on August 13, 1980, an informant stated
  that he'd picked up a white female who'd been badly
  beaten and dropped her off at Taylor Road and I-95.
  The report indicated that the victim's name was Sheila
  DeKitler. No birth date was given.

- A Port Orange resident reported that in June or July, a
  white female by the name of Laurie M. McCoon had
  left their place of employment at the Daytona Beach
  Dog Track and had not been heard from since. A check
  with a Keith McCoon revealed that Laurie was in California, that he had talked with her the night before, and
  that she was fine.

- An Altamonte Springs resident advised that approximately six or seven years ago, when she was about fourteen or fifteen years of age, a white female by the name of Debbie Hachett had been reported missing to the Daytona Beach Police Department and had not been heard from since.

- A Titusville resident indicated that a white female by the name of Irene Foulks had been missing from that town since approximately August 8. Investigator Hudson contacted Foulks's husband in Pennsylvania, who stated that his wife had had three teeth extracted, which did not match the dental records of the unidentified woman found on I-95.

- A Belleview resident called in that a Carla Mixon Burkes, age twenty-three, five feet six, weighing 110 pounds, with blond or light brown hair, had been missing for nine days—too short a time given the skeletonized remains, and she was therefore was ruled out as being Jane Doe.

Several months later, on March 12, 1981, Sergeant Paul Crow, of the Daytona Beach Police Department, interviewed Gerald Stano to determine if he knew anything about the unnamed victim who'd been found on I-95 in Volusia County on November 5, 1980.

Stano had told Crow that about two years prior, he had picked up a white female on Main Street in Daytona Beach, during the annual Bike Week invasion that occurred each March, when both permanent and itinerant vendors lined the beachside street selling souvenirs to the thousands of black-jacketed bikers who descend upon the city.

"Do you recall this incident?" Crow asked, taking Stano

back to a previous admission that he had knowledge of the case.

"Yes, I do, sir," Stano replied.

Crow then asked him if he remembered the girl in question and the location where he had picked her up. Stano referred to a bar on Main Street called Blackbeard's. The year was in 1978 or '79, he added. It was past 9 o'clock in the evening when he encountered the young woman.

"Was she hitchhiking, walking down the street, or what?" Crow inquired.

"No. She was, uh, inside the bar, and I sat across the street at a Laundromat, and she come walking out of the bar and approached the car and asked what I wanted, and I told her what I wanted, which was to have sex with her, and she climbed into the car willingly."

This was Stano's usual way of implying that the young woman in question was an agreeable participant to his advances.

"Where did you go then?" Crow proceeded.

"Well, we took a short, we, we, we took a short drive down Main Street, across the bridge to US-1, came down, down 92, and then down 92, or Volusia Avenue, whatever you want to call it, to I-95."

"Did she ever ask you where you were going or why you were going that way?" Crow did not wait for an answer and pushed further. "Gerald, what you're telling me then, did you end up on Interstate 4, Interstate 95, or where did you take her to?"

"No. We ended up on Interstate 95 going southbound towards the Taylor Road exit."

This spot along the interstate was in the same area where Sheila DeKitler, one of the victims, reported to Investigator Hudson that she had been beaten and abandoned. Later, she said, a man picked her up, and she survived her injuries.

Then Crow asked Stano the most telling question.

"Gerald, how do you describe the clothes on this victim?"

"Uh, she had, she was wearing a dark shirt with, uh, in color, with some type of writing on it, and red shorts. And also very distinctly on her shirt I remember either on the front or the back was either the saying, 'Do It in the Dirt' or an emblem, or a picture of it, one of the three." As it turned out, it was all three.

"Okay, did you ever find out her name or anything?" Crow asked, already guessing that the answer would be negative. Gerald Stano never opened the door to any kind of personal relationship with any of his victims. His small talk often focused on music, which was his personal passion.

"No, sir, I never did."

"At what point did you kill the girl?"

"When we hit, uh, the Interstate down there in between I-95 and that little crossroad by Taylor Road, in between the median of I-95."

"Gerald, do you recall how you killed her? Think hard now." The detective knew well enough that this girl was just one among many others.

"I believe she was strangled." Again, Stano used the passive tense, as if the act of murder were only a casual event not having anything to do with his own action.

"What brought this on?" Crow now pointed to the trigger effect.

"A hot and heavy conversation that was brought on between the two of us over some, uh, money that was being transacted from having sex with the girl." Once more, the conversation was "brought on" and the money was "being transacted," a casual, cold, and objective reference to murder.

"Okay. Then she was a prostitute?"

"Yes, sir."

"Gerald, to the best of your recollection, you did choke her to death?" The investigator wanted to assign blame.

"Yes sir, to the best of my recollection," Stano gave up somewhat reluctantly.

"Do you recall taking her clothes off or did you leave them on her?" No answer. "Gerald, think back, do you remember if you took all her clothes off?" Crow insisted, knowing that the girl's shorts and T-shirt had been found at the crime scene, near but not on the body.

"I think it was removed, the blouse, her shirt, and left her shorts and shoes on. Because it was dark at the time." And again, "it was removed."

"Okay. And did you recognize her on Main Street before as a prostitute? Is that right?"

"Yes, sir, I did."

"Have you seen her often walking up and down Main Street?"

"Yes, a number of times."

"Okay. And how would you describe her physically?"

"Physically, uh, shoulder length hair, uh, built so-so, you know, no Marilyn Monroe."

"Okay. Is there anything else you can tell me about this case that you recall now?"

"Just that she used to hang around Main Street and from what I can understand from a couple of other guys, I don't know their names specifically, but I know she was a rip-off for a prostitute."

For Stano, it was another confession, but for investigators, it was another frustration. Because of the body's decomposition, there was no opportunity for fingerprints. Their only hope was that if a missing person was reported with her description, perhaps dental records could be compared. The Main Street Jane Doe was someone's daughter, or sister, whose life on the streets ended violently—perhaps she had even received that dire warning from her parents when she left home in some faraway city.

Yet in Daytona Beach, she had blended in with the crowd, never making the kind of connection with anyone who would bother to report her missing.

FIFTEEN
So Many Girls, So Little Time

> My relationships with women I can say was not exactly the best. It was good up north, cause you have a different type of girl. Down south, they think you got money to burn on them. Besides, I was very picky at my girlfriends.
>
> —Gerald Stano to Kathy Kelly, August 21, 1985

Sixteen-year-old Linda Hamilton, the oldest of four children, left her home in Millbury, Massachusetts, on June 27, 1975, and her parents, Robert and Marion Hamilton, never saw her again.

Linda's photo makes her look sweet, serene. Her striped shirt fit demurely around her neck. Her shoulder-length hair was parted in the middle per the style in 1975. But Linda was no stranger to trouble, as Volusia County Sheriff's Office reports would indicate. She had been assigned to a juvenile court counselor in Worcester, Massachusetts, and her background was very familiar to one Millbury police sergeant. An "ideal child" until she was thirteen, Linda started running away then, usually to Rhode Island, her father would later tell lawmen.

She packed lightly for her last trip. Her father told investigators he believed that she had only taken her silver Timex watch with a wide leather band, a sleeping bag, and two bathing suits.

It was shortly before 9:00 a.m., July 22, 1975, when G. C. Bradshaw, a member of the police department in DeKalb County, Georgia, found Linda's body. She wore pierced earrings, nothing else.

The last time her father would see her was on a slab at a morgue when he arrived in Volusia County, Florida, to identify her on July 30, 1975. Her nude body—heavily tanned from the sun and bearing the outline of a two-piece bathing suit—had been found a little over a week earlier at New Smyrna Beach, three-quarters of a mile south of Turtle Mound.

Sheriff's investigator Bud Eaton and medical examiner Dr. Arthur Schwartz came to the scene. Investigators began to work the crime scene, measuring ninety-two feet from Linda's body to a row of vegetation along the shore. Along a cutoff just south of where the victim was found, investigators found what they believed were signs of a struggle. They made plaster casts of tire marks and footprints discovered at the scene but found nothing else of value.

The first story about the discovery of the body appeared in the *Daytona Beach Evening News* the same day the body was found, a four-paragraph account that offered few details.

Over the next few days, reporters covered the slow process of identifying the victim. In an unusual move, investigators enlisted *News-Journal* artists Rafael Torres and Steve McLachlin to create sketches based on photos of the dead girl.

Worried parents from several parts of the nation called to inquire about the girl with the bikini tan. Investigators had determined she was about fifteen years old. Her body lay unclaimed in a Holly Hill funeral home as, again and again, parents from other areas learned that this was not their child.

Eventually, in a rare move, investigators released to the press the actual photos of the dead girl as efforts to identify her intensified. On July 29, 1975, the *Daytona Beach Morning Journal* ran two photos—one from the front, the other a side angle, by *News-Journal* photographer Bob Pesce. Promising leads from anxious families were evaluated and discounted until Linda's father made the positive identification.

But the grim image of a young dead girl on the pages of the local paper—not a pleasant sight for residents getting their daily news at the breakfast table—finally gave investigators the break they needed.

Linda Hamilton, a high school freshman, had met up with seventeen-year-old Scott Henne in the first week of July. "They became traveling companions and eventually traveled to Daytona Beach together," according to an official sheriff's office report by Deputy R. J. Baker.

Once they arrived in town, they met up with some of Henne's friends and later shared a dwelling on North Oleander Avenue. Henne and Linda were allowed to share the front part of the house. She soon met three young men spending some time at a vacation home in Flagler Beach. The registered renter of the property, Edward O'Leary, told investigators that Linda had stayed at the condo several times. "He further stated that he had knowledge of her status as a runaway and also, that she was 16 years old," said deputies. For those reasons, he didn't approve of her staying there but didn't object strongly to his own brother staying there while he was vacationing there with his friends.

Wherever Linda stayed those weeks she was in town, she came and went at her leisure. She talked of making contacts so that she could get mushrooms for use as a hallucinogenic drug.

Somewhere on her aimless ramblings around the beachside, Linda Hamilton's path crossed with Gerald Stano's. In a March 12, 1981, interview with Sergeant Paul Crow, Stano recalled the details.

CROW: Mr. Stano, I'd like to refresh your memory and take you back to 1975. I believe the day will be July 21st. And what I'm talking about is a young lady by the name of Linda Hamilton. Her body was found in New Smyrna Beach on the beach. Do you recall this incident, sir?

STANO: Yes, I do sir.

CROW: Do you recall when you picked this young lady up?

STANO: Uh, yes I do.

CROW: Where did you pick her up at?

STANO: Somewhere around the amusement park or on A1A in New Smyrna Beach.

CROW: You say New Smyrna Beach; do you mean Daytona Beach, the amusement park A1A area?

STANO: Yes. In Daytona Beach.

CROW: Okay, when you got her in your car, did you drive around Daytona? Tell me what you did.

STANO: Well, we drove around for a while and, uh, we just took a ride down A1A towards New Smyrna Beach and smoked, smoked a little bit of pot and everything and I was drinking at the time, as I usually do, and uh she got a little upset because I wanted to have a little sex with her and she didn't, and I did. And I just put my arms around her, put my hands around neck and strangled her in the car down there at New Smyrna Beach and choked her.

CROW: Gerald, this incident took place in the car?

STANO: Yes sir.

CROW: And when you took her from the car, how did you get her down to the beach?

STANO: I dragged her down to the beach.

CROW: Did she have her clothes on or was she nude at the time? Do you remember, Gerald? Think back real hard. Do you remember if . . . When you took her down to the beach, when you left her, did she have clothes on when you left her?

STANO: No. No. She was, no, she was completely naked when she, when she left in the car with me under my power. She was under my power when she left.

CROW: Okay. And you say you drug her down to the beach. Was it close to the water's edge?

STANO: Uh, where I buried her, yes. It was close to the water's edge. Yes.

CROW: You say where you buried her, uh, how did you bury her?

STANO: I buried her about two feet down in the sand.

Stano related that he "took off," cleaned the car, and went back for another beer. Six years after the slaying, he recalled the small talk they engaged in, how she had told him that she was staying in Flagler Beach for a few days with friends.

After he drove away, Linda Hamilton died in her watery grave. A postmortem examination would show she had ingested seawater and sand into her stomach. The autopsy further revealed evidence of strangle marks around her neck. She had been asphyxiated and drowned, just as Susan Bickrest had been.

Whether prowling the streets of Daytona Beach in the late hours amid a backdrop of flashing nightclub signs or cruising around during the day, Stano showed no hesitation in approaching his "marks." Some encounters ended badly for him, such as the time he grabbed a young woman's purse when she refused to return the money he had paid her for sex. She called police, but investigators discounted her story because she seemed to be mentally unstable. Again, Stano escaped close scrutiny by police.

SIXTEEN

Mary Carol Maher, the
Final Murder Victim

I kind of look over the girls, because of my weight problem I
have. If they snicker at me, forget it. But, if they take me for
what I am, that's a different story. Besides, I am not what the
girls call a hunk. I am just an overweight nobody.

—Gerald Stano to Kathy Kelly, August 21, 1985

Mary Carol Maher's baby book was a labor of love for her
mom, Gerry. Following the birth of her first daughter—
just about twelve months after her first son—on January 17,
1960, Gerry began documenting all the important moments
of Mary Carol's life.

The scrapbook, now over fifty years old, recorded the
milestones in the life of the young woman her mom called
"MCM," her initials. Carefully written down were the names
of guests at a baby shower in her honor. A birth announcement from Gerry and her husband, Jack, proudly proclaimed
to family and friends the arrival of their daughter, born at
7:55 a.m. on a Sunday, weighing eight pounds, ten ounces.
She was twenty-one and one-half inches long.

"Mary Carol had a slight bruise over her right eye but
she's a beautiful girl," her mother noted. Gerry's second child
proved to be athletic and artistic, a girl who made her own

greeting cards for her mom, all of which were saved. An accomplished pool player, she loved the thrill of the game and frequently vanquished her male opponents. Pictures from family gatherings and newspaper clippings about Mary Carol's swimming prowess and her graduation from Mainland High School in Daytona Beach, Florida, were affixed to the pages. The happy occasions such as Christmas were there in Gerry's book of memories, too—indeed, among the last photos of Mary Carol were pictures of an idyllic family Christmas gathering in 1979.

In a perfect world, Mary Carol would have shown this compilation of her life's achievements to her own child one day.

But the book that had started so joyously with a little girl's birth instead became a tribute to her life, all twenty years of it. The happy project took a dark turn when Mary Carol was reported missing, then found dead. The scrapbook reflects the life of a happy child well loved by her family, the documentation of the dramatic events until the end of her twenty years, her disappearance, then murder. In the first story that appeared in the paper, Mary Carol was merely reported missing. Her body was discovered about three weeks later; it would be about six weeks before investigators were able to determine that she was the last young woman not to survive a ride in serial killer Gerald Stano's car. With a sharp object, he had killed her by striking her again and again, breaking her sternum.

Gerry's children, her two sons and two daughters, were the foundation on which her life was built. She also called upon her deep faith, which she had relied upon to steer her through troubled times, including her divorce and becoming a single mother in the 1970s.

It was that abiding belief in a higher power that brought her through the darkest time of her life: Mary Carol's murder. Some thirty years later, she could recall with certainty the last night she saw her daughter, and the ragged fear that overtook her when Mary Carol wasn't at their appointed meeting place the next day.

"I came home from work very tired," said Gerry, recalling the night of January 27, 1980. She spoke quietly, eloquently, as she sat in the house in Ponce Inlet, Florida, she shares with Leonard Friedman, her second husband of more than twenty-five years.

In 1980, Gerry was a Realtor, an occupation for which she had a real calling, which was a bonus since it helped support the family of five.

That evening, Mary Carol asked to use her mom's car to go out with friends.

"I had an appointment in Gainesville the next day to have dental work done and I needed to be on the road early," Gerry said, explaining why she couldn't fulfill her daughter's request.

Instead, she agreed to drive Mary Carol to the Holiday Inn, where a lounge on the highest floor—the Top of the Boardwalk—was a popular gathering place for young people. There, Mary Carol said she planned to meet two longtime friends.

Once they arrived at the hotel in Daytona Beach, Mary Carol tried to convince her mom to come upstairs for a while to say hello to her friends. Gerry declined, reminding Mary Carol she had to be up early the next day. Mary Carol had decided to accompany her mom to Gainesville, so they agreed on a time to leave in the morning.

Their last few moments together were marked by the closeness the mother and daughter shared.

"She put her arms around me and gave me this pat on the

back," Gerry recalled. Gerry drove away about 10:30 p.m. She never saw her daughter alive again.

The next morning, she awoke to discover Mary Carol had never come home. Her room was just as she had left it. Gerry wasn't overly concerned, since her daughter would occasionally spend the night with a friend if she was out late, so Gerry drove to the subdivision where Mary Carol's friend lived.

But when Gerry arrived, there was no Mary Carol. She drove back home, thinking her daughter might be waiting there.

"Meanwhile, I've wasted thirty minutes," she recalled, concerned about being late for her dental appointment. She left for Gainesville, a two and one-half hour drive away. When she got back that night, she discovered that Mary Carol was still not home.

Mild concern was starting to set in. Mary Carol and her mother enjoyed a close relationship, but she was, after all, twenty years old. She worked at a restaurant in Holly Hill and enjoyed going out with friends several times a week.

Gerry began trying to track her daughter down, but all the promising leads to her whereabouts proved fruitless. Calls to acquaintances turned up information that only increased Gerry's concern: Mary Carol's friends had never made it to the Top of the Boardwalk.

"One had to work late and one was sick," she said. A bartender later told police that Mary Carol had sat alone and seemed "melancholy," her mother said. When she disappeared from the bar, an employee thought she had gone to the restroom.

"Keep her safe and in a warm place," prayed Gerry as the hours turned into days, then weeks.

* * *

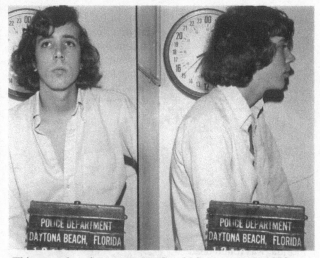

This mug shot shows a young Gerald Stano c. early 1970s.
DAYTONA POLICE DEPARTMENT

Gerald Stano, staring intently during court proceedings in 1983.
FROM THE FILES OF
THE DAYTONA BEACH NEWS-JOURNAL

LEFT: In 1973, New Smyrna Beach High School student Barbara Bauer went shopping for fabric in a trip that ended in her death.

FROM THE FILES OF *THE DAYTONA BEACH NEWS-JOURNAL*

RIGHT: Linda Hamilton, a young woman visiting Florida, was found dead on the beach on July 22, 1975, her nude body bruised and beaten.

FROM THE FILES OF *THE DAYTONA BEACH NEWS-JOURNAL*

LEFT: An accomplished woodworking student, Mary Kathleen Muldoon was shot first and then drowned in November 1977.

FROM THE FILES OF *THE DAYTONA BEACH NEWS-JOURNAL*

RIGHT: Toni Van Haddocks, a young mother of three, was out on the street hustling men, police said, when she was murdered in February 1980.

FROM THE FILES OF *THE DAYTONA BEACH NEWS-JOURNAL*

LEFT: This T-shirt bearing the image of a man on a horse and the message "Do It in the Dirt" was found with the remains of one of Stano's victims. Her identity was never established.

DAYTONA POLICE DEPARTMENT

Stano (in glasses) accompanied Police Sergeant Paul Crow (in white shirt and tie) to the site where he claimed to have left the body of Susan Basile, his youngest known victim, in Port Orange, Florida.

FROM THE FILES OF *THE DAYTONA BEACH NEWS-JOURNAL*

Twelve-year-old Susan Basile, the only victim Stano was believed to have known personally, had skated with him at a rink near her home. Her body was never found.

Susan's grief stricken father, Sal Basile, talked about his daughter just after she disappeared after getting off the school bus near her home in June 1975.

Mary Carol Maher was a championship swimmer who disappeared after her mother dropped her off at a bar the night of January 27, 1980.

COURTESY OF THE MAHER FAMILY

Mary Carol Maher's mother, Gerry Friedman, successfully sued Stano over the murder of her daughter, but the big cash jury award was only a moral victory.

COURTESY OF THE MAHER FAMILY

RIGHT: Security was heavy for Gerald Stano's June 7, 1983, court hearing after several death threats were called in to the courthouse where he appeared.

FROM THE FILES OF *THE DAYTONA BEACH NEWS-JOURNAL*

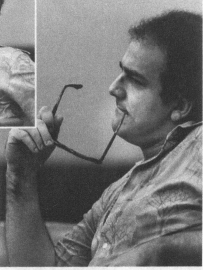

ABOVE LEFT: Stano appeared amused in court the day his fate was decided: two death sentences.

ABOVE RIGHT: A pensive Gerald Stano put his glasses in his mouth as he listened during a court hearing.

FROM THE FILES OF *THE DAYTONA BEACH NEWS-JOURNAL*

The circuit judge who sentenced Stano to death, James Foxman, heard a total of twenty capital cases in his career on the bench. "I try to put them out of my mind," he says now.

Gerald Stano looked over at paperwork held by his attorney, Don Jacobson, a former FBI agent, during a court hearing.

Paul Crow, c. 1995. The former Daytona Beach police sergeant who headed the Stano investigation was later named chief of police.

FROM THE FILES OF
THE DAYTONA BEACH NEWS-JOURNAL

Reporter Kathy Kelly, seen here in a 2010 photograph, drew Gerald Stano out into telling her why he'd killed and killed again. She received more than forty letters from the convicted murderer between 1985 and 1986.

AUDREY PARENTE

Gerald Stano was no stranger to the disco room at the Holiday Inn Boardwalk. A devoted fan of disco queen Donna Summer, he occasionally went there with a group of friends, said at least one young woman in a later deposition.

Gerry Friedman now thinks Stano had been stalking her daughter. She believed Mary Carol might have had a passing acquaintance with Stano through a friend who worked at a Howard Johnson's Hotel with him.

"They were outside one night talking after work and Stano came by and asked if they wanted a ride," said Gerry. The girls declined.

Gerry firmly believed her daughter wasn't hitchhiking that night. Anytime that was suggested in a newspaper story, she complained to Police Sergeant Paul Crow. Thirty years later, she's more convinced than ever that Gerald Stano had singled out Mary Carol and was tracking her.

According to Gerry, she learned through police reports that the night he approached her daughter at the Top of the Boardwalk Lounge, Stano asked Mary Carol if she needed a ride home to Ormond Beach, Florida. Mary Carol's hesitation about accepting a ride from someone she didn't know well, if at all, may have been tempered by his indication that he knew where she lived.

After exhausting all possible leads as to her daughter's whereabouts, Gerry finally reported Mary Carol's disappearance to the police on January 30, 1980, but she recalled the nonchalant attitude of the officer working behind the complaint desk.

"She's probably off having a good time," the officer told her.

"I went everywhere," Gerry Friedman said. By then, she admitted, she was "panicky. I went to work less; I did less."

By that time, Mary Carol's older brother John, and their younger sister, Celeste, were both attending Clemson University in South Carolina on swimming scholarships. Indeed, all of Gerry's four children, including the youngest, Mark, were regular water bugs. Their love of swimming no doubt came from Gerry, who was a member of a synchronized swimming group at Chicago State University. At a young age, when they were bored at home, a family friend who coached swimming suggested they take up the sport. Later, they got swimming lessons as birthday presents.

"We swam all day, ate, then went to bed," recalls John Maher, oldest of the Maher children. He and Celeste had worked hard to recruit Mary Carol for the Clemson swim team because of her strong showing as a swimmer at Mainland High School. She, her mother, and their younger brother joined the other siblings and spent a festive weekend when Mary Carol went to check out the campus. A group family photo in Mary Carol's baby book documents the South Carolina trip. Although she was offered a scholarship, she decided to stay at Daytona Beach Community College for her last semester before transferring to the South Carolina school in the fall.

"She wanted to stay and enjoy the beach," said John.

On February 3, 1980, the facts were noted in a news release issued by Sergeant Roy G. Willis:

"Missing person: Mary Carol Maher, W/F, 20 years old. Subject is 5-6, 125 Lbs. and has long sandy blonde hair which she wears in a pony tail on the right side of her face. Subject has blue green eyes.

"Last seen wearing tan slacks with a possible pink blouse with floral designs. Last seen at the Top of the Boardwalk

Lounge, located at the Holiday Inn 400 N. Atlantic Ave., at 10:45 p.m. on the 27th. Day of Jan. 80."

A small story appeared in the newspaper about her disappearance. Leads, if any, were few and futile. Mary Carol Maher had simply disappeared without a trace.

The mystery of her whereabouts ended two weeks later, on February 17, when two young men out "dirt-dogging" in a remote area off Bellevue Avenue thought they had discovered a dead animal because of an unpleasant smell.

Investigating closer, the sight of a watch on an arm convinced the two it wasn't a dead dog. They discovered it was actually a woman's body covered with a foam material and some tree limbs, "so we jumped in my car and headed for the police station," said one of the men in a statement to police.

Sergeant Paul Crow responded to the scene. The victim appeared to be a white woman, wearing a black-striped long-sleeved silk shirt with blue jeans. He soon discovered holes in the front and back of the shirt, as well as her right thigh. "The body had what appeared to be multiple stab wounds," he wrote in a report dated February 17, 1980. Returning to the police department, Crow searched missing reports for a possible match to the human remains. Aside from the differences in clothing, the description of the victim matched the missing person report, 80-01-8046, prepared on Mary Carol Maher. Crow later confirmed that Mary Carol had been wearing her mother's blouse, rather than the one described in the missing person alert.

Mary Carol was a strong swimmer; she was athletic, fit. Yet she was no match for the man intent on harming her. Her body showed no indication of defensive wounds during the attack in which Stano struck her again and again with a sharp object.

Crow contacted Gerry, then went to her home, where she

identified some of the jewelry found at the scene. "As soon as I saw the watch, I knew it was hers," she recalled later. The family's vigil of waiting was over. Mary Carol was dead. "That was the beginning of the end," her mother believed.

Three weeks after Mary Carol hugged her mother good-bye, Gerry learned she would never see her alive again.

The hours and days of prayer for Mary Carol's safe return ended with the news that the body found off Bellevue Avenue was hers. Individually, her family suffered in their own private hells.

"There was some guilt on my part for not pushing her into coming [to Clemson] in January," John Maher said. "It took me a few years to see that it wasn't my fault," he said, admitting to a "lot of rage."

For Gerry Friedman, her daughter's death was proof of her mantra: "It's up to God. He knows when you're going to be born and when you're going to die." She suffered greatly after her daughter's death, both mentally and physically. She had what she termed a nervous breakdown as she struggled to cope with the loss of her daughter and the horrific details of her death; and Gerry also suffered cancer and chronic back problems. But the pain in her heart was an unremitting one.

In 1983, she sued Gerald Stano for more than $100 million in Circuit Court in Volusia County, Florida, seeking to be compensated for the mental pain and suffering she experienced from her daughter's death and the loss of her services and companionship.

Six months later, a jury awarded her more than $200 million in what was then believed to be the largest money judgment ever handed down in a wrongful death suit. "I don't expect to collect any of the money," Gerry Friedman told reporters after the jury returned the verdict. "I did it for my daughter and all the other victims' families. Mary Carol can rest in peace now."

For this mother, years of attending bereavement support groups may have eased her pain a bit, but the murder of her daughter left her with permanent scars more painful than any surgery or cancer treatments.

On July 21, 2008, she wrote:

I have been wounded in my heart and soul for over 28 years. The scars will remain with me, my children, family and friends forever.

As a single mother of four outstanding academic and athletic children, I have always been proud of them as well as their achievements. Mary Carol was on a full scholarship when her untimely death occurred.

The least victim of Gerald Stano had to have been a better person than this demonic individual.

Some may have forgiven the despicable deed—yet God must deal with his soul.

Perhaps we may now have some closure and peace of mind that this nightmare of 28 years is coming to an end.

Once a heart is pierced, all that remains are the scars.

The injustice of it all are the years of anguished waiting.

A copy of that statement is tucked inside Mary Carol's baby book, now filled with newspaper clippings of her untimely death. It has become a tribute to a daughter whose life ended way too soon, and a testament to the suffering of a close family for whom Mary Carol's death would always be raw.

SEVENTEEN

Profile of a Serial Killer

"HERE COMES THAT OLD RED AGAIN"

> I thought I would never get caught, and everything would be alright. But it didn't work out that way at all.
>
> —Gerald Stano to Kathy Kelly, November 3, 1985

Nobody should have been surprised by Gerald Stano's murderous path. Devoid of any kind of bonding experience with his mother, he spent a lifetime feeling rejected by his adoptive father and scorned by the women who didn't like his taste in clothes or music.

Court-appointed psychiatrists spent hours analyzing Stano. When all was said and done, it seemed murdering women was something for which he was predestined. Finding his prey "would turn me into a different person altogether," he would claim. For Stano, his driver's license was also a license to kill. It gave him mobility, just what he needed to stay under the radar of law enforcement officers, who weren't operating with any of today's investigative tools, such as DNA testing.

Stano's first appointment with the electric chair was made in June 1983 when Circuit Judge S. James Foxman gave him two death sentences for the murders of Susan Bickrest, the bar waitress found dead near Spruce Creek in 1975, and

Mary Kathleen "Katie" Muldoon, the Daytona Beach Community College student and part-time bar employee found shot to death in 1977. Before sentencing Stano, Judge Foxman said, "I see no motive in these killings."

Furthermore, he said, "Normally we see passion, greed, the need to eliminate a witness; I don't see that here. These murders are completely senseless."

Almost three decades later, when discussing Gerald Stano, whose claims of killing more than forty women would place him among the most prolific serial killers in the country, Foxman recalled, "He seemed to be the most ordinary person."

Conceding he didn't think the former short-order cook was highly intelligent, Foxman had no doubt that Stano committed the crimes he confessed to. "I think there was more than enough evidence to conclude he did those murders. He did recall a lot of details at great length."

Within six months, Stano received a life sentence for the murder of Cathy Lee Scharf, the young woman he had picked up at the Anchor Bar on Merritt Island. His first murder trial in her death ended in a mistrial; the second ended with a guilty verdict in December 1983 and a recommendation by the jury that he be sentenced to die.

He walked into the courtroom there already facing a life sentence for the murder of Nancy Heard, twenty-four, found strangled in Ormond Beach in 1975. In 1981, he received a life sentence in her death in Volusia County. In Brevard County, Circuit Judge Gil Goshorn rejected a last-minute request for a new trial before sentencing Stano to die by electrocution, the method of court-ordered death as mandated by Florida law.

The next month, a Seminole County jury convicted Stano in the 1974 stabbing death of an unidentified woman dubbed "Madame X." Stano claimed to have picked up the short, stocky woman with bad teeth in 1974 as she was hitchhiking in Altamonte Springs, a suburb of Orlando, Florida. Her body was found three to four weeks later. A set of engagement and wedding rings was found nearby and an autopsy indicated she may have had two children.

She was never identified and earned the nickname of "Madame X" from a radiologist. Her family never knew her fate. Just minutes after the jury convicted Stano, Circuit Judge Robert B. McGregor sentenced Stano to life in prison.

By that time, Stano had also already pleaded guilty to the murders of Mary Carol Maher, twenty, the pretty blond former high school swim star who died from multiple stab wounds; Toni Van Haddocks, twenty-eight, the black prostitute with the broken arm whom he had viciously attacked; Nancy Heard, twenty-four, the motel maid whom he had strangled to death; Linda Hamilton, sixteen, whom he had killed in nearby New Smyrna Beach; and Ramona Neal, nineteen, whom he had picked up while she was in town celebrating her high school graduation.

Gerald Stano had first been arrested on April 1, 1980, for his assault on Donna Marie Hensley, the prostitute whose escape made her a "live victim," a critical witness for investigators. Through Hensley, investigators connected Stano to the murder of Mary Carol Maher. After he was charged with Maher's death, Stano was examined by psychologist Ann McMillan and psychiatrists Robert Davis and Fernando Stern.

Dr. McMillan's report concluded June 23, 1980, included her interviews with Gerald Stano's adoptive parents for three and one-half hours and subsequently Stano himself for six and one-half hours.

Dr. McMillan detailed Stano's early development and the neglect he suffered from birth and his behavior in childhood and later years, from lying and stealing to petty theft and vandalism. The Stanos described their son as a "lifelong pathological liar."

As a young adult, he worked at the Burroughs Corporation, where he was fired for being "totally incorrigible." While drinking heavily, his behavior was described as ranging "from a happy, silly drunk" to "a violent, deranged madman."

Dr. McMillan concluded her report by summarizing her initial impressions, that Gerald Stano had never been a "normal" personality, nor had he ever had a pattern of normal male-female relations.

Now, as to what made him "kill and kill again,"* as Stano once was asked, it wasn't just the fact that he would be alone in his room and lonely, and would "see all the couples having fun," and then he would go out in his car and "find a girl walking." The stressor, or trigger, would occur once the "young lady" (as he called his victims, as if to depersonalize them) said something that set him off. It could be anything from a disparaging remark about his weight to a slight dismissal of his taste in music.

Interestingly, all of the girls whom Stano had ever been seriously involved with had some type of abnormality. For example, his first girlfriend was mentally disabled; the second was epileptic and had undergone brain surgery; the third one was a fifteen-year-old runaway who purportedly had emotional and behavioral problems; and the fourth, his former wife, supposedly had emotional problems, including compulsive overeating. His only other relationships with women were with prostitutes or with young women whom he believed to be prostitutes.

Dr. McMillan's final and most compelling conclusion

---

* Writer Kathy Kelly posed the question to Stano: "What made you kill and kill again?"

stated that "Gerald Stano's abnormal behavior and antisocial acts have followed a consistent progression from infancy to adulthood that makes the act of murder a logical, rather than an illogical event."

The psychologist based these findings on what she termed the "three most logical bases for mental disorder," which she deemed present in Stano from at least six months old:

1. Neurological impairment because of either head injuries or severe malnutrition or both

2. Childhood schizophrenia (now paranoid schizophrenia), again because of physical and maternal deprivation, brain damage, or biochemical alterations

3. Asocial personality

Dr. McMillan went on to examine the characteristics of the schizophrenic murderer and the differences between the psychopathic and schizophrenic personalities.

The report also characterized the schizophrenic's murders as ones of "unnecessary ferociousness and senselessness" in which the killer committed more than one crime, using the action of murder as a way of discharging an "intolerable schizophrenic anger."

In keeping with these observations, the antisocial behavior of the schizophrenic murderer caused him to not only disassociate himself from the killing or killings, but to also enjoy a sense of calm or even gratification.

Psychiatrist Dr. Robert Davis sent his report to Circuit Judge James Foxman as well as to Gerald Stano's court-appointed attorney, Donald Jacobson; Howard Pearl, the assistant public defender; and Larry Nixon, the assistant state attorney.

Dr. Davis also recounted Gerald Stano's early childhood and then detailed Stano's activities back in the early 1970s, when he was living in Daytona Beach with his mother. Even back then, he had begun to pick up girls on the Boardwalk and along the beach area. He admitted to getting involved with a fifteen-year-old and taking her to Georgia on one occasion and to New York on another.

Stano told the psychiatrist of a confrontation at a school in Daytona Beach with a gang member whose girlfriend operated as a prostitute, and he said that one of the gang members cut his chin with a knife.

Dr. Davis deemed Gerald Stano competent to stand trial, and he stated that the accused did not qualify under the criteria for any sort of psychiatric hospitalization or treatment. But, said the psychiatrist, Stano *did* exhibit chilling characteristics in his murderous spree, with total strangers as his unwilling victims:

"This man has little or no conscience. He is grossly selfish, callous, and irresponsible. He is very impulsive. He has a very low frustration tolerance and can fly into a rage at a moment's notice. He blames the violence of his behavior on the belligerence of his victims."

During his many interviews with police investigators pertaining to the murders, Gerald Stano always faulted his victims for mouthing off to him, arguing, or making disparaging remarks.

Sergeant Paul Crow pointed out the randomness of Stano's method of operation in his attacks. He would stab some of the victims, as he had Donna Marie Hensley and Mary Carol Maher; he strangled others, such as Barbara Bauer and Susan Bickrest, whom he also drowned, as he did Linda Hamilton. With still others, he would use a combination of attacks, such as stabbing, shooting, or beating, as with Ramona Neal and Katie Muldoon.

* * *

Dr. Fernando Stern, the other psychiatrist who examined Gerald Stano, also delved into Stano's early years and failed marriage, during which he was physically abusive to his wife. Dr. Stern noted that Stano stated he'd always been violent toward the women he dated, especially when he was intoxicated.

Alcohol was a key factor in Stern's analysis of Stano's mental state. He believed Stano wasn't sane at the time of the murders, during which Stano had claimed to always be under the influence of alcohol "probably due to decompensation of a chronic psychotic condition due to alcohol abuse."

Stano threatened to beat his wife on several occasions, always insisting her sisters or other family members be around when he was present. As for Stano's current mental state, the psychiatrist deemed him "perfectly able to stand trial."

Dr. Stern referred to Stano's vivid memory, whereby he was able to tell the doctor the particular details of several of his crimes. The psychiatrist classified the cold, calculating manner in which Stano described all of these incidents as a highly inappropriate behavior. As with atypical schizophrenic disorder, Stano went through these episodes during which he was unable to control himself while under the influence of alcohol.

"Here comes the old red again," Stano recalled thinking when he demanded sex from one woman and was told, 'Hell, no!'"

This psychiatrist also referred to Gerald Stano as "utterly remorseless."

Dr. Ann McMillan compared Gerald Stano to other sociopathic killers.

Citing *Classifying Criminal Offenders: New System Based on MMPI (SAGE Library of Social Research)*, by Edwin I. Megargee and M. J. Bohn, published a year earlier, in 1979, Dr. McMillan listed ten subtypes of criminal offenders, among whom the "Charlie" profile—named for Charles Manson, who sent his acolytes, Charles "Tex" Watson, Patricia Krenwinkle, and Susan Atkins, to butcher actress Sharon Tate and her companions at her home in Los Angeles on August 8, 1969—was "the most malignant." These were the criminals who committed "senseless crimes," which were, Dr. McMillan pointed out, basically "anti-social acts." The criminal who fit the "Charlie profile" was a sociopath who became psychotic over a period of time.

A sociopath, according to various definitions, was someone whose behavior may be superficially charming, like Ted Bundy's,* or as Stano could also be when he was engaging young women in casual conversation. The sociopath felt absolutely no empathy for any other human being. Other convicted murderers who fit into the "Charlie profile" category were Sirhan Sirhan (Robert F. Kennedy's killer) and David Berkowitz (aka "Son of Sam").

After examining Stano, Dr. McMillan concluded:

"The best single predictor of violence and of determining the true degree of psychopathology is past behavior. In tracing Gerald Stano's case history from the prenatal stage to the present it can be clearly demonstrated that Mr. Stano has never been normal; and that in his progression from childhood to adolescence to adult abnormalities it was logical to predict that 'murderer' would inevitably be added to his labels.

---

* Ted Bundy had not yet been convicted when *Classifying Criminal Offenders: New System Based On MMPI (SAGE Library of Social Research)*, by Edwin I. Megargee and M. J. Bohn, was published, but he would have received stellar marks on Dr. Megargee's "Charlie" scale.

Primary diagnosis: Paranoid schizophrenia
Secondary diagnosis: Sociopathic personality."

In recent years, the practice of criminal profiling has evolved into an infinitely more sophisticated science. Certain rules, however, still apply when examining the causes and early factors of criminal behavior.

For instance, a large number of serial killers seem to have been either adopted or severely neglected as children, or from apparently functional families where one parent was the controller. Many were illegitimate.

Charles Manson's mother, Kathleen Maddox, was sixteen when Charlie was born and was a sometime prostitute and petty criminal. She married a man called William Manson and changed Charlie's last name to the one that has now become infamous.

Ted Bundy was born in a house for unwed mothers. He grew up believing that his mother was his sister and his grandparents were his parents.

Gerald Stano, too, was illegitimate, and severely neglected as an infant. His adoptive parents were seemingly functional, but he often referred to his father as cruel and controlling—at times, even abusive.

As youngsters, these criminals find the socialization process difficult if not impossible. Bundy was inept with women as an adolescent, and Stano was not at all liked by his peers.

As for what makes them "kill and kill again," it's some form of unfairness they perceive to have suffered, or have suffered, from childhood and into adolescence and at the hands of some authority figure, especially women.

Bundy pined after a society girl who dumped him unceremoniously, and then, as has become known, he murdered young women with long brown hair parted in the middle, as if to kill her again and again.

Stano first blamed his ex-wife for his drinking and prowling for women, and then the behavior of his "young lady" victims for his violent acts, stating that they were talking too much or making fun of him. Some he killed when they refused his advances or ridiculed his clothing or choice of music.

But the bottom line was, these criminals found perfect justifications for their heinous acts, and there was no point in trying to find any logic in their behavior. The very aberrant and abhorrent nature of their crimes defied all logic.

EIGHTEEN

Life on Death Row, Waiting To Die

> Kathy, this waiting period now, is really taking it's toll on me hard. I wish he (the Gov.) would tell my attorney what he wants to do further, or to sign my warrant.
>
> —Gerald Stano to Kathy Kelly, April 17, 1986

> They think I have turned all of my cards over. I have held a few back Kathy. Because, two people can play a card game. And, they have to make a very good offer, if they want my cards totally turned over. Maybe they could care less about what I have card wise. But, it would really turn some heads if they knew what it is. I will convey these cards only, at the right time and place. It will do no good trying to find out what it is, cause they won't come out till the right time.
>
> —Gerald Stano to Kathy Kelly, November 3, 1985

Waiting to die was hard for Jerry Stano.

For eighteen years, his days were ruled by the tedium of prison life. His inevitable date with death, however, was planned right down to the last minute, his last meal, his last phone call. The pretty young women who climbed into his car didn't have that luxury. They thought they would be back in Sunday school the next weekend, back behind the counter serving drinks, or in class at college. Their time was up, too, but they didn't know it.

The days in a cell at the Florida State Prison death row, not far from the electric chair, moved slowly. The routine of prison life—rising at his customary 6:00 a.m.—was a comfort. He could smoke, make a cup of instant coffee, or listen to his favorite music on his headphones.

Appeals on his murder convictions made their way through the courts. Appeals are mandatory, and public defenders who handle only death penalty cases pore over copies of trial testimony looking for that one little error that will give the prisoner a reason for a new trial. These appeals add years to prisoners doing their time. Their hopes rise with news a witness may have been asked to change testimony or the outcome of a forensic case is in doubt.

The days, months, and years of waiting were broken by occasional "callouts," summons from a prison official to tell him an appeal had been denied, or his execution had been delayed.

Visits from his parents—his only regular visitors—were often painful. He was happy to see his mom but often returned to his cell frustrated by his father's cold attitude and the effect it had on his mother.

He also deeply resented the constant pejorative comparisons to his younger and also adopted brother.

Stano's one attempt at athleticism—a prison volleyball game during one of his limited outside hours—met with failure. He sprained his ankle, and it swelled badly. Better for him to keep his sports interests limited to the small television in his cell. He took up crocheting, making baby blankets for the children of fellow inmates or friends. His former public defender, Chris Quarles, would bring yarn to him for these projects.*

---

* Under current Florida prison guidelines in 2009, that hobby is no longer permitted.

Goading from guards and fellow prisoners about the stack of sentences he faced nagged him. He had high blood pressure, as he reminded me in one letter, and that type of stress was harmful.

"You know, I hate when the guys start talking about my time—5–25 years and 3 Death Sentences. They don't know when to back off. All I do is put on my headphones and stereo, and block them out. I refrain from talking about it with hem cause of my temper, and, I would end up in a fight over it on the yard, and loose [*sic*] all my privileges for 30–60 days. . . . Follow what I am saying? They don't seem to realize I am nothing to play with."*

The monotony of prison—interrupted by occasional court appearances or visits to the prison doctor—was also broken by visitors who toured the prison hallways with guides, seeing firsthand the most dangerous prisoners of all, the murderers.

Ron Word, an Associated Press reporter based in Jacksonville, toured the prison and said that his "most vivid memory of Stano was during a tour of death row." The serial killer, Word recalled, was "sitting in his underwear, doing a paint-by-number of *The Last Supper.*"

Although the anticipation of death permeated the cellblocks, prisoners depended on the jailhouse pipeline for word when their population has been reduced by one.

"It looks like Gov. Graham got one of us the other day at 12 noon. After it was over, they have the nerve to bring visitors by for a tour. They don't care about our feelings when they have an execution. All they care about is themselfs [*sic*]. But, we have to stick with each other, and hope for the best." †

---

* Gerald Stano to Kathy Kelly, September 16, 1985

† Gerald Stano to Kathy Kelly, April 17, 1986

At one point, Stano thought it might be useful to apologize to the families of the victims, though actual remorse seemed a foreign emotion to him. The "bitchin'" girls got what they deserved. He never would have shot, stabbed, or strangled them if they hadn't asked for it by being disrespectful.

Although this seemed to him like a good idea at the time, he thought maybe someone else should write the apology:

"Kathy, what would you say to an article printed in the newspaper? It would be a type of apology to all the relatives of the victims. . . . What do you think? If you want to do it, let me know, and I will formulate the letter for you. But, I would want it word for word as I write it. I trust you more than anyone to write it. It's the least I can do. Cause, the public has me labeled as "having no remorse or feelings." . . . But let me know what you think, okay? I would like to verify a few things, and put a point across to someone and their family.''*

Even from his prison cell, Stano was still conniving and thinking of ways to manipulate people and the situation in his favor. Did he have any idea how transparent it seemed to have a prisoner facing death suddenly begin to feel sorry for all those murders and the lives they had ruined? Did he know people would see it for what it was, a ploy for sympathy, a reprieve from that last walk to "Old Sparky"?

In some letters, he seemed resigned to his future and his fate:

"As you know, I go for the pre-clemency hearing Friday, Sept. 6. I am a little nervous about it too. But, we all (us men on D.R.) have to go through it once. Then, our case goes to Gov. Bob Graham for his consideration. After that, he signs a warrant for us, and we go to death watch for 30 days. I haven't been there yet, but I might be there before this year

---

* Gerald Stano to Kathy Kelly, October 10, 1985

is up. It all depends on how fast he rules on the case. But I have a feeling he will rush mine through."*

Again and again, the Florida Supreme Court denied appeals from Stano's legal team. During 1997 alone, three execution dates for him were stayed. Five days before Stano was scheduled to be executed, a Brevard County jurist, Judge Tonya Rainwater of the Eighteenth Circuit in Viera, Florida, denied his last appeal on March 19, 1998.

She dismissed claims in a forty-seven-page brief that a prisoner to whom Stano had supposedly confessed had now recanted his story. The last-minute appeal also claimed to have statements from four Daytona Beach police officers accusing Sergeant Paul Crow of lying to protect his cases.

The round of allegations was ill-timed and ill-founded, she wrote. The prisoner's claims of recanting his story amounted to hearsay; inadmissible evidence, she wrote in dismissing the appeal. As for accusations against Crow, state and federal courts had dismissed similar claims in the past.

The night before his planned execution, Stano requested a deluxe meal, not unlike one of the repasts he had enjoyed during his carousing days in Daytona Beach. With great care, he invoked a happier time in his life. His bountiful dinner selections at fine dining spots were definitely not on the prison menu, but an exception was made for his final meal. Before being strapped in, Stano consumed a Delmonico steak, bacon bits, baked potato with sour cream, some French bread with butter, and a tossed salad topped with blue cheese dressing. For dessert, he requested a half gallon of mint chocolate chip ice cream and washed down the big meal with two liters of Dr. Pepper.

After Stano's death, his attorney released a final statement, dated March 23, 1998:

---

* Gerald Stano to Kathy Kelly, September 5, 1985

LAST STATEMENTS OF GERALD EUGENE STANO

I want to thank my family, my many friends, and my legal team for all their love and support. Know that I love you all and cherish your love. Thank-you for sticking with me even when you were attacked, made fun of, and criticized.

People on death row need good people to help them. Whatever people feel about the death penalty, surely everyone agrees that innocent people should not be executed. When people on death row do not have good lawyers who are allowed to do their jobs without fear, innocent people get executed.

I am innocent. There are good police officers and there are bad one. Many police officers have come forward and said that I was put on death row by a police officer who lies under oath. That is true. I was frightened, I was threatened, and I was held month after month without any real legal representation. I was not strong enough. I confessed to crimes that I did not commit. It is hard for a person who has never been held in jail, completely isolated, and without any help, to understand that a person will confess to something awful that they did not do.

My heart goes out to the families who believe that I am responsible for the death of their loved one. My team presented my innocence, but today courts seem to want vengeance more than justice. The result in my case was that no one listened. Now I am dead and you do not have the truth. This is tragic. Sgt. Paul Crow created the story, but all other police officers know I am innocent. Crow should be held accountable.

In the end, Paul Crow became the target of Stano's venom, some eighteen years after the two had first met and formed an unlikely alliance. Crow had been father confessor to Stano, tripped up in his killing spree by the one who got away.

"All of the people I met have told me: 'you're crazy to have trusted a cop.' That's them. Not me. I wasn't like that. They never hurt me, so why should I not trust them. . . . All during this, Paul was like a person I could talk to, and confide in. I didn't look at him like a policeman. I saw him as a real person, who cared what happened to me.'"[*]

His letters referred time and again to the special relationship he had with Crow, one of trust and understanding. Yet, when his final days neared, Stano turned on Crow.

"I don't think it was him," said Crow, referring to Stano's final statement. "I think it was his attorney."

Stano's attorney for the appeals process, Chris Quarles, a public defender, continued to be bound by restrictions of the bar even years after Stano's case was closed via his execution. It was his job to give his client the best legal representation he could, to fight the charges.

"He clearly wanted to please Crow," said Quarles when discussing whether Stano had been coerced. "I think there's no doubt he pleaded falsely to some."

But did he think Stano was telling the truth when he admitted the multiple killings?

"I would have no better take on that than anyone else," said Quarles.

Quarles had been a public defender in the appellate division since 1980, and there was no doubt that Stano was one of his more interesting cases, he said.

"He must have had a certain charm," said Quarles of Stano's prolific approaches to women. The longtime public defender encountered people who knew Stano before his arrest, and they commented on the killer's affability and easygoing nature.

---

* Gerald Stano to Kathy Kelly, November 3, 1985

Abused as a child, Gerald Stano went to his death saying he had been used by a police officer and a court system for crimes he didn't commit. Despite detailed confessions to law enforcement agents in several jurisdictions, multiple stories of how his rage could be ignited by something as simple as criticism of his music, Stano said it was a lie.

When he was in custody all those months and years, Stano believed he had the upper hand. As long as he had information investigators wanted, they would have to play the game his way. A few hints here and there, then he would sit back in the chair and prolong the agony, making detectives work for every scrap of information they got.

Until then, the stocky man in the polyester shirt and pants who'd lured women into his car over and over again had gotten away with murder. Years later, he would sit for hours telling and retelling the killing tales.

"After eight hours of talking to him, you were drained," said former Volusia County Sheriff's Office investigator Dave Hudson.

Although Crow had heard chilling details of the murders of the pretty young women and was convinced Stano had killed them, he said he had given the confessed serial killer one last chance to clear his conscience.

"Jerry, I don't think I'm gong to be able to talk to you any more," he said he had told Stano when he visited him at the Florida State Prison. They were put into a small room that served as a guard's booth, all glassed in. The appeals process was counting down, and Stano's date with the electric chair loomed; although ultimately it would actually end up delayed again and again—for another twelve years.

"If there is anything you want to recant right now, here is the time to do it," said Crow. "I'll do anything to help you."

"I'm okay with it," Crow quoted the condemned killer as

saying, referring to his lengthy string of confessions. "Suddenly he appeared cocky," Crow said. "He said no, that he would see me in court."

And, although Stano's final statement referred to love three times in the first paragraph, that was another foreign emotion to him. He adored his adoptive mother and claimed that he cared about his brother, Arthur, but showing affection was not something that Gerald Stano did.

On the morning of Monday, March 23, 1998, uniformed officers brought Gerald Stano to the death chamber and seated him in the seventy-five-year-old electric chair.* The macho Jerry was gone. His head was shaved and coated with gel. The top buttons of his shirt were open and an electrode was attached to his right calf.

In the audience, his attorney mouthed words of encouragement, while siblings of some of Stano's victims waited to watch his final breaths. Within fifteen minutes of being strapped in with a leather headpiece and an apronlike mask, the first jolt—eight seconds of 2,300 volts and 9 ½ amps—coursed through his body.

"Die, you monster," Ray Neal said aloud, punching the air with his fist for emphasis. Afterward, Cheryl Ramona Neal's brothers, who had witnessed the execution, rejoined the rest of their family, who had not, filling them in on the details of Stano's final minutes. The family member of another victim had brought cigars. The stogies were usually a celebratory measure for a birth, but these families were cheering a death,

---

* It wasn't until January 2000 that the Florida Legislature passed legislation allowing lethal injection as an alternative method of execution in Florida.

the end of life for a man whose circle of victims spread far beyond the women he beat to death, or shot or strangled.

If the moral victory of the $200 million judgment—never collected—brought Mary Carol Maher's mother Gerry Friedman comfort, Stano's execution did not.

"I don't believe in the death penalty, abortion or euthanasia," she said emphatically.

But her son, John, and his sister, Celeste, were at the Florida State Prison in Starke on March 23, 1998, to watch Stano put to death.

The Maher siblings sat in the audience with family members of other victims as the jolts of electricity coursed through Stano's body. John Maher's eyes met Stano's briefly as he looked for any sign of remorse.

"In the end, he was a coward as I expected," Maher said then. "I've got a sense of relief. I can't hate like that ever again. It's not worth the toll it's taken on me."

Stano's body was released to a local funeral home, then cremated. A funeral home spokesman declined to disclose the disposition of the ashes.

Stano went to his grave without uttering a word from death row about his victims.

Were there more? Was he still holding a few cards close to the vest?

In the eighteen years between his arrest and execution, Gerald Stano enjoyed the feeling that he was in charge. He picked out Paul Crow for his mentor, almost a surrogate father figure. He called all the shots on when he would be interviewed and just how the information these investigators so desperately wanted would leak out. For hours on end, he tantalized them with small hints of what he had done before actually admitting the heinous crimes for which he became so famous.

He alternated between owning up to cases long before police had any inkling he was involved or reluctantly giving up facts, such as about the murder of Susan Basile, his youngest victim.

In the end, he turned on Detective Paul Crow, the only person he had said he could trust. He walked the tightrope to the electric chair by himself. But eventually, Stano's time ran out. If he had one of those proverbial cards up his sleeve, he didn't show it.

APPENDIX A

Stano's Letters to Kathy Kelly

Gerald Stano's first letter to me arrived in my work mail August 20, 1985. The clerk who sorted the letters brought it to me with a puzzled look, saying, "That killer is writing to you." She had no idea I had asked him to write, to tell me his story.

After that, to avoid conversations at work, I gave Stano my home address, knowing full well—I hoped—that he would never show up at my door. I had made one visit to the prison, at that point, and we'd agreed that I would write him a series of questions about his life and the cases, and he would answer.

Quickly, his letters took on a personal tone, asking what kind of music I liked and what I planned to do over upcoming holidays. The assortment of letters and several get-well cards have been stored in a shoe box in my closet, waiting for the time I could write about the murder cases and what Stano had to say—in his own words.

In some cases, I have changed the names of women Stano had become involved with. Their youthful infatuations with a man whose dark side they knew nothing about should not scar them again now.

August 15, 1985

Dear Kathy,

Hi! I want to thank you for coming up, and wanting to take time to write about me. I am sorry about you having to take time off from work to come up. Wish there was some way for me to pay you back.

If you want to get on my visiting list, please contact Mr. Dayan, my Classification Officer. Explain to him what we are doing, and that you can only get weekends off to do it. If need be, ask Don for a little help.

Also, please don't forget about your family, and devote all time to me. Your family comes first Kathy.

I really don't know where to start except, one incident in Penn. where Angela's* step dad (Richard) threatened me with a .22 caliber gun. It was after I had to pay for an abortion for Angela. That is when I started drinking and running around. It was the beginning of a different Jerry that had to rely on booze and beer.

I would drink very rarely until I moved to Florida. The reason for that is because of Yvonne,† whom I dated for two and a half years, before moving to Fla. She was an epileptic, and I cherished the ground she walked on. But, the threat with the gun was always in the back of my mind. That is why I always never took advantage of her anyway.

When I moved to Florida in 1974, I saw girls getting in and out of cars. After awhile, they were getting in my car too. After a while, the girls said they were going to

---

* Denotes pseudonym

† Denotes pseudonym

*have their "old man" get me. That triggered my memory
of the threat. So, I would go out and get some beer and
booze, and get drunk, and than pick up one of the girls
and kill her, knowing I wouldn't have to worry about her
getting the "old man" on me. Plus, I was also thinking
what my child would have been, if I didn't have to pay for
an abortion. All of the murders were the same way, and I
thought I would never get caught.*

*But, one night it was only an aggravated battery type
deal. It totally backfired on me. I was arrested, and now
I am on the Florida's Death Row.*

*But, I was also married down here. It was one day at
the station that my ex-brother-in-law swung at me, and I
came at him with my belt. That gave me a flashback of
that incident in Penn. I took out my anger on my ex-wife's
dog and her. Once, in front of her aunt and uncle; and
that started the divorce proceedings. She moved to her
mother's house and left me with our trailer (24'x 60').
After the divorce, I had a small relationship with one girl
and that was the last time before I was locked up.*

*This is basically what started the change of Jerry, to
the Jerry that people call a "serial killer".*

*My childhood was the usual. If I wanted to buy some-
thing, I had to have a good reason. If I wanted to talk to
my father, I would cringe at the sight of him. I was afraid
of him, and to this day, I still am afraid of him. Even my
brother is afraid of him to this day also. My mother
would take charge of us during the week, and tell him
(dad) what we did wrong on the phone. When he got
home, he would march us both into the bathroom and
beat us with a leather razor strap. When I cracked up the
family car, he came after me with a straight edge razor
opened up. When I had accidents with my cars, he would
always go into a rage, and say "Why couldn't you have*

been killed?" He has always carried a grudge for my
brother and I. Probably, because all of his brothers had
kids who got straight "A's", the honor roll and now sup-
porting themselves. My brother and I never had a chance
to do that before we were married.

Kathy, I am trying to touch base on things that might
be of help to you. I am waiting for your questions. Maybe
I have answered a couple, maybe not. But, you have my
full cooperation Kathy. When you said you were 38, I fell
over. I thought you were 30–32. I really didn't know what
to expect at first.

I will continue this over the weekend and mail it on
Sunday night. Our mail goes out on Sunday–Thursday,
but we receive mail on Fridays.

Well I am back again.

I was trying to figure out what I was going to say, but
caught myself in Pennsylvania with my last girlfriend. It
usually happens when I talk about her.*

You probably have a list of my qualifications, but if
you don't here they are.

1.) High school grad.

2.) Certified Computer operator-programmer.

3.) Cook

4.) Outboard Marine Mechanic- apprentice

Married June 21, 1975 till July 16, 1986 have taken
[lessons on] the following musical instruments.

1.) piano

2.) violin

3.) clarinet

4.) guitar

5.) organ

---

* For Stano, the requests in my letters to recall details of his early life caused his
mind to relive those early days, as if they were happening again.

Music I like is all types, esp: the oldies, dance music (disco), and todays music of the 80's.

I use to like to dance, go for rides, and play the organ (which my mother still has), roller skate.

As I said before, everything I had was in beautiful condition, from my clothes to my car. At home, everything was put in its proper place. I learned that from my mother's father. He was more of a father the two years I was with him, than my father. My grandfather trusted me, where my father never did. It was like, he never wanted children. He would beat us; as far back as I can remember. He would always find fault at what I would do and the same with my brother.

He tells me now when he comes to visit: "Why don't you hang yourself, or cut your wrists and throat." He also says "I am killing him slowly." My mother tells me to keep fighting, and that she is behind me 100 percent all the way. Mom and I have both said that if something happens to her or me, it won't be long before the other goes. Now my mother is the one with the bad heart, and has had cancer surgery. Dad is the one who is failing real bad. I believe my mother will outlive him. But he has to stop riding my mother's back. He is the one who is driving her to her grave. Mom is very much afraid of him now also. All he wants to do is run, run, run all day long. When it comes time to come up and visit me, he turns very hateful. Paul can confirm this and also Don. Dad lives for his clubs and the real estate office. It was the same way before he retired. Always worrying about the company and salesmen. Forget about the two boys at home.

Kathy, I will close for now, but please write when you get a chance. Also have Paul, drop me a line.

Take care, and drive carefully when you come up next time.

Also, make sure you get permission to bring your tape recorder next time. And try to get on my visiting list as a friend. Not a reporter. They might even give you a special pass for one Saturday or Sunday. We can find out when you come up next time.

Respectfully,
Jerry Stano

P.S. I hope your not afraid of me, or coming up here to see me.

I felt that he was trying to turn it all around right off the bat and trying to make it seem like something it was not.

August 18, 1985

Dear Kathy, I was thinking back, and I remember you sitting in the center office of Paul's. I believe I also have read some of your articles in the paper.

I would like to touch on the subject of police questioning suspects. Most people are playing games with them. They don't see they have a job to do. First, the detective has extensive work to do in the research department then, they take a list of suspects and look through their m.o.'s. Then when they find a suspect with an m.o. like they are looking for, they follow that person very carefully. When they finally catch the person, he lies about everything not realizing that the background work has already been done. If the suspect would just put his cards on the table, the detective will do the same thing.

You see, Paul and I had and still have a communica-

tion not like others. Some of the counties Detectives are
real back breakers. They put you in a cell, and wait for
you to talk your head off. They want you to clean all of
their homicides for them, besides, the one they are questioning you for. If you don't play well with them, they get
very nasty and treat you very rough.

Paul set up a good thing for me while I was in Daytona Beach City Jail. He was the go-between for me, because he knew what the other counties were going to do
to me. When we were on the road, he was always present.
Even the other counties didn't like it, they had to confirm
what we wanted. One County even came and got me from
here by plane without Paul knowing it. I knew what to
expect before that happened. You see, I wanted to help
Paul as much as possible, and he knew it. But, the other
counties thought we were working too closely together. If
Paul didn't care about me and my family, he could have
handled everything differently. But, he saw what I was
doing with, a person that was not your average run of the
mill type. Even his boss was very cooperative, along with
the city jail for two months.

What other Det. do you know would work with a person the way Paul worked with me, and vise versa. Nobody at all. That is why I respect Paul very much. Even
his detectives' co-workers are great people. If Paul
wanted to know anything about a case, we would talk
about it, and lay ground work, than we would get off the
track for a few minutes. But, it was strictly business between us. If the other people would see us lying around
laughing or clowning around, they thought that we were
setting up something. But that is the way we were, and no
one can take that away from us.

Kathy, I sure hope that this is helping you to formu-

late your book. I am waiting for your letter with the questions, so I know what to talk about. But, aside say this may help in some other way.

I didn't know if you like music, but I do. While I am writing this, I am listening to my stereo with the head-phones on, to the oldies. Most of what I have on records at my parents' house. Do you like music if so, what type? I hope you don't think I am being nosey.

I forgot to ask you Kathy, but what do I get out of this? You and Paul will harvest the most, but what about me? I was wondering about that. Besides, I would appreciate it if you would not tell any other reporters about this. I would only refuse them Kathy. You are the only one I will talk to. If you get a chance to talk to Don, please tell him to come up with you next time. It's been many moons since I saw him last Kathy. He is really a true friend of mine, as is Paul. I would also like to see Paul, if you could tell him for me please.

Well I can't think of anything else at this time. Please write soon with those questions Kathy. But, don't forget your other duties at the News-Journal. They come first, as does your family.

Sincerely,
Jerry

* * *

August 21, 1985

Dear Kathy,

I was really happy to get your letter.

Before we go to far, I must tell you that the Parole & Probation Commission have me scheduled for an inter-

view on Sept. 6, 1985 at 1:30 p.m. After that, my case
goes to Gov. Bob Graham, and it might bring a warrant
signed for me. Don is aware of this also. But, I wanted to
let you know before it happens Kathy. This may put a
dampener on what we have here. Also, please try and see
if they will let you get on my visiting list. It could be very
helpful in this project.

I don't mean to be noisy [sic], but do you have any
relatives working on the police force in Daytona Beach?
I was only wondering. Cause, they treated me very nicely,
while I was there for 2 mths.

Hope you had a nice weekend. It was the same old
thing up here.

You said for me not to worry about offending you with
language. I have always given respect, when it is given to
me. Especially nice young lady's like yourself. When the
men get together by themselves, that is a different story.

Well, let's get down to business, and answer your
questions for you.

Well, my first girlfriend was named Angela. She was
in High School at the time. Good looking, but she wasn't
smart. She was slow learning, and that had her qualified
as retarded by my parents. We met at a Junior Achieve-
ment Program. It started the two of us seeing each other.
I had my first car, and would drive up to see her on Fridays, Saturdays and Sundays. We started dating pretty
regularly, and I brought her a ring too. So that was a
commitment so to speak. I started taking advantage of
Angela by saying how much I loved her. She let me do
what I wanted to her. It started with only her blouse, then
it was everything. So, one night, we were at it in my
car, we had sex and that was the moment she got pregnant. When she had morning sickness, her mother approached my parents with—"Your son Jerry has gotten

*our daughter pregnant. We want him to pay for the abor-
tion." So, my parents told me what happened and what
they wanted. That was the end of about 1 ½ years together.*

*By the end of the year, I thought no one wanted me for
a boyfriend until I met Yvonne on New Years Eve 1971. I
will get into this later after I answer the rest of your
questions.*

*My relationships with women I can say was not ex-
actly the best. It was good up north, cause you have a
different type of girl. Down south, they think you got
money to burn on them. Besides, I was very picky at my
girlfriends. Like Yvonne up in Pennsylvania. If the young
lady is a respectful type (no running around) I will take
to her, and treat her with respect. But, if she is a tramp,
she won't get any respect from me. I kind of look over the
girls, because of my weight problem I have. If they snicker
at me, forget it. But, if they take me for what I am, that's
a different story. Besides, I am not what the girls call a
hunk. I am just an overweight nobody.*

*As for my childhood, it was not exactly a happy one.
Cause I was raised by my mother, and only saw my father
on Friday nights, and Saturdays. Friday nights after supper, we would get marched into the bathroom and get
beat with a leather strap and sent to our rooms. They
tried to compensate by getting two of everything. From
as far back as I can remember, I was never trusted to
do anything. It was always a sheltered life. Couldn't do
this, couldn't do that. That was a mistake, cause it would
have helped. They wanted me to carry an "A" average in
school, cause my mother was that way, and my father,
held a grudge, cause he put his other brother through
school, then he wouldn't help my father.*

I first got into trouble (minor scrapes) in Mt. Vernon,

N.J. in 1965. It was the type of people I had to be with. All street wise. They had me pegged from the start, cause of my clothes, etc. So, I had to prove myself to them. That is when I thru rocks at cars (off the walk bridge) and turned in fire alarms. But they still thought I was not one of them.

I have mentioned before, that when Richard pointed that .22 caliber at me, that was the turning point. The first time I wanted to hurt someone, was when my father came at me with a 2' x 4' and hit the windshield of my car. I got out and grabbed a tire iron from the garage, and wanted to beat him with it, because he hit part of me, my car. It was my 1970 Impala Custom which I cherished very much. It even had a plate on the front with Yvonne's name. This was in 1971 or 1972.

It wasn't easy trying to tell my parents what happened. My father was very nasty towards me, and would always tell me "why don't you just kill yourself." He has always been that way Since April 1, 1980 when I was arrested. Even to this day, he is very nasty, and he says practically the same thing to me. My mom is the one who cares a lot. She took it very hard, and said "she would stay by me, no matter what." Mom takes care of getting all my packages, and comes to see me every two weeks. If my father had any say (if mom wasn't here), he wouldn't come up or even get me any packages.

Well, Kathy, I have answered your questions, and I await more.

Please feel free to write when you want to. Also, try and bring Don with you when you come up next time, or even Paul. Then you could see what I was talking about Kathy. It would probably be very interesting for the book, cause people could see how Paul and I handle one another.

By the way, don't forget to try and get on my visiting list Kathy. This is only if you want to. Besides, you were the one who brought it up. And it would be a good thing too, for what we are doing. If it happens, you can bring $20 cash in $5 bills (4). That is for sodas, sandwiches, ice cream, o.j., etc. They take you to the main part first and you can get coffee to bring in, along with sodas, o.j. Then, when you get in V.P. park, they come around for hot sandwiches, and bring in more sodas, and ice cream. I thought I would pass this on to you just in case you get on my list.

Hope to hear from you soon.

Sincerely, Jerry

* * *

August 24, 1985

Dear Kathy.

Was very happy to receive your letter Friday. Glad you got the letters I wrote you. You have a good idea about not sending my letters to your office. Best be safe, and sound, than have a lot of talk in the office. That is why it would be a good idea to try and get on my visiting list. You won't have to worry about losing any time from work. But that is up to you Kathy.

Sure hope you are enjoying yourself on weekends, cause all I have is my stereo and t.v. to help pass the time. I am not complaining, but I miss my freedom. At least I don't have to listen to my father all the time.

Forgive me for asking "what was in it for me." I want people to see the real Jerry, and what he went through growing up, and what happened to him, and where he is now. With your help, Kathy, we won't leave any stone unturned, OK?

Now for the questions you asked.

I can remember my parents telling me one day, I was adopted, but not the year. It didn't register until one day when I was in high school. It hit me like a ton of bricks. Why would my real mother and father put me up for adoption? Did I do something wrong when I was a baby or what? Plenty of questions like that were running around my head. I would sit and look at my fathers (adopted) picture, and it would look like me. I even had thoughts that my father's first wife was my real mother, and he was my real father. Reason for that is, I look to much like my father now. Everyone has said "that you can tell, that is father and son." If you look carefully, why else would my father ignore me while growing up? It brings into the pictures of being "unadoptable" the doctors told my mother at 13 mths of age. This makes me wonder, if that was why they frowned upon all of the girls I dated. I still have my doubts about my father being my real father. Sure, they try to match you up real good, but, not like my father and I. We have too many things in common. I also found out from Don, that I was the baby of 5. One was "stillborn, one was born blue," and three of us were okay. That made me wonder why my parents didn't want my other brothers or sisters. Besides, finding out that I was "unadoptable" really hurt me. My parents kept that, and the fact that 2 others of mine were out there. This was pointed out to me in the county jail. If my parents knew this, why did they want me to begin with, and spend so much time getting legal papers, and doctors to say "go ahead and adopt him." Why didn't they just put me back in the agency for someone else? That is the question. And it probably won't be answered.

See, my mother was married before also, and can't

have any children. So, that brings up the fact I was the first one to come along that my mother liked. So, she got her doctors, and supervisor, to go along with the adoption, cause she was a registered nurse at the time.

Also, it brings up why they never told me about any of this. They were probably afraid that I might just want to go looking for the others and if they told me I was "unadoptable," I might do something. Sure, that crossed my mind, but I would always stop and say. "Why do I want to hurt my parents?" So, I never pursued it any.

But, what has me wondering is why my parents never let me run with the other kids. Probably, because of the label that was put on me, by the doctors. Besides having motor problems too. They thought I wouldn't fit in with them. So, they got me interested in music, playing the piano, violin, clarinet, guitar and finally the organ. Plus I loved music (records). I was in the Marching Band in Junior High and High School. They always kept me sheltered till I got in my car. Then, it was all new to me from then on. I could go places by myself or with one of the girls I went with. But, I even had a curfew. Even after I graduated from High School. They stopped my curfew when I got married, cause I wasn't living at their home.

Everything I had was considered theirs. Even my cars had liens on them. They never [gave] me a chance at anything. It was always what they wanted me to do. If I wanted to take my girlfriends to the shore (N.J.) I had to have their parents talk to mine, and confirm it. Even after I got divorced, my parents took control again. I took care of two houses for my parents, and never once, could I have any friends over. That is why I spent my Friday and Saturday nights at the Skating Rinks. Cause I enjoyed myself and was around people that enjoyed having me there. All of this stems from my being "unadoptable."

You see, most people think, "Why is this guy roller skating and things like that." He should be in bars, dancing, etc. But, they don't realize I was making up for lost time.

Kathy, my life is very different from everyone else as you know. But, you don't know what it's like to be told what to do, and when you can do it. And you're 25–28 years of age. The others that age are calling the shots for themselves. From what I have told you so far, I feel a little better. You are the first person I have been able to talk to about this. Don't think I am trying to get even with my parents, or old girlfriends, or ex-wife, but I am telling you about the real Jerry, and what he went through growing up and what he was confronted with all the time.

I am telling you everything that happened from 13 months of age til I was arrested. When we get all of this completed, I can tell you what it is like to be locked up for the first time in my life.

Kathy, you can send me stamps in your letters if you like, or get a money order made out to me if you like. But they allow stamps to come in though.

Well, guess I'll close for now, please write soon, and please take care of yourself for me. See you soon.

Respectfully, Jerry

* * *

August 27, 1985

Dear Kathy,

I thought I would start another letter to you. I sure hope you don't mind. I hope I don't bore you with my letters, but the people want to know about the real Jerry.

It's funny, but I have always felt, I got the worst of everything growing up. What I mean is, my brother could do no wrong. If he did, I would pay the penalty. But, I loved him like a brother, even though we were both adopted. I would take him here and there if he wanted. Sure, we had our differences, but that's normal though.

My brother thought I was crazy keeping my room clean, my car clean. He never did anything like that. He looked like a "rag-a-muffin." Always wearing holey jeans, leather jackets, etc. I would always have pressed pants, ironed shirts, wing tip shoes, etc. If we went out with the family, he would put on some good clothes, but it always rubbed me the wrong way. I knew my father wanted his boys to look good, and I would always do it, cause I was the oldest, and knew I would get balled out later. So, I always pacified my father that way.

You see, Kat, I learned more from my grandfather than my father. Plus, we did more together at home. My father always tried to play my grandfather's role in Penn. I knew the way to do things, and he always wanted it his way. So, it would always end up in a big argument. Even to this day, it's the same way. He knew I was a work horse, and always wanted to see me make a few dollars. So, he would pay me to do things like cutting the lawn, waxing the family car. But, if my brother wanted any money, he would give it to him with no questions asked. That would rub me the wrong way too.

Kathy, even when they came up Sunday, he had an attitude, cause he was missing one of his clubs he belongs to. All he does is pick, pick, pick and complain to me how he hates coming here. But, my mother is very concerned, and is always full of life, joking and telling me what is new at home, or where she has been, or what she is reading now.

You can probably see what I am talking about, by visualizing what I am saying. If you were to meet him, he would put a different attitude out. But, leave, and he is back to normal. He is used to handling salesmen 12 hours a day, and then taking his frustration out on me. That may be where I got my quick temper from. All fathers should keep their work in the office, and never bring it home. But, my father is an exception. He would always bring paperwork home, and never pay any attention to me or my brother.

But, if an argument started with family, and he would go into a rage because we were interrupting his train of thought. I don't see how my mother has stayed married to him all this time.

Kathy, this is a portion that I thought would be of importance to you, for our project we are working on.

I will write more tomorrow, before I mail it tomorrow night.

* * *

August 28, 1985

Well, here I am again. Looks like a lousy day ahead. So I can write, read, and watch t.v.

Kat—I have a neighbor that thinks he is king. Wants to talk all the time, and is trying to play "the nut role." If I get off track any, that is why, cause he calls me all the time.

You asked about Angela. Well, yes her parents forced her to have the abortion. She was the one that was retarded. You see, she was my first girlfriend. But my next girlfriend is whom I loved very much, and so she loved me the same way. If I stayed up north, I would be married, and have a family by now. If I haven't mentioned

anything about her, let me know please, and I will ex-
plain. You see, I don't know the format you wish to por-
tray of me and my girlfriends. But, I can say one thing,
you look like a girl I knew at my church that was very
cute, and I dated her a few times. You also look a little
like my mother, Kat. If you're are going to put pictures in,
you might want a shot of me when I was little, and grow-
ing up. If so, let me know, and I will send you a few of
each to pick from.

Kathy, what I would like to know is, "Why do people
draw conclusions without looking at the person's back-
ground?" This has always stayed with me, [and] I would
like an answer.

Guess I'll close for now, write when you get a chance.
Be careful where you go and hope to see you soon.

Respectfully, Jerry.

P.S. Kat, I just got your letter of Aug. 27. I will start
working on your question tomorrow morning. I will rack
my brain for that question.

As for you not going to try for my visiting list, I can
understand. You do it the way you see fit.

It may take a while for me to formulate this next letter,
so don't worry Kat. I'm working on it.

See you later,
Jerry

How ironic! Speaking from experience he warned *me* to be
careful about "where I go." He also started calling me "Kat,"
which no one except close family and friends has ever called
me. It was his way of trying to ingratiate himself to me. It

was also the technique called "forced teaming," typical of con men, rapists, and serial killers as well as police officers appearing to be a friend, not an inquisitor.

August 29, 1985

Dear Kathy,

I just received your letter of Wed. pm.

I too am shocked at that being declined.

I have written inmate requests to Mr. Dugger (Superintendent) and Mr. J.R. Reddish (Assistant Superintendent of Programs.) This was done before I wrote to you.

I want you to contact Don Jacobson, and tell him to call here and find out what happened. Nobody can refuse an interview but me, and believe me, I wasn't even notified you called this time, like I was last time.

If you call again, please ask for Mr. J.R. Reddish or Mr. Dugger. These are the two you should talk to.

These people really have me upset over this, and it's not good cause I have high blood pressure and take medication for it.

Kat, no one has pressured me about talking to you. Not even my father. No one knows except us. That's how I want it until I'm ready to tell others.

This problem will be worked out if I have to file legal papers on them. But we (you and I) won't give up on this. You keep calling for an interview with me and I will stay on these people with inmate requests.

But, don't give up Kat. We have something working, and I know you and I both want it to work out.

Kat, please keep trying on the phone. Maybe even have Paul try calling for the both of you.

Things are going along real well now. That is why we can't give up on this.

Kat, I am being honest with you also, about everything. As I said before, you are the only person in your field I have consented to do this with.

I knew something was wrong, when I got your letter written by hand. Just sit tight, and do what I said—keep calling here for an interview and have Paul try also. Because I want to see you again, Kat.

Let me know who you spoke with when you called here, and they declined our interview.

Please write me back on this Kat.

Also, be careful and stay calm. Let me do the worrying for us. Okay? Besides, I worry about you now cause of this.

Yours truly,
Jerry

P.S. I am working on that assignment for you, but will take care of this matter at hand first.

Jerry

* * *

August 29, 1985

Dear Kathy,

As I said last night in my letter to you, I will be formulating all the facts I can remember about it.

It was rough last night cause I saw the whole thing all over again. Think I got about 3 hrs. of sleep. Luckily I have coffee and cigarettes, cause I was at them last night.

Let me start by describing the car I had. It was a light green 1973 Plymouth Duster. It was a small about six engine with a 3 speed on the column, with Avenger 60's with chrome slotted mags and high-jack air shocks, am/fm stereo eight-track, anti-theft door locks, and always in immaculate condition. It even had two chrome mirrors I put on. I was really proud of that car. I got it brand new from Cheltenham Chrysler in Penn.

I was working at Burroughs Corp. running computers in Paoli, Penn. We had a new # 7700 I was running for demonstrations to different companies.

It was one night when my Dad and I got a call that my Grandfather died. After that night, I was never the same. I loved him very dearly. So, one night after work, I decided to drive to Florida. Figured I would make it straight through. You see, I was upset about my grandfather dying, and also the fact I was going into the Navy, and I would probably lose Yvonne (my girlfriend) too. All of this was playing on my mind while I was driving. I got as far as Gainesville and I figured I better turn back, cause I had a job, and girlfriend who needed me, and my grandfather would have wanted me to keep both. So, I drove around Gainesville for a few hours, and came upon two girls hitchhiking. I stopped and asked if they needed a ride, and they got in. I told them I was thinking of going to college here. I was drinking beer and the girls were a little nervous about that.

The subject turned to sex then, and I was wanting to get into bed with one or both. But they took a negative attitude cause I was a little overweight, and that triggered something in my brain, and I pulled out my hunting knife from under my seat. All I wanted was sex, I wasn't out to murder them. But it ended up with me stabbing both girls to death. I even had to chase down one of the girls. I carried that one to a wooded area off the road, and went back to my car, and the other one was slumped over moaning. So I stabbed her a few times in the back and carried her almost as far. After that, I cleaned up my car, and myself, and headed back to Pennsylvania and my job.

You see, Kat, there was another that was close in months, but these two were the first. I ought to know which ones are which, I was there when it happened.

When I got back to Pennsylvania, I went about my business like nothing had happened. I didn't even have to worry about taking a day off for travel time. I went home, cut the grass, and then went over to Yvonne's house. No questions were asked where I was last night, cause she trusted me, and knew I was upset about losing my grandfather.

That is what happened with the first case I ever did.

Kathy, it was even worse when I lost my grandmother. I was married at the time and all my (ex) was interested in, was how much money was left to me. She learned that none was left to me, and took an entire different outlook at me then. She was spending more time at her mother's and less time at our house. This can be discussed later, Kat.

I am going to try and get a few hours of sleep now, cause I have put down what happened with that case.

Please forgive me for cutting this short, but I am a walking zombie. Will write more this weekend.

Sorry I took so long writing back to you, but I was waiting for an answer on those inmate requests I filled out about our visit.

I got a real nice letter from Paul last night. It was good to hear from him. Kat, he will help us get our interviews.

*Well, I want to get this in the mail tonight. Please
write soon—and be careful where you go.*

Yours truly,
Jerry

*P.S. Don't give up on our interviews, Kat—keep trying,
and have Paul try also. Will let you know when I hear
from them, or why they refused our interview.*

The "trigger" was the put-down about his weight from one
of the girls, or both. And here it was, in black and white, how
he "went about his business like nothing had happened." The
first murders were obviously out of frustration, and perhaps
also triggered by the girls being lesbians. After that, he knew
that he could kill again.

September 1, 1985

Dear Kathy,

*I thought I would drop you a line, since there is nothing
happening up here.*

   *Besides, I am still steamed at these people for what
they did to you on the phone. If I didn't care about getting
visits from my mother, and you, I would go off on them.
Then, I would be placed on a disciplinary report with
nothing (no visits, etc.) But you and mom are the only
reason I haven't done that.*

   *I am also worried about this hurricane that is brew-
ing on the West Coast. If it comes East, it will hit here,
and you will have severe winds and flooding in Daytona.
I hope you are in a high area like my parents. But they*

have a pool with screening and that would be torn to bits. If it comes your way, please make sure everything is tied down, and you take shelter. I don't want anything to happen to you or my parents.

Bet your going to have a good time this weekend. Have fun, but be careful, okay?

We have a 3 day holiday up here, which holds our mail up one day.

Kat, let me know how long it takes for you to receive one of my letters. They like to read mail here on the way out, cause we can't seal our envelopes. They do it for us here.

What I was thinking was, these people don't like to let reporters, news people in too much, cause they know what some of them do. But don't worry. Just keep calling, and have Paul try too if need be, Kat. I want to see you again, and also Paul too. With both of us working on these people, they will see what we mean.

Let me explain something, when a lawyer calls for an interview, they don't contact us. They just call us in when he comes. But when a newspaper calls (mag, paper, tv) they contact us before for approval. I wanted you to know that. You see, they were to contact me before they gave you an answer. They took it upon themselves to answer for me, which is not right. But I have caught them at their own game. That is why I filed those inmate requests to these two people. Call again, when you get my last letter, but ask for one of those two people I mentioned, and find out why they declined our visit, and I will do the same here. Cause I will get to the bottom of this problem.

If you get a chance, please have Paul tell Sgt. Charles Connelly "Hello, and I am doing fine." Charley and I went to jr. high together and was in the band. His mother knew my grandmother through the band. That was when Frank Northrup was band Director of Seabreeze Jr. High School. But that is history now.

Guess I will close for now, I don't want to keep you from anything.

If you get a chance, drop me a line, and please tell whom you talked to when they declined our visit. That way, I can file a grievance request on the person.

Be careful on Labor Day Weekend.

Always,
Jerry

Again, he warned me to "be careful." Anne Rule, who wrote *The Stranger Beside Me*, a firsthand account about her having worked alongside serial killer Ted Bundy, also recalled how, after she and Bundy finished their shift at a crisis-intervention center manning phones, Bundy would walk her to her car, advise her to roll up her windows and lock her doors, and say, "Be careful."

September 5, 1985

Dear Kathy,

Hi! Thought I would start a letter to you. As you know, I go for the Pre-Clemency Hearing on Friday Sept. 6. I am a little nervous about it too. But we all (us men on D.R.) have to go through it once. Then, our case goes to Gov. Bob Graham for his consideration. After that, he signs a warrant for us, and we go to death watch for 30 days. I haven't been there yet, but I might be there before this

year is up. It all depends on how fast he rules on the case.
But I have a feeling he will rush mine through, Kat.

I am still waiting to hear from those people whom I
wrote about why our interview was declined.

I am listening to I-100 here in Daytona while writing
to you. They are playing my artist, David Lee Roth "Cali-
fornia Girls" and "Just a Gigolo." The one song, "Just a
Gigolo," is my theme song. It fits me to a tee. Paul knows
what I mean, Kat.

I wrote Paul a nice letter the other day. It was good
to hear from him. At least Paul and I see eye to eye on
some things. I am talking about questioning of different
detectives.

Kat, I wrote you a letter in response to your question
you asked. I wanted you to have the answer before I went
to the Pre-Clemency Hearing on Friday. Write me, let me
know what you want answered, Kat. I also told Paul to
help out with our visits if need be.

And now I wonder why he told me about the songs in
the context of all he did: "California Girls" and "Just a Gigolo." After "Gigolo" there is too much information, another
telltale sign of conning: "[It is] my theme song. It fits me to
a tee. Paul knows what I mean." And then again, of course,
"Kat."

Sunday, September 8, 1985

Hi Kathy,

Back again. I got responses to the inmate requests you
sent. Both of them were worded the same. Am enclosing
a photo copy for you, I have the originals.

*I am waiting patiently for your next letter, and our
next visit together.*

Well, Friday is over.

*My Pre-Clemency Hearing, they wanted to have three
cases at once, but my lawyer was only prepared for the
last case. I have to have a lawyer from Volusia County
represent me for these 2 cases. I'm not looking forward
to it again.*

*My parents were up today. Mom was really happy but
the old man was a real snob. Sure would like to know why
he has the attitude he has. I have enough problems on my
mind than to have him bitch for 4–6 hours.*

Guess I'll close, Kat.

Please write when you get a chance.

Yours truly,
Jerry

P.S. Photo copy enclosed for you.

While I was in the hospital for major surgery (I had part of
a lung removed), he expressed concern for me.

September 9, 1985

Dear Kathy,

*I received your two letters today. You better take care of
yourself, cause we have a lot of work to do. Please take
care of yourself for me Kat. While your in the hospital I
will give you some time to rest. All you do is run, run, run
every day.*

See you heard from the prison here. Some mixup,

huh? At least, they know that we were both aware of what happened, and I took the necessary measures here, and so did you. We won't have any problems now, hopefully. But, you get better first okay? That's more important Kat.

I am writing now to learn when my case goes in front of Gov. Bob Graham. I have to have an attorney from Daytona represent me on these 2 cases for clemency. Hope I get someone I know from there. That would help a lot Kat. But, I have to wait and see who Judge Foxman appoints for me.

Football season opened, so I have been watching football all weekend. I won this past weekend, and have another bet on tonight's game. Keep your fingers crossed for me.

Wish I had a phone in my cell, cause I would call, and wish you well, and also talk to my cousin in New York.

Kat, you know I have been having dreams about Pennsylvania and my old girlfriend there.

Guess writing about my life has triggered my memory. It's funny cause I have been asked by many news reporters, etc., to talk to them, and I have refused. But, you're the only one I want to talk to. Besides, your friends of mine are my friends too. You know who I am talking about.

Well, this Thursday I will be 34. It seems like 54 to me. I would love to go to "Julian's Rest." on A1A in Ormond Beach for supper then go to 600 North for some dancing, or to "Troddus Shore Bar Lounge" and listen to the "Better Way." That would make my night, or go to dinner with a young lady to the Hilton, and then where she wanted to go. But I will have to settle for a cup of coffee and a cigarette and one apple pie.

Guess I'll close for now. For me—please get well, and

take care of yourself. Don't want anything to happen to you Kat. I will wait for a few days, then write to you again around Thursday morning and mail it Thursday night.

Yours truly,
Jerry

P.S. Get Well soon okay! I am listening more to WKTZ 96fm. It's just like WWLV 95.5 in Daytona. Guess my taste is changing in music. But I like it.

* * *

September 12, 1985

Dear Kathy,

Hi Kat! Hope your feeling better. I have said a few prayers for you. Hope they helped. You take it easy at home, and get better. Don't worry about coming up, till you feel much better. I just hope that it's nothing serious, Kat.

I am waiting now for oral arguments in Tallahassee for my Clemency. It's very nerve racking at this time, plus I am worried about you in the hospital. But I know you will come out with flying colors, Kat.

Today is my birthday. Guess I will make a cup of coffee, smoke a cigarette, and listen to the stereo. Got a beautiful card from my mom.

I will write more this weekend, you take it easy, and rest up, I want you to get better real soon. Be back later.

* * *

September 15, 1985

Sunday—

Well, what a change in the weather. Feels good though, Kat. I am used to this kind of weather.

How are you feeling? Back on your feet yet? Sure hope it was nothing serious.

Guess I will watch t.v. today. All football (NFL & college games). At least we yell at them, and get some steam let off.

It's funny, but when I start to correspond with someone and that person gets sick, I worry about them. The only people who write me are my mom, my brother, Paul Crow and you Kat.

Have you ever listened to the stereo and a certain song comes on, and it starts you thinking about the past? Well, it happens to me every Saturday night from 7–12 pm when the Oldies come on. I find myself up in Pennsylvania with Yvonne. Never with Angela (retarded one.) I don't know why, but it always happens with Yvonne, my Impala, and we are going to the store. It's funny how that works, but it does. Plus, I usually find myself crying sometimes about it. I've tried to block it out, but it doesn't work, Kat. You see, I didn't have any flashes of Daytona, like I do with Pennsylvania.

Well, I have to do laundry now. Wish I had a washing machine but I have to do them by hand. I will finish this in the morning. Please take care of yourself for me.

Stano took up knitting, and claimed to worry about his health, as well as his mother's and mine. Aside from the way he described each and every car he had ever owned in painstaking detail, and the condition in which he kept them, here he also described the way he kept his cell: "immaculate," and "everything has a place." That began in childhood, when young Gerald would throw fits if anything was "out of place" at home.

Monday, September 16 p.m.

Hi Kat! How are you feeling today?

You know, I hate when the guys start talking about my time—5–25 years and 3 Death Sentences. They don't know when to back off. All I do is put on my headphones & stereo, and block them out. I refrain from talking about it with them cause of my temper, and, I would end up in a fight over it on the yard, and loose [sic] my privileges from 30–60 days. I don't need that type of headace. Follow what I am saying?

They don't seem to realize I am nothing to play with.

I have other things to worry about than them and their mouths, like my mother's health, my health, and you being in the hospital.

I am enjoying this cool weather we are having. I made an afghan for my bed and it looks nice. Have also made some hats and scarves for my family. I made them all by knitting. I have a pair of plastic size 8 needles. If you were to take a tour of where I stay here, you would see how I keep my cell. It's immaculate every day. Everything has a place. That's the way I was outside, and nobody can change it.

Well, I want to get this in the mail tonight. Sure hope your home, and taking it easy. Get well soon. Write, when you get a chance.

Yours truly,
Jerry

P.S. Get well soon Kat!

He sent me a "Get Well" card, trying to reinforce what he believed was a friendship—or, in his mind, even more—with me.

September 21, 1985

Dear Kathy,

Bet it feels good to get home. Sure wish I could be home for just 24 hrs, and have some good Italian cooking. Plus, go swimming in the pool and play my Hammond organ again.

They have fixed HBO for us, so we can watch the Holmes vs. Spinks fight tonight. Should be real good to. Everyone is placing bets but I haven't placed anything on it. Don't think I will either.

My uncle just got out of the hospital in Penn. He lives by himself, and has never told anybody he is a diabetic. So, I was upset about that, when I heard it. If I knew he was like that, I would have stayed up there. Besides, he can't drive now, and he has a new Caddy, and I think the world of him. He reminds me of my grandfather who died.

I am waiting for that clipping from you that your sister has. My parents saw it Wednesday on the "Today Show," and nearly went through the ceiling. It was the name "Eugene Stano" that did it, cause that is my father's first name. He is really furious, and wants it changed immediately. I have to agree with him cause of the names.

They are coming up tomorrow and I just can't see my father now. Mad at the world, and me. He will never change, Kathy. His attitude is why my mother is sick. Mom told me if she could get her hands on a gun, she would kill my father, then herself. It's all due to the way my father is. I would like to know what makes him like that. Plus, he always likes to be on the run, away from the house. Paul can verify what I mean about him. But I guess you can't change him now.

I would like to see my brother, but he won't come up. I asked a friend if he would talk to my brother and explain the situation to him. How I am waiting for clemency and then comes a warrant. I am praying that it comes after the first of the year. I have made a list of everything I have (inventory), cause they also inventory my stuff. I like to be double sure of everything Kathy.

Before I forget, the card I am sending you is a Get Well card. It's nothing fancy, just something I thought would cheer you up.

Guess I will close for now, please write when you get a chance, and I am waiting for our interview.

Respectfully,
Jerry

* * *

September 26, 1985

Kathy,

I am happy to hear that you have gone back to work. You must have a lot of paperwork to catch up on. Hope you got your card alright.

In my letter of Aug. 29, I thought I was pretty well-versed, when I told you all of the things that led up to the killings. But, it seems I must have been pretty lax on some stuff. So, I will have to recall again the evening, even though it is really painful to do so.

Kat, I am working with a very painful right ear. I have an inner and outer ear infection. They have me on ampicillin, Sudafed and ear drops. I can barely hear out of it. It has kept me up for the past 3 nights. Sure hope this medication works, cause it is driving me crazy.

Well, I was never in the habit of picking up hitchhikers. The girls looked pretty good (not Miss America material). It was just one of those on-the-spur-of-the-moment things. I couldn't stand to see the two of them walking. So, I gave them a ride.

After they got in, we were talking awhile. They asked where I was from, and I told them. Besides, I had been in the car and offered them each one. Well, to the best recall, they didn't want to get out, cause of the music and free beer.

The subject did turn to sex after a while. You see, the one girl next to me was rubbing my right leg with her hand, and I was doing the same to her, with my right hand. She looked like she wanted to have sex, but the other one was the nervous one. I think the two girls were lovers. By that, they kissed a few times, and that is when the one girl started to rub my leg. That is when I made the suggestion of having sex. Then, the other one by the door said, "not with a big hog like you." That is when I went over the edge. As for them being prostitutes, they were two "lovers." You see, I have always had a weight problem Kat. But, my ex-girlfriend, YVONNE, never mentioned that once, when [we] were together, or did her family. But, my ex-wife's family would always say something about it.

Kathy, it really hurts to recall these events, but I will do my best for you. I told you I would help you with things for your book, and I will. But bear with me okay? You see, I am also bearing the weight of Clemency in Tallahassee coming up.

I also want to talk to Paul in person before it's too late. Before I forget, Paul has a box of things that belong to me. Please ask him to give them to you, as I can't have them up here. You might also enjoy listening to them, (the box of tapes.) Then you could see what type of music I used to listen to.

When you come up next time, we can clarify some things in person better. You know they scan the mail going out of here. But, I don't care if they read mine, cause, what could they do to me? Nothing.

By the way, you know I can receive stamps in my letters from you. They don't object to that up here.

Kat, I am going to stop for a while, cause my ear is really hurting a lot. I will write later on.

Well, I'm back Kathy. My ear is feeling much better now. Guess the medication works. I still have to take it for 10 days, then see the doctor again.

I received a letter from my attorney who is handling my clemency. We have been granted a motion for a new psychologist to examine me. You might want to contact him and come up when the doctor examines me Kathy.

Please contact him if you want to do this, cause it might help you write your book. I have no objections if you do this. But you have to have the approval of the Dr. and Mr. Bardwell. Explain to Sam what you are doing and tell him you have spoke with Christopher Quarles too.

Kathy, please ask Paul if he got my letter, cause there are some important questions I asked him I need answered. I would appreciate it very much.

This is all I can remember about that evening I question Kathy. I have tried to remember everything and come up with the same answers. I have made notes from the beginning to end three times, and come up with what I have told you. There is just nothing more I can remember about it. I'm sorry.

Don't think I'm not trying Kathy. I really am doing my best for you. I know you want to portray what I was like before, during and after the killings. I realize you have previous notes from different sources, and now you want to get my side of what happened. Kathy, you will have a book to be proud of, and I will have a clear mind knowing I helped. I have never told anyone about myself (except for Paul) and now you in detail. Everyone was getting their facts on reports from the Police and F.D.L.E. Nobody took the time to ask my anything, the way you are. That is why, I am giving you my full cooperation and courtesy.

Guess I will close for now, write when you get a chance. I am waiting for our interview also.

Respectfully,
Jerry

P.S. Kathy, I was wondering about your typing the envelopes. I took typing in High School, and the envelopes look to be Double Spaced. Are they? Wish I had a typewriter in here. It would be a lot easier than writing. But that is not permitted here.

* * *

October 2, 1985

Kathy,

Was glad to get your note Tuesday night. At least they got things right this time. They know I will file another Inmate Request form on them.

Kat, I am receiving mail from people I don't even know, concerning pictures of myself. It all started with that Art Museum, and my picture. These people want to send me everything from money to items I need (clothes wise.) All they want in return is my picture. Nobody has mentioned anything about a book yet, but I wouldn't put it past them. As far as I am concerned, they can "fly a kite." You are the only one I want to talk to about this. I will keep you posted on what they have to say, and offer me.

I will try and find out why they wouldn't let Paul come up with you. He might have to come up by himself. My ear is much better than it was. Guess the medication really works. I still have to take it till Friday.

We have been having thick fog up here this week, but it's burned off by 10 am, so you won't have any trouble driving up next Thursday.

Kathy, are we going to put anything in about my ex-wife, and her family? Or my other girlfriend (Yvonne) and her family? So far, we have hit lightly on my parents, and brother. It has mainly been about the first murder, and it has me wondering why you want so much detail. You know I already have two (2) mandatory quarters for that. If you must know, you would have made a great detective, instead of working for the News-Journal. Guess being around the station most of the time, has rubbed off a little on you. Also knowing Paul the way you do.

Why would he say that I "would have made a great detective" only because "being around the station . . . has rubbed off" and also because of "knowing Paul?" And then he proceeds to talk about the female detective who had a "bad attitude" because her boss "was an S.O.B. and it rubbed off on her." Apparently women didn't stand on their own for Gerald Stano. They never did.

Paul can verify this Kathy. There was a female detective from the West Coast who had a boss who was an S.O.B. and it rubbed off on her. She had a bad attitude that rubbed me and Paul the wrong way. They even came for me by plane once (her and her boss, an FDLE person.) Treated me like dirt for 2 weeks in their county jail. All of the others (det's) were up and above board. Paul and I could talk to them real easy. I have never seen such an extensive background check as the FDLE did on me then. They even went and located my old 1073 Plymouth Satellite Custom we bought in Pennsylvania. Plus, they took my 1977 AMC Gremlin totally apart in the Sanford Crime Lab. They even contacted a few girls I knew in Daytona too. And they were very nice girls too (NOT Prostitutes.) Even old bosses I worked for too. They all gave good references of me, even the girls. I thought they (all of them) would talk bad of me, but I was wrong. I always tried to make a good impression on my bosses at work, and never give any problem to them.

Kathy you wouldn't believe how much I want to be out of this place. I go to thinking of my old girlfriend Yvonne, and it brings tears to my eyes. I should have put my foot down to my father before I left Pennsylvania. But this is what happens when you lead a sheltered life and can't fend for yourself. I should have seen the writing on the wall 13 years ago. But I never had the courage to do anything to hurt my parents. All of that is in the past now, and has been coming back quite regular now that I have been talking to you about everything.

I will continue this Monday morning, after my parents' visit on Saturday. They sound upset about something. I have to find out what it is. See you later—

* * *

Sunday P.M.

Hi again:

Well, I had a nice visit for a change. My parents went to see my attorney this past Friday. Said, they can see where my attorney is coming from and gave him a lot of background material on tape too. Mom wants me to see she is working for me.

I received your letter with the stamps and new questions. Thank you.

Kathy, I would like to point out that the subject you want to discuss is very sensitive.* I have to give this a lot of thought Kathy. I have my reasons for this, and I hope you can understand what I am saying. But I want to give this a whole lot of thought before I answer the question about this subject. Please forgive me Kathy, but as I say, I have my reasons.

I am looking forward to this Thursday's visit. See you then Kathy.

Respectfully,
Jerry

---

* He was referring to the only victim that he knew, which is why the subject was "sensitive"; also, her age was twelve.

P.S. Thanks again for the stamps you sent. Now I can write more than 2 pages at a time to you.

* * *

October 7, 1985

Dear Kathy,

This letter I am writing to you is in reference to your letter about Susan Basile.

I have written to Paul about it, and showed him where F.D.L.E. messed up on their part. They were interested in clearing their books, than taking time to verify where I was, what I was doing, etc.

You see Kathy, I was in the old County Facility (before the new one) til 6/3/75. Then, I was put on probation for 1 year, with my father-in-law being in charge of me. I even had to have permission to leave the county for my honeymoon which was for 2 weeks. I stayed in Orlando at the Ramada Inn Southwest for 1 week then my wife and I went to Pompano Beach for 1 week. We even called from each place to her mother, so they knew where we were.

I was given a job at my father-in-law's station the same day I was released from the County Facility (6-3-75). I even had reports once a month filled out for my probation officer. I have papers to prove where I was for the whole month of June Kathy. So, you can see where the false confessions come in to play.

I am trying to show you exactly how much I want to help with this project. We don't want to print anything that isn't true Kathy. That is why I am explaining this to you this way.

The reason I was locked up was for the following:
11-07-74

A.) Ct. I –Forgery

B.) Ct. II-Uttering a false or forged instrument.

A.) Ct. I Nolle Prossed [not prosecuted]

B.) Ct. II 1 year probation 6/3/75

I also did 2–3 months time at the old County Facility, besides the 1 year probation.

Sure hope this doesn't hurt the way you wanted the project to go. But I want you to know the truth about everything Kathy. There will be no lies or fabrications of the truth on my part.

Some law officers don't care about the person who committed the crime. Like, if he has an explanation, of where he was, the night in question. All they care about is "cleaning up their books of that particular crime." I can also tell you something that will shock you about the West Coast investigations. A detective promised me and Paul a steak dinner in return for clearing up a case of theirs. Guess what—they bought Paul and I that steak dinner Too. Even Robert Smith of F.D.L.E. got one too. I hope you can see, how they pay a person for clearing up their books of crimes.

I can explain in person better about this.

See you Thursday at 1 p.m.

Respectfully,
Jerry

* * *

October 10, 1985

Kathy,

Hi! I was really glad to see you today.

Now, I want you to listen for a minute. I know your

doing this on your own—not company time. So please worry about work first, then our project. We are in no rush to do this, are we? Let's get most of the paper work done by writing, but that is time consuming on our parts. When you visit we can clean up loose ends that need to be clarified more. Just like we did today. As far as your tape recorder, you can bring it any time you like Kat. I am used to those things, as you know.

Before I forget, I hope you made it home safely. It was raining when you left. I was worried about you driving up this morning, due to the tropical storm we had.

Kathy, you can see why I want to keep this from mom and Dad. It's between you and me and Paul, okay? I don't need any problems with the family now. They have been through enough stuff.

I am waiting for your girlfriend to tell you who is working at the 7-11 store. If it's my ex-wife, I wonder what happened at the beauty parlor? But there is no love lost there. I was happy to get out of that family, the way I did.

Please tell Nancy not to give any information out to her either. It's none of her business what and where and who is handling my appeals. She never cared before, so why should she care now. Am I right? Besides, she can read the newspapers to find out.

Kathy, what would you say to an article printed in the newspaper? It would be a type of apology to all the relatives of the victims. I would want you to write it though. What do you think? If you want to do it, let me know, and I will formulate the letter for you. But, I would want it word for word as I write it. I trust you more than anyone to write it. It's the least I can do. Cause, the public has me labeled as "having no remorse or feelings." But let me know what you think, okay? I would like to verify a few things, and put a point across to someone and their family.

You caught me off guard with your questions today. I was centered around what we have talked about already. Also, I didn't mean to bore you about Yvonne. But she meant a lot to me at the time. I still think about her at times.

By the way Kat, I have some yarn left over that I'm going to make you a hat and scarf combination. It will be a while before I start it, cause I am making Christopher Quarles and his wife each a matching set too. It will be my Christmas gift to you. It is the least I can do, for now, cause you take time to come up here to talk to me, and most important—you take time off from work to do this.

Kathy, remember I told you I was receiving mail from people who wanted my picture? Well, I got a letter tonight from a man in Wisconsin who sent a $20 money order and said he would send more if I send him a picture. Well, I told you I wasn't going to send any pictures, and I'm not going to. I am tired of these people doing this to me Kat.

Well, I will stop for now cause my show is on— "Cosby Show"—will write more this weekend.

* * *

October 12, 1985

Another boring weekend again. But I have my stereo to help me out.

Please help Paul get a visit set up, cause he wants to come up. I would appreciate it Kat.

Doesn't it seem funny—you got sick and went into the hospital for a week, and I got my ear infection at the same time? That's how it used to be at home with my mother and I. One would get sick and the other would follow.

Well, I am waiting for your line of questions. I am ready with pen and paper. Again, I apologize for getting wound up about Yvonne. Forgive me Kathy.

One question Kathy, have you listened to Aretha Franklin's new song, "Freeway of Love?" That is one of my favorite songs right now along with ZZ Top's "Legs."

If you get a chance, catch them on the radio. If I had a phone—I would have Bob Mitchell (I-100 FM) play them for you.

Waiting for your letter,

Yours truly,
Jerry

P.S. Don't forget to look at the box of stuff Paul has of mine. See you soon—

I now wince at the thought of him identifying me with his mother. I was young at the time, but I suppose that, unknowingly, I satisfied that nurturing need he had, and a need for acceptance he never received from women.

October 21, 1985

Kathy,

Hope you had a safe trip, even with all the rain. Besides, have a safe trip for the two weekends you go out of town.

Here is the best I can do with the questions you ask about.

Well, I had just been fired from the Burroughs Corporation in Paoli, Penn., and I wanted to be alone for a while. So, I got into my 1973 Plymouth Duster: (green over green with avenger 60's and slotted disk mags, 3 speed on the column, and a beautiful stereo system. It was also jacked up in the back with air shocks.) I made it as far as Holly Hill Plaza, where I wanted to buy a few tapes for my car. While in the parking lot, I saw a Duster's hood up, and thought I would help. It turned out to be a young lady with a Duster like mine, but only an automatic. Hers was blue on the bottom with a white vinyl top. She had a dead battery, so I took my jumper cables and gave her a jump start. I told her I would like to make sure she was charging the battery alright, and to let me drive her car for a few minutes. Her motor had a slight knock coming from it, which didn't sound right to me. So, I locked up my car, and we drove off in her car.

It seemed to me she liked the way mine looked. But hers was a mess though. We talked for a while, then she started to act a little strange. Like she was nervous, and then asked, "When are we going back for my car?" I believe at that time I hit her with my right hand, and said something like, "If you do what I say, you won't get hurt." By that time, I was in a place I wasn't familiar with. She was also complaining a lot at that time, and was getting on my nerves. I stopped the car, and then tied her hands and feet together with either rope or something like that. I then choked her till she passed out I thought, and I carried her from the car. I'm not sure if I had sex with her before this happened. Maybe, maybe not.

When I left her, I believe I covered her like the others were, I'm not sure though. I then thought, I have to leave Florida, and get back to Pennsylvania. My car had slipped my mind till I got to Georgia. I got as far as Valdosta, Georgia, and left her car in a motel parking lot. I went back to the interstate and thumbed a ride back to Florida, and got in my car and left for Pennsylvania.

I had stated first that Sammy Henderson was with me during this ordeal. Well, he wasn't at all. It was all fabricated about him. You see, we went to Junior High School together here in 1965. We were friends at one time but his parents would treat me very nasty. They bought him everything he cried for, no matter the cost. That really rubbed me the wrong way from the start.

I really felt nothing about Sammy getting arrested, cause I already had 75 years mandatory. Besides, I hated him, I wanted him to suffer like I did.

But later, it started playing on my mind—why should I involve someone else when I was alone for the murder. I also said that I was staying at his parents' motel while I was down here then. That also was fabricated too. It was just to get even with Sammy after all these years.

Kathy, as I said before, it's not easy to remember everything to a tee. I know you have copies of the confessions I wrote for Paul, and it makes me wonder why you want me to relive all of these homicides again? But for you, I will. Nobody else as far as I am concerned. You have my full cooperation, as you know.

Well, my parents were up Sunday. Everything went pretty well. Dad seemed in good spirits too. They know nothing of what we are doing, which is good. I am still waiting for the paperwork from up north, I told you about.

See you soon—write when you get a chance.

Yours—
Jerry

Why had he implicated Sammy Henderson: because Sammy had the sort of family life he longed for, and envied?

October 29, 1985

Dear Kathy,

Hope you had a nice weekend. Mine was the same thing, except my parents weren't up. Next weekend for them. If you wonder about the new paper, I buy it from the canteen. That way I can use both sides of this.

Well my contact up north said there was no way to locate the files from before my parents got me. So I am back to square one again. And still wondering what the answer is.

Got a letter from the judge last week. He has appointed an attorney for my two Volusia Cases for Executive Clemency. I should be hearing from this attorney shortly, as I wrote him, and told him to get a hold of my attorney from Brevard County. That way, they can work together in the same issue together.

I thank you for your opinion on that subject. I had plenty written down, but threw it all away after I read your letter. By the way, I'm going to make you something for Christmas, Kat.

I am waiting for Paul to come up. He and I have a lot to catch up on, and there are a few questions I want to ask him.

It may sound funny, but I would like to have a copy of the book when it is finished. I would like to see how you put everything together, and what Paul had to say. Hope you don't mind, Kat.

I'm still waiting to hear who is working at the 7-11 store in Daytona.

Sorry it took so long to get an answer to your last questions of the Bauer case, but I wanted everything just so. If you saw my notes as I write them down, you couldn't make anything out of them. That is why I rewrite them twice.

I saw that Dr today my attorney had appointed. Gave me a battery of tests to do, plus wants to have a brain scan. (EEG)

Guess I will make myself a cup of coffee, and relax with the stereo.

Kat, the next time you come up I am going to show you a picture of Yvonne and my ex-wife. That is, if you don't mind. Even Paul hasn't seen the picture of Yvonne. You will be the first.

I'm waiting for a letter before I mail this one. Bye for now Kat. Be good.

* * *

October 30, 1985

Hi again Kathy,

I am a little worried tonight. Got a letter from my mother saying she put her back out. It's very painful for her and she has to take Soma pills for the spasms. Sounds like she won't be able to come up Sunday. Hope she feels better. But that used to happen when I was out, and it usually lasted about 2 weeks.

Bet you are busy at work these days. Don't let me interfere with your work, Kat.

I just finished a baby blanket for my neighbor. Light blue, pink and white. Looks cute. I made a little hat to match for the little girl too.

Looks like I won't be playing volleyball for a while. I twisted my ankle today. Very painful right now and it is swollen twice the size it should be.

Well, I will mail this tonight. Write when you get a chance. But remember, work first, me later.

Respectfully,
Jerry

*   *   *

November 3, 1985

Kathy,

Got your letter Friday.

I am up early today cause my parents are coming up today. Sure hope my mother's back is better. I'll find out, if they come up.

Well, you asked about a good topic.

I was arrested on April 1st, 1980, and was brought to Daytona Beach Police Dept., where I met Paul for the first time. It was a very trying time for me. I didn't know what was going on. Here I was, handcuffed in front of my employer and co-workers. When I got to Police Headquarters I was a nervous wreck. Here I was, taken upstairs to a room where I met Paul. He saw right away that I was very upset and to the limit of going out of my mind. He was considerate and asked if I wanted a cup of coffee. That made me take a different look at Paul. He started some idle talk about something, and I picked up on it. After about 4–5 hours of questions, I was being booked for Murder One.

Before being taken to the jail, I took Paul to where I put a body behind the airport. Little did I know, that was the beginning of the end of me. All during this, Paul was like a person I could talk to, and confide in. I didn't look

*at him like a policeman. I saw him as a real person, who
cared what happened to me.*

*There is a side to Paul I saw that really knocked me
out. You never want to cross Paul at any time during an
investigation. Especially if he is leading the whole operation. You see, you have a Det like Paul, and then you have
Bozos out there, and you also have Blockheads. The difference is very noticeable. The Bozos are: always having
talks with their bosses, and are real timid to ask questions.
They have their bosses ask the questions. Then comes the
blockhead. These idiots think they can make you talk.
Plus, if someone else (a Det) starts and heads an investigation, these idiots try to take the bull by the horns. Little
do they realize whom they are hurting. Then these whackos
try and pick you up on their own, and hi-jack you to their
counties and say, "You can't call this or that person."*

*Whenever Paul had me in his office and I was in his
custody, I was allowed to send mail out, talk to my parents
on the phone, and also have visits with my family. Plus,
receiving small packages from home, cause he knew who
was buying and bringing them to me. Paul is a person
who will work and help you.*

*All of the people I met have told me, "You're crazy to
have trusted a cop." That's them. Not me. I wasn't like that.
They never hurt me, so why should I not trust them? I have
been honest with Paul, and he has been honest with me.*

*Besides, Paul and I have a rapport nobody under-
stands. We can joke around, or be serious, and if we are
in the presence of a Bozo or Blockhead, we know it.*

*The reason I decided to be honest and tell of the mur-
ders is this:*

*I had taken a trip up to Pennsylvania to hopefully find
my ex-girlfriend and ask her to marry me. But I was too
late. She had gotten married and that really hurt me. Be-*

sides that, I was divorced, and no girls wanted me. They always had their reasons why they didn't want me. So, I came back down to Florida, and tried to hold jobs, but never could. If a girl went and looked at me twice, I would ask her out, and get turned down. Then, the day came when I was arrested for Aggravated Assault and Battery. That there was the turning point for me. Got everything off my chest at that time. Here I thought everything was done with, but never really gave the thing any thought till I was on Death Row. Then, everything hit me at once.

Some of the guys say I should of stayed up north, moved to another state, or anywhere but stayed here. I thought I would never get caught, and everything would be alright. But it didn't work out that way at all. To be honest with you Kat, I'm scared. But I can't show it, cause I'll get ribbed by the men here.

There was two (2) times I thought I was seen. I was really scared one night I was seen. I took a round about way home, and finally figured out that I wasn't being followed. But it put a good scare into me. The next time I was drinking after it happened, and was scared cause I thought someone had followed me all the way home. It took me about 2 hrs to figure out no one had followed me. But a girl I knew came knocking on my door, and got me all nervous again.

As for the question, "What made me kill and kill again," I can't really answer that, except like this. I would be drinking, and lonely, and thinking about all the couples having fun together, and here I am single having no fun at all. Then I would go out riding around, and I would find a girl walking, and hopefully she would get into my car, but she would end up making some kind of remark about my weight, music or looks. That would turn me into a different person altogether. I really don't like to

*talk about that person, cause it gets me very upset. But
for you, Kat, I will. Cause you want to know everything.
Other people have tried, but to no avail on their parts.*

*Kathy I can tell you one thing. I would trust Paul be-
fore any other Det. I have been around plenty and have
seen how they work. They went as far as to promise me a
steak dinner with all the trimmings. That one person did
keep his promise too. Took me to a Steak Restaurant
along with Paul. I had everything from salad to dessert.
Plus, they took the handcuffs off me for this also.*

*Paul and I thought this person was kidding, but he
was serious. This is how some Dets say "Thank you for
clearing my books." But Paul is entirely different. He will
put his cards on the table, and hold back a few. Then, the
other person puts his cards on the table. Then, you discuss what has been put in front of both of you. But you
never share your last card. They think I have turned all
of my cards over. I have held a few back Kathy. Because,
two people can play a card game. And, they have to make
a very good offer if they want my cards totally turned
over.*

*Maybe they could care less about what I have card
wise. But, it would really turn some heads if they knew
what it is. I will convey these cards only, at the right time
and place. It will do no good trying to find out what it is,
cause they won't come out till the right time.*

*Besides, everyone is entitled to some privacy of his or
hers.*

*Well, I hope this answers your questions about Paul.
If I need to elaborate some, let me know.*

See you soon—

*Respectfully,
Jerry*

Now that I look back and read, again, his initial acknowl-
edgment as to "motive," or what made him "kill and kill
again," I still get a slight chill because he would simply "find
a girl walking," and that would provide him with an excuse
to take her. He also clearly conveys that he will take some of
his crimes to the grave when he writes about the "cards" that
he is "holding back." And which card would have "really
turned some heads" I wonder.

November 21, 1985

Dear Kathy,

Just thought I would drop you a short note.

Hope everything is going very well for you.

*I haven't heard from you in two weeks. Is there any-
thing wrong? Have I said something to frighten you? If
so, I am sorry.*

*I have finished your present, and will send it as soon
as I see the property room officer. Sure hope you like it.*

*Maybe today you might be up to see me. Next week is
Thanksgiving. Hope you have a beautiful day. As for me,
I will faithfully watch the Macy's Parade. But I wish I
was out of this place. It gets me a little upset at this time
of year, cause I'm not with my family.*

*Got a letter from my attorney, who said it will be at
least February or later before I go in front of the Gov for
clemency.*

*I am still waiting to see Paul. He is probably busy at
this time.*

Well, I've got to shave, Kat.

Hope to see you soon.

Very truly yours,
Jerry

Two weeks without a letter had convinced him I was upset about something, as if we had a lover's quarrel. Our relationship as inmate and reporter was never real to him; he always wanted more. My gift? A garish orange and white scarf and hat he had knitted.

November 22, 1985

Friday pm

Dear Kathy,

I was very relieved to receive your letter. As least you're not mad at me.

Wish I was out to see Kenny Rogers at the Civic Center. I like his music. Would have liked to have seen Heart when they played there. Besides, the skating rink there looks nice. It's been quite some time since I have been on ice skates.

Well, bet you are going to have a beautiful dinner for Thanksgiving. They will serve us a tray of sliced turkey, salad, vegs, dressing and dessert (pie.) But not enough.

Kat, as for the interview with 20/20, we could try. All they could say is no or yes. They don't have to know everything we are doing.

As for Dec. 3, I didn't know there was an execution set for that day. But I will be waiting for your visit anyway, cause I don't think it'll happen that day.

Thank you for the stamps, Kat. I appreciate them very much.

Well, guess I'll close for now—write again when you get a chance, Kat.

Yours truly,
Jerry

P.S. Happy Thanksgiving!

* * *

December 2, 1985

Dear Kathy,

Hi!

   Hope you had a beautiful Thanksgiving! Have plenty of turkey and the trimmings? They try up here, but it's not the same as home cooking.

   I saw Macy's Parade, and both football games. Won one—lost one. Tonight, I have a bet on the Chicago Bears. Hope they win for me. My Phila. Eagles lost Sunday.

   They gave that man a stay today from Miami Federal Court. He was really close too.

   Kat, I hope you will enjoy yourself this week. You probably can get some Christmas shopping done.

   I hear that Alabama played at the Ocean Center. I really like their music, Kat. Did you see "Dick Clark's American Bandstand" last night? Really brought back some memories. I remember dancing to some of the music in high school.

   Well, guess I'll close for now. Hope to see you this week. But if not, it will be soon.

   You have fun this weekend, and be careful.

Jerry

(p.s. over) Thanks for the short note. You have nice hand-writing too.

* * *

December 10, 1985

Kathy:

I got your letter tonight written Saturday.

I will try to find out about you being put on my visiting list. When you come up next time, ask for an approval form for visiting. Better yet, write to Mr. Dayan my classification officer. He will be the one who will take care of that.

As for bringing your tape recorder in the visiting park, that will be out of the question Kat. Too many security measures for that.

Your working schedule will play a big factor on this too. It seems you can only get weekends off to come up to visit me. We don't need any problems with your work. It will be better seeing you on weekends. That way, we won't be cut short on time.

I was only going on what my mother told me about the Alabama Concert. Had a feeling it was full. But, people do make mistakes Kat. Sounds like you are ready for the Kenny Rogers Concert. I would like to see him in person myself. The only concert I saw was up in Pennsylvania at the Spectrum. It was the Commodores, and a little group trying to get a name for themselves.

I am going to try my best to get you on my visiting list Kat. Keep your fingers crossed. You know when you come to visit, you can buy things to eat, coffee etc. They even have microwave sandwiches too. I can fill you in when I see you.

Well I want to enclose this in the last letter to you. Please drive safely when you come up.

Respectfully,
Jerry

* * *

December 12, 1985
Thursday a.m.

Dear Kathy,

Well, bet your ready for the Kenny Rogers Concert to-night. It will be a good concert too. He always puts on a beautiful one. Probably do all of his songs, plus his new one.

I am happy that you came up today. It's usually a Thursday when you come up. Probably will be a little hassle for you. I am trying my best to get you on my visiting list. You have to fill out a questionnaire, get it notarized and enclose a small picture of yourself. That's the way they work things around here. I sure hope this can be done, cause it would be a lot easier on you, what with work. We will have to see how things work out, and what they have to say. All we can do is keep our fingers crossed, Kat. You would probably like it better on week-ends. We could cover a lot of ground then.

Sounds like we are going to have some cold weather coming our way this weekend. I have my sweatshirt out ready for it. I like the cold better anyway. Probably cause I lived up north all of my life.

Did I tell you they have a church group coming in from Jacksonville on Sat. Dec. 21 to deliver Christmas stockings, and socks, plus homemade cookies for us? They take care of the Florida State Prison, plus the Old Unit. They have been doing this for 10 years now. Very nice people, to do this for us.

I was wondering what they did with the cells down-stairs at Daytona Beach Jail. It used to be the County and City Prisons. Boy, could I fix up one of those main cells for myself! It would look like an apartment, Kat.

Besides, there would be no noise to put up with like here.
I would really enjoy it there too.

I am picking up Daytona (I-100) very clear this morn-
ing. Wrote to Bob Mitchell last night. Sure hope he gets it
alright. Haven't talked to him for 2–3 years. The last time
was when I was in Daytona Beach City Jail for 2 months.
He is a good friend of mine I met while at the service
station in Daytona. Plus, he used to be a D.J. at Starlite
in Ormond every now and then. They were the good old
days, Kat.

I can remember all the good old days very clearly.
Even the ones from up North too. Especially the ones
with my old girlfriend in Pennsylvania. We used to have
a lot of fun at this time of year. No sense in going into
detail, cause it is old hat now, and we can't relive the
past. But it's nice to think about it, though.

I'll close for now, will write more during the weekend,
Kat. Sure hope to see you today, if not I know it will be
soon.

* * *

December 12, 1985

Well, guess you couldn't make it today. Probably next
week. I am waiting very patiently Kat.

I got some information about you being put on my
visiting list. All you have to do is write to my Classifica-
tion Officer Mr. Dayan and ask him for the necessary
forms for being put on my visiting list. He will send
you the forms, and you fill them out, get them notarized,
and put a small picture with it for the record. Then
we wait for approval from his boss. I was told that it
should be no problem, cause I don't have any young la-
dies on my list, except my mother. So, go ahead and write

to Mr. Dayan as soon as possible. I have wrote him a letter having my ex-sister-in-law taken off my list. She never came up anyway, Kat. So, that will let you get on my list. I was also told that you cannot bring any tape recorder in, except for weekday interviews. But you can bring up to $20 in $5 bills, so we can have something to drink, eat, etc. The visiting hours on Saturdays and Sundays are 9 am to 3 pm. We can figure out when mom and Dad come up, every two weeks on Sundays, and you can come up on Saturdays. Nobody will know you work for a newspaper (inmates that is.) Before I forget, you need your driver's license for I.D. purposes when you come up to visit. My mother has one of those clear plastic purses she carries in with her. You might want to do the same Kat. They won't let you bring your pocketbook with you. I can fill you in on more, if you have any questions about visiting.

Bet you are ready for the concert? Wish I could see it. He was in Jacksonville last night. Have fun Kat. Be careful where you park, cause there are a lot of people who steal, and bang their doors into others.

Have you gotten your present yet? Let me know when you do. Sure hope you like it.

I am still waiting to see Paul. He probably is very busy, and can't get any time off to come up. Also, the Holidays are coming up too. That has a lot to do with it. But we write to one another though.

These people must think we are made of money here. They have increased the prices on most of our canteen (store) items. I feel sorry for the ones who work on $5 a week. At least I keep myself in coffee, cigs, toilet articles, etc. Most of the floor I'm on is the same way. We try to keep this side looking up to snuff, because of the tours come down to look.

Well, I want to put this in the mail for you, Kat. Again,
I hope you enjoy the concert tonight. Be careful.
See you soon—

Yours truly,
Jerry

P.S. Don't forget to send off to Mr. Dayan all the neces-
sary papers for you to be put on my visiting list.

I now believe he began to view my visits as "dates," since he
wanted us to be able to buy snacks from the machines.

December 15, 1985

Dear Kathy,

I was just listening to the radio, and thought I would
write you a letter.
How was the concert? Bet the place was packed. Was
his band there also?
I am making lounging slippers now. Just finished an
afghan for my bed. Mom wants me to make one for her
bed, with shades of blue that will match her walls.
It's cold up here this morning (27 degrees.) Feels
good though. This is the weather I am used to. But with
snow too. Saw some yesterday while watching the KC
and Denver game. They have the heat going but this con-
crete holds the cold in.
What I would give to be in front of a fireplace with the
t.v. on, and a young lady sitting next to me.
Kat, we have covered everything I can think of. Is
there anything you want elaborated on? If so, let me

know. I would like to have everything perfect for you. That's the way I am Kat.

I was thinking you might be up this week. Probably Tuesday, Wednesday or Thursday. I am ready whenever you come up. I am up at 6 am every day. That was the time I used to get up when I was going to work, Kat. My neighbor and I are the only ones up at that time. Everyone else stays in bed, cause they watch t.v. all night long. It's funny, when you get into a routine, and your body is used to it. I'll always be like that. Even on weekends too. Here it is 8:05 am, and I haven't shaved yet. Better get to it, cause I don't feel right with whiskers on.

Well, I will leave for now, but will return later to finish.

Throughout his interviews and confessions, he refers to each of his victims as "the young lady." In doing that, he gives them a respect he never showed them when they disliked his music or clothing.

December 16, 1985
Monday—

How are you today? I am feeling pretty good. The cool weather makes me feel good. Feel even better if I was home now.

Bet you have been pretty busy at home and with work.

I am trying to get my brother to come up for the holidays. It's not easy Kat. For some reason he doesn't want to see me anymore. Why, I don't know. It could have been from an article a reporter wrote from Sanford. She said I hate my brother. That is not true, Kathy. I love my brother very much. Sure we had our differences growing up, but that is only normal. Especially for two boys.

They are playing all of the old rock'n'roll I heard while in high school. Sure brings back some memories. We even used to dance to those songs.

I'm sorry if I spread my letters out, but I have others to write to.

It's nice to have a young lady to write to, and have her write back with advice, Kat. I thank you for that.

Have you heard of the new group "Wham," from England? They are really good, I like their music a lot. If you get a chance, give them a listen. Also, have you heard the new Christmas Song Medley on the Country Western station? It sounds nice Kat. What about Al Jarreau? That's my type of music for listening. Did I tell you we have to use headphones for our radios up here? Well we do. I always do cause I have a small GE stereo and it sounds better with headphones on. I had my stereo head-phones sent from home, cause they were almost new.

Guess I better close, or you'll never get this other-wise. I am waiting to see you and to have you approved on my visiting list. Please do that as soon as possible, Kat, so you can start coming up on Saturdays and not take any more time off from work.

Very truly yours,
Jerry

And here he also refers to me as "a young lady."

Merry Christmas
December 25, 1985
Christmas Day p.m.

Dear Kathy,

Merry Christmas! Sure hope you had a real beautiful day! As for me, it was just great. I was crying for about an hour with my parents. Had pictures taken too.

It has turned really cold up here Kathy. Even though the heat is on, the wind is blowing 20 mph out of the n/w. Plus, these windows don't close all the way either.

Kathy, I was thinking, what questions do you have in store for me now?

I can only figure out that they may pertain to my clemency appeals, and the other parts of my appeal process. If that is the case, I want to be very careful about what I write, cause some of the process is still going on at this time. No offense Kat towards you though, but it's confidential at this time.

Well, I want to get this in the mail to you before they pick it up tonight.

Have a nice New Year's.

Be careful if you drive anywhere. Hope to see you soon.

Best wishes for a Prosperous and Happy New Year.
Jerry

* * *

January 2, 1986

Kathy,

Happy New Year.

Sure hope you had a beautiful time on New Year's Eve. As for me, I had cup of tea, and a cigarette, and watched Dick Clark's "Rockin Eve."

It's been six years without a drink for me. If I took one now, I would probably pass out. But I can do without it. I will settle for a cup of tea, or coffee, any day of the week now.

They had a special on HBO this week, with Dolly Parton and Kenny Rogers. It was really good too. Now I can see why there was a sellout crowd at the Ocean Center when Kenny Rogers was there.

For Christmas, they gave us all brand new lockers. Now I can put all of my stuff in the steel locker. It also serves as a nice table. I can also keep my yarn and needles in there too.

Kathy, I was asked if I wanted to be interviewed by you 2 weeks ago. I wonder what the problem is. Maybe you were busy, and can't get any days off till the New Year.

Remember how I used to bite my nails? Well, you're in for a surprise Kat. I stopped 2 weeks ago biting them. For the first time in 34 years, I have fingernails. My fingers feel funny too. Probably cause there are nails on there now. My parents cannot believe their eyes. This is also one of my New Year's resolutions.

I go before Gov Graham March 20, 1986. I'm not looking forward to it either. But everyone gets one trip, free without worry. I can't see it that way at all. There is always a first time for everything. I might be the person he gets on the first trip. So I hope you will come up before then a few more times.

Well, guess I will close for now.

Sure hope to see you soon. Write when you get a free moment, but work comes first Kat.

Sincerely,
Jerry

*   *   *

January 9, 1986
Thursday p.m.

Kathy,

Got your note last week. I was looking forward to seeing you today.

They asked me yesterday if I wanted to talk to you. Must have been busy, cause they signed (2) warrants Tuesday. It will probably be set up for next Thursday. I am waiting patiently for it.

Sounds like the Ocean Front Center is doing good. The "Miss Teen U.S.A. Pageant" should be really nice there. Sure hope they televise it. Then I can see it real good, instead of pictures from the paper.

Well, I don't want to keep you from your work any longer. When you come up, please drive carefully.

Respectfully,
Jerry

P.S. If you get a chance—listen to Aretha Franklin's "Freeway of Love."

* * *

January 12, 1986

Well, thank you for sending back my pictures. As I said before, the last three are in this letter.

My thoughts proved right. I always strike out when it comes to a girl.

I realize you have copies of the reports of various cases, and have read and reread them. It doesn't bother me, but I don't like rehashing them. They are over and done with, plus I am serving time for them now, and also awaiting the Electric Chair on three of them. Maybe I might be better off going off that way than the other way I had planned. I will never see the streets again, so what have I got to lose. Nothing.

Guess I will close for now. Please send the pictures back when you get a chance.

Respectfully,
Gerald Stano

* * *

January 19, 1986
Sunday p.m.

Dear Kathy;

I was going through my photo-album for you today. I found some pictures you might want to use. Would you please send them back. I have them labeled with letters A-G.

Letter A—4 years old. Schenectady, New York

Letter B—4 years old—12/25/55 mother and brother N.Y.

Letter C—5 years old—1st fish in Hampton, N.H.

Letter D—5 years old—ocean—Hampton, N.H.

Letter E—17 years old—Jr. High—Pennsylvania

Letter F—19 years old—Sr. High—Pennsylvania— Claudia

Letter G—19 years old Sr. High Pennsylvania— Band

Let me explain the pictures for you.

A. I am at my grandmother's garden in Schenectady, New York.

B. This is my first bicycle at age 4. Brother's rocking horse and mother looking on.

C. Deep sea fishing trip. 1st one with father, and I got a 5 ½ pound haddock. Age 5.

D. Swimming in the ocean at Hampton Beach, New Hampshire. Age 5.

E. First dance at Junior High in Ambler, Pa. Christmas Dance. 17 years old.

F. Christmas Dance at Wissahickon Sr. High in Ambler, Pa. The girl is Claudia, whom I went with for 2 ½ years before moving to Florida.

G. Me in a band uniform in High School.*

Kat, I tried to space the photos from young to old. These are the only ones without my family. I would like to keep them out of the pictures. I also have some pictures of my wedding, which I don't think would be good taste to put in. Besides, want to keep her out of the book, as I said I would. I'm sorry I don't have any pictures of Angela but I'm asking my mother if she does.

As you can see in the two casual photos, I am no slouch when it comes to clothes. The blue suit was my first one. Both of my shirts were French cuffs, the shoes were (wing-tips) cordovans. I didn't start growing a mustache till my senior year.

I am writing for your questions before I mail this letter, with 4 pictures first, then 3 pictures next. Hope these pictures can help you. Let me know what you think of them. Sorry I didn't have any more. Also, you can see, I was always on the heavy side from 4 years of age—till the present.

---

* The original photos were returned to Stano after being copied but were not located for this project.

I'll write more later Kat.
I sure hope you had a safe trip home.

*   *   *

January 28, 1986

Kat, sorry I took so long in finishing this letter, but I was waiting for the stamps. Thank your for sending them. I really appreciate them.

I watched the "Miss Teen USA" pajent [sic]. Was very nicely done. (from start to finish).

Well, today Paul came up. It was really nice too. Had a beautiful visit with him. We talked abut everything, Kat. It seems, I have been away for so long.

When you say, "computer problems"?—What do you mean? What type of computer is it?

Now, to answer your questions.

1. Young women should go out in 2–4 girl groups. Never go out alone, cause that is asking for trouble. I don't care where it is, that is trouble for one girl.

2. It's what a girl wears, and carry's [sic] herself, that "makes a girl an easy victim." If she wears clothes that are tight, revealing, etc., and the way she carries herself—like, the way she talks, walks, etc.

3. As for the theory "ask for it." I feel the same way the women's groups feel. They are 100 percent right. * *Just like I said above.*

Now, as for what I say at the end of my letters "be careful." Well, it's like this—I happen to care about you. It may sound funny but it is true. I know, you have a job to do (plus, writing the book), but, that's not it. I like you

---

* On the contrary, women's groups vehemently deny that the manner in which a woman is dressed can be blamed in any way for unwanted attention.

as a very good friend. It's something like Paul and I but different Kathy. I hope you can see where, and what, I am saying. Hopefully, this hasn't put a different light on anything. I don't want to cause any problems. If I were out, you would be the young lady I would like to be with. You strike me as the "old fashion type." That's what I like Kat. We could have plenty of fun together. But, you probably have a boyfriend. So I will just be a business oriented person to you. Please give me your opinion, on what I just said. I would appreciate it very much, Kat.

Well, I want to get this in the mail tonight to you. Glad to hear you got home safe.

I'll write later to you.

Respectfully, Jerry

P.S. The first (4) pictures are enclosed. Before I send the others, let me know if you get these.

GS

*   *   *

February 2, 1986

Dear Kathy,

You have probably received the four pictures by now. The last three will be in this letter. Please make any comments on the pictures you like. I have had comments before, about my pictures, so I'm ready for one more comment. It won't bother me at all. I take most of them in stride.

Paul gave me a nice compliment. Said I looked good for being incarcerated for that long. I really enjoyed see-

*ing him that day. He also brought up a question about
the day I go to the chair. Wanted to know if my parents
were coming. I told him no. I can't have him see me go
out like that. Then he asked me if I wanted you there. I
said, No cause you're a young lady and I don't want you
to see me like that. Just remember me from our visits we
have had. I told Paul to go see my parents the day it happens. Kathy—please don't ask to come up that day. I just
want to go out by myself. It will be easier for me to take.
They usually ask if you want to have a last media (tv)
interview. I am going to refuse it. They would love to have
a party with me at that time. But I won't give them the
chance. If I see anyone, it will be you only. No one else.*

*By the way, when I am down on "death watch" I get
to use a phone every week. But I would need your home
number. Maybe it is up to you though Kat.*

*Also, I hope I haven't embarrassed you in my last let-
ter. You did ask for an explanation of that one sentence.
So I told you exactly what I feel and think.*

*Kat, what I want to know is, how are you going to get
across to the public the way Paul and I communicate?
People won't believe everything they read. You know that,
and so do I.*

*Have you seen the house my parents have in Ormond
Beach? It is a beautiful home. If you get a chance—drive
by it. Then, you'll see what I'm talking about—the way I
used to live.*

*I am getting a little nervous now, cause of March 20,
1986* coming up next month. I will keep you informed on
what happens, Kat.*

* * *

---

* The date of his next court hearing

February 26, 1986

Dear Kathy,

Forgive me for not writing earlier. I sprained my finger playing volleyball, it is fine now.

Thank you for letting me call when I go to Death Watch.[*]

It would be a good idea to purchase a personal computer. They are easy to operate too. When you purchase one, get it with multi-storage and multi-program capability. That way, you can use it for more than just writing the book. Everything from balancing your check book, grocery items, etc.

As you know, they got Ted Bundy on Death Watch. Also, Roy Allen Harich (Volusia County.)

It is the first one for both of them. But it doesn't look good for Ted Bundy, though. It will be the same way with me Kathy. The Governor wants both of us very badly before he leaves office.

Well, Guess I'll let you go for now. If you think of any questions, feel free to ask them.

Sincerely,
Jerry

*   *   *

March 3, 1986

Kathy;

Thought I would take a few minutes to write to you.

---

* Death Watch is the cell prisoners were moved to when they had a date to be executed. Prisoners were allowed telephones there, and I told Stano that he could call me.

I have just finished an afghan for my mother, and one for my attorney (Chris Quarles.)

Now, I am working on one for myself. It's all orange, and looks beautiful so far. I am taking my time with it, cause I want it just so. You know how fussy I am about things. Besides, it helps me pass the time away.

I am waiting for a neurologist now, to examine me. He was appointed by my trial judge in Titusville. If it helps, I am all for it. Besides, they might find something that will help in future cases. Maybe, I can be the turning block for this.

Bet you have your work cut out for you, with all these notes, and stuff. It will probably take you quite a while to get everything together.

It seems that one of the maximum wings had a slight problem last week. They had to bring in "pepper gas" to quiet them down. "We" could hear the machine running, and wondered what was happening. You could hear a pin drop on my floor. Stayed like that for the whole day and night.

They're changing things around so up here, it makes you wonder what to expect next.

Kathy, could you tell me what part you are going to put the pictures in?

They put my old radio station back on the air this morning. It's WAPE 95.1-FM. They went to FM now and are using one of the old D.J.'s from the 60's. The "grease man," is up North somewhere working for a radio station. Sounds good, but I'm hooked on "I-100" D.B.

Well, I don't want to keep you any longer. You are a very busy young lady. Drop me a line when you get a chance.

Respectfully,
Jerry

P.S. Bet Daytona is really hopping with the Easter crowds there? Plus, the motorcycles too?

* * *

April 2, 1986

Dear Kathy,

Thank you for your letter today.

Yes, I am waiting on bended breath about my clemency answer.

It's not easy sitting here now. Every time I hear the plane come in and take off, my heart stops. I know it's just another part of Death Row, but it really shakes you up knowing the Gov is in control. I can handle it, but it's my mother I'm worried about. It could put her back in the hospital, in intensive care this time. Also, Dad is working around people who talk all the time about me. But he doesn't let it bother him any cause he would surely go off. Even my brother has it hard out there.

I'm sorry it took so long in writing to you, but I know you can understand my position here. If I hear anything, my parents would know first, then I would notify you and Paul next.

Sure, practically everyone wants to see me executed. But at least let the Doctors run some tests on me first. This is what we have asked for from the Gov.

Sounds like the place will be jumping on Friday night. I've heard them talking about it on I-100. That is my station I listen to. It must have been something to see Mr. Mister and Starship at the Bandshell. MTV had the right idea too. Doing it during Spring Break '86. Plus all the free concerts there. When The Pointer Sisters play the fol-

lowing: "Neutron Dance," "Jump" and "Automatic,"
think of me skating around the rink and dancing too.

I will never remember Gerald Stano skating or dancing
without thinking of Susan Basile and Cathy Scharf. It would
only bring back a flood of awful memories.

You realize that is my type of music you are going to be
listening to Friday night, Kathy. Please let me know how
it is, and if the News-Journal takes any pictures—please
pass them on to me.

Kathy, I would give anything to be there for that con-
cert. Even if they put me in a straight jacket, shackles on
my feet, and armed sheriffs on each side of me.

Please give me your phone number so I may call you
when I go to Death Watch. You know it could be any day
now. So I would appreciate it very much. Also, have Paul
give me his number also.

As for the inmate that dropped dead—he had a heart
attack. They waited 45 minutes before the ambulance got
here, plus an officer was very nasty about calling for help
for the inmate. If it was an officer there would have been
a helicopter here in 5 minutes. As far as we go—they
don't care one way or another.

Well, how are things coming with the outline? Bet
your up to your ears in notes, and files. But that is what
it's all about when you take on a project like this.

Kathy, please have Paul drop me a line. I know he has
been very busy during Spring Break, but maybe he can
take a few minutes to write to me.

You take care, and enjoy The Pointer Sisters. Don't
forget to tell me about the concert, and send me some
pictures of it.

Bye for now—
Jerry

* * *

April 13, 1986

Dear Kathy,

Sorry I haven't written much to you, but I am somewhat nervous lately.

It seems the Gov is taking his time in making a decision about my case. But that's good in the long run though.

Also, I have received numerous letters from all over. They are from Doctors who want to exam me. If only the Gov would go for it. Then, the Drs could use what they learn from me, to help others before it's too late.

But there are a handful of people who think it's a waste of time and money to do that to me. They just as soon see me killed in the chair. But they don't realize how beneficial it could be to other people, before they do what I did. That's the way I see it Kathy. Maybe you see it differently. The Doctors see it my way though, and my attorney does too. Who knows what the Gov may do or say about my case. But there is one thing though, he—Gov Graham, wants more proof about the doctors before he says anything. So it might happen.

Guess you had a good time at The Pointer Sisters concert. How many was there? Bet both shows were a sellout.

I'm surprised you went to see them, cause you told me you like Country Western.

Guess everything can get back to normal, now Spring Break '86 is over.

I have made myself a blanket/afghan for my bed. It's orange and light rose trim. Really sets my cell off good.

Well, guess I'll close for now. Please drop me a line when you get time.

Jerry

I now realize that Stano was using the same tactic as Ted Bundy in prolonging his stay of execution. Bundy, too, argued that justice would be better served by having physicians examine his brain.

April 17, 1986

Kathy,

This is just a note to say "thank you" for the picture of The Pointer Sisters. I really appreciate that very much.

It sounds like you are on call 24 hrs a day with your job. But they couldn't find a better person for the job though.

Kathy, this waiting period now, is really taking it's toll on me hard. I wish he (the Gov.) would tell my attorney what he wants to do further, or to sign my warrant. It is got my mother very upset also. I worry about her, due to her bad heart.

By the way, how is the book coming? Getting anywhere?

If you remember, please tell Paul to drop me a line. He is probably very busy these days. Paul is one heck of a nice person, Kathy.

It looks like Gov Graham got one of us the other day

at 12 noon. After it was over, they have the nerve to bring visitors. They don't care about our feelings when they have an execution. All they care about is themselfs [sic]. But we have to stick with each other and hope for the best.

Well, I better let you get back to work. I know you are very busy these days, and I appreciate a note now and then.

Respectfully,
Jerry

*   *   *   **

May 22, 1986
Thursday PM

Dear Kathy,

I wanted to write you because of what happened today.

It was 11:00 a.m. when they came to my door, and said I had a "call-out." I was then escorted to the office, where I was then told that the Governor signed my warrant.

They talked to me about the news media, and if I wanted to talk to them. As it turns out, I can't even call you. Just my family and my attorney. Visits are for my family only, and my attorney too.

It seems we will have to write to each other, until I get back to the regular wing.

When I called home, my mother took it better than I figured. They are allowed to visit 12 hours a week, and I can call them only 2x's a week.

It was a shock when they came to my door, but it wasn't as bad as I thought it would be, Kathy. I have all my property, t.v., and especially my stereo with head-

phones. But I can't have any contact visits with my family, except for my attorney.

Please tell Paul to write me. I don't want to send him a letter because they might think that something is up.

This is not what you call "having a good time."

I am a nervous wreck right now. But I am trying to make the best of it, Kathy.

If they put anything in the paper about me, would you please send it to me? I am quite sure they will have a big article in there.

Well, I've got to close, don't want to keep you any longer. You are a very busy woman.

Please write me soon.

Truly yours,
Jerry

P.S. Tell Paul to write me soon.

* * *

May 28, 1986
Wednesday p.m.

Kathy,

I thank you for your letter and the clippings.

As for my cell, I am only 30–40 feet away from the electric chair. I am with Ted Bundy. There are only three cells on each side. The middle one is empty at all times. I have all of my property, radio, headphones and t.v., plus we get canteen every night too. We are allowed to make 2 phone calls home per week, and can call our attorneys when needed, and they can call us any time.

I just got my attorney today from CCR [Capital Collateral Review]. I am waiting to hear how they want to proceed with my case.

It sounds like you had a beautiful 2 week vacation. What part of Pennsylvania did you go to?

Kathy, as for our interviews, like before, please call Mr. D.H. Mathis. He is in charge of Death Watch. Explain that we used to have interviews, and maybe something can be worked out. But I doubt it very much, Kathy, because they are very tight on us now at this point.

When I visit my parents, it is behind glass now. Only my attorney is allowed a contact visit.

Please tell Paul to write to me. It would be better this way, cause I don't want them to think I am doing something.

I want to apologize for the short letter I wrote, but I had just found out about the Gov signing my warrant that morning. It took me 2 days to calm down from that. Even my parents took it okay. I was worried about my mother.

Well, guess I'll close for now—write soon, please, Kathy.

Respectfully,
Jerry

* * *

June 3, 1986
Monday

Kathy;

I was very aware of the interview you called in about, but I am not granting any more.

I have had my share of insults, news media portraying me the wrong way, etc.

Plus, they hound my family to no end also.

Kathy, I am in a position now, that is very crucial in my life. Most people could care less about me. But, I can't go down without a fight.

It seems to me, I should have never talked to any media to start with. But, Paul Crow and Donald Jacobson started all of that some 6 years ago.

This has nothing to do with you, but I have to put my foot down now. I'm sorry, but that is the way it has to be. This goes for everybody (all news media) included.

Besides, some man has already written a book from the West Coast, and it is going to be published in September of this year. What can I say Kathy.

Well, guess I'll close at this time.

Jerry

* * *

June 4, 1986

Kathy,

I got your letter today, thanks for writing.

I am sorry, but I am going to have to stop writing, and ask you not to arrange any more visits. It is my decision and my attorney's too. I'm sorry but it has to be that way Kathy.

I am on Death Watch with Ted Bundy. Yes, we talk to each other. Plus, we have our t.v.'s, radios and property.

As for Paul, I am not talking to him either. My lawyer is handling that (Paul.)

By the way, somebody has already beaten you to writing a book. I found out through the mail about it.

You are a very good reporter, Kathy. And I acknowl-
edge you for it. You are also very cute, too. If your boy-
friend cannot see that, he is crazy.

Well, I've got to run. My song is on the radio—"Just
A Gigolo," by David Lee Roth.

Jerry

His favorite song was about a gigolo, which is how Gerald
Stano seemed to perceive himself. He described me as "very
cute." But those women who climbed in his car and never
got out fell in another category—bad girls. After all, would
they have been out there alone if they hadn't been "asking
for it"?

Gerald Stano never wrote me again after this last letter,
and I don't know if he ever quite prepared himself for death.
From his letters to me, I don't think he ever believed that he
deserved to die. He only thought his victims did.

APPENDIX B

Stano's Letters to Investigator Paul Crow

You see, you have a Det like Paul, and then you have Bozos out there, and you also have Blockheads.

—Gerald Stano to Kathy Kelly, November 3, 1985

Gerald Stano desperately wanted to maintain—from behind prison walls—what he felt was an important relationship he had with Sergeant Paul Crow, the lead investigator into the multiple murder cases. He would complain to Crow if he didn't feel like he was getting fair treatment in the jail or seek his help in trying to improve his relationship with his brother.

Long after he was out of Crow's custody, Stano continued to write him friendly letters, telling him proudly of his efforts to stay in good physical shape since he knew the police officer was a physical-fitness buff. The letters were chatty in tone and rebuked Crow in a joking manner for not writing more often.

For Stano, the bond remained with the man he looked up to as a father figure, even long after the cell door on death row had clanged shut.

October 7, 1982

To Sgt. Paul Crow

Paul, these past 2 days have put the topping on the cake. What I am trying to say is that I will probably not make it through the night.

I have already started the process so I figure it will be tonight when I leave this world.

Paul, sure we used to clown around, but I was serious about this last case. (You know which one.)

Paul please advise my mother and father of the situation and please give them their letters.

This is the last request or favor I am asking you to do for me Paul.

Please get my brother here to see me before tonight.

I can't put up with any more of this stuff, papers, news, etcetera.

Yours truly,
Jerry

* * *

TO THE NEWSPAPERS:

I, Gerald Eugene Stano, would like to say at this time, I probably won't make it through the night.

I have had enough news coverage. I can't take any more of it. Let alone my parents whom I love very much. Especially, my mother.

I have tried to be above board with everybody but they won't believe me. God knows how I have tried.

That is why I am going to leave this world. I have

*already started the process of killing myself. So I figure
by tonight it will be over for me.*

*Any information you might want you can get it from
Sgt. Paul Crow DBPD, Detective Division.*

*Respectfully,
Jerry*

No way Stano would've gone through with it, taking his own
life, said Paul Crow. "The bottom line is, he was a coward
and an attention getter," he said. Crow pointed out an earlier
instance of these failed or faked attempts: when the sergeant
first arrested Stano, he was in a holding cell at the Daytona
Beach Police Department, and he attempted to cut his wrist
with a tube of toothpaste, the old hard metal type. They were
only faint cuts, though, Crow stated, and part of what the
detective referred to as Stano's "mind games."

Tampa Area (no date)

Girls were from the Dale Mabry Boulevard area.
    They were prostitutes.
    *Usually picked up within a 3 block area from the Alibi
Lounge*
    *Most of the girls were wearing slacks/pants with
blouses. Some had dresses on.*
    *What would happen is, I would pick up the girls and I
would get asked the question of (What did I have in mind?)*
    *Then I would argue about the price and try to talk
them down.*
    *That would start another heated word session. At that
point I would say, "Let me get my wallet from under the*

seat." *I would bring forth (with force) my knife and stab the girls at least 2x. If I had my gun (borrowed) I would hold that at them until they gave me a head job, then I would get out of my car, and have them get out. Then I would tell them to take off their clothes, or I would kill them. By then I would have pulled the trigger or finished stabbing them.*

I used the gun to scare them, even though I would stab them to death.

The girls were deposited on secondary roads, just off main highways.

Some of the pants were designer jeans.

Some were just plain slacks with blouses.

Some were dresses or shirts.

Some or a couple of the girls that had dresses or shirts on would have no underwear on.

Some had no bras under their blouses or shirts.

Some of the girls had sandal type shoes and some had loafers (maybe a pair of boots on.)

Their hair would vary in length, never past their shoulders. Usually was not held back. A couple would have their hair tied or held back with barettes [sic].

Most of the jewelry was costume (looked fake)—rings, necklaces, bracelets, etc.

One or two had ankle bracelets, which I took.

Most of them had handbags which I left or took with me and threw out on my way home.

The girls that were stabbed had numerous stab marks above the chest, and a few to the head and back area.

Some were also strangled by my hands around the throats.

A couple were laid down with their blouses part way up and their pants unbuttoned and pulled down about 2–3 inches. Never fully undressed.

A couple of that had dresses on were pulled up about waist high, but the dresses were never taken off.

Some were killed during the holidays and some during the years.

They were put off the roads about 15–30 ft. 5 covered (maybe)—not all of them.

Jerry's cars and clothing—

My clothes were usually a pair of slacks, sports shirt, and brown or black ankle boots (zipper on the side.) Sometimes a blue (light colored) leisure suit with shirt to match.

73- Plymouth Satellite Custom green on green—4 dr.

77- Gremlin—Red—tag # CMR-804 FLA

Black inside—2 dr.

Tinted windows all around. (Black)

The bodies were taken about 30–40 min. in either direction. Never over that.

Also, my jewelry consisted of a gold Timex digital, gold I.D. bracelet with "JERRY" engraved, gold w/blue stone class ring (on right ring finger), gold chain and a gold ring on my left hand ring finger with the letter "G" on a black stone.

This gold ring with a black stone was lost somewhere around the Tampa Area.

My glasses were brown with lens that change in sunlight. Aftershave was usually Musk-Oil or Brut.

I don't think any of the girls had any tattoos. Didn't see any.

*   *   *

Paul—

Please read this carefully.

I want to explain something that I can't say in person until you know about it first.

The facts are "Yes," I am "GAY."

I have been like this for some time now. I always used to wear tight pants, shoes with the heels 1 ½", cut off shorts (shorter than normal,) and always a gold chain-silver charm with a skate, plus lots of aftershave or cologne and a gold I.D. I always wanted to stand out in a crowd whenever I went anywhere. Even with my parents.

As for Sammy* he had thoughts that I was gay. But I never showed anything to that effect.

Elmo Massey knew I was gay along with the rest of the "L" wing at FSP [Florida State Prison]. Because that's where we all went for protection of ourselves.

I was afraid that something might happen about me being gay. I wanted to tell you before it went any further but was afraid to say it.

Paul—that is why I never had any friends. I guessed they sensed that I was gay. But what puzzles me is why my girlfriend and wife went with me. All I can say is that I let them rule. Whatever they wanted I would do.

Also, my apartment was always clean. No guy (normal) would keep up his place the way I would. If one thing was out of place I would know it.

That is why I also used to ride around with the stereo up, and the windows down. Not necessarily looking for a girl.

Plus, when I took the girls, wife and girlfriend, shopping in the malls, I would look at outfits with them, trying to help them pick out dresses, while the other men stayed outside and smoked cigs and talked.

Well, now that it is out and off my chest, I feel better.

---

* Henderson, the teen he falsely implicated of complicity in the Barbara Bauer kidnapping and murder.

But, if this hits the paper, I will be in big trouble up at F.S.P. or Raiford. Because that is what the BLACKS like to see or hear about, so they can get them as their BOYS.

Please help me out in this problem, Paul.

Jerry

At one point, Stano sent Crow a letter confessing that he was gay. Crow believed that the "outing" was really for Stano's family's benefit, and another one of his many mind games. Why would he have killed female prostitutes, Crow imagined Stano theorized, if he was gay?

September. 4, 1985

Dear Paul;

Hi guy! I thought you forgot about me being here.

Figured you needed time to unwind. I had two visitors in July. Lee Baker and Robert Smith.* They were trying to get some information from me by talking about some people I went to school with. I was very disturbed at both of them. Mainly Lee Baker, because he is an asshole from the word go. Bob was trying to ease the tension between us, but didn't succeed cause I got up and walked out on both of them. Paul, they figured they hit a brick wall with

---

* Lee Baker and Robert Smith were investigators from Tampa, whom Stano didn't like from his time at the state prison. Paul Crow had warned Stano that his was an "open case," which meant that the officers from the West Coast could come and get him at any time. That set him on edge.

you. Well, they are barking up the wrong tree by coming to me. I am through with those people, and the way they treated me for 2 weeks over there.

Thank you for talking to [my brother] Arthur. If he doesn't watch his step, he will land in here too. The family doesn't need any more trouble. But, it stems from my father. He is the agitator, and the one who causes everything. Paul, please help keep an eye on my little brother for me. If you have to talk to him again, tell him I told you to do it, and get his mind right.

I am my own person in here. Nobody messes with me Paul. The Spanish men treat me like one of them, plus I am learning Spanish.

I have done a lot of searching on myself and it has paid off.

We have a weight pile on our yard, and I bench press 175 lbs. I also use a belt when I am working out. Usually I work out about ½ an hour, then play volleyball for the remainder.

Paul, do me a favor, please give those tapes of mine to Kathy, so she can see what music I used to listen to.

I listen to I-100 every night. Very happy to hear about Bob being promoted. He is a good friend Paul. The only one who was kind to me and to show me how to disc jockey at S. Daytona Starlight on Nova.

Now, about Kathy Kelly. As you know she is the only one I have consented to talk too [sic]. Reason is, she is a friend of yours and Donald Jacobson. Is she married Paul? Let me know okay? Our first meeting was touch and go. But we are writing each other and it seems to be going very well. Kat called for an interview with me again, and these people declined it. So, she wrote me a letter and told me they declined our visit, and yours too. Please give her a hand in getting this righted, as I want to see her again Paul. I am the only one who can decline an interview. NOT THEM. But maybe they see what I am doing. Please help with this, and tell Kat that you will help us get our interviews started.

I understand Kat hangs around the police station. Keep an eye on her for me Paul. And please help with our visits. Thanks—

As for my thoughts on helping potential victims, I will give you help Paul. Somebody has to do it. And I might as well be the one, with your help and Kat's help. Paul, your [sic] right about you and I having the inside track of about the real me. But, I am covering it with Kathy too. People would fall over if they knew what type of relationship we have. That is why everyone (dets) was pissed off at us in the motor home, and they wanted it changed. But we stuck to our guns Paul. They came to us. I am being level with Kathy, cause she can portray it on paper. Then, the people can see what it was all about.

Mom and Bozo have been coming up every two weeks. I don't know if you heard, but mom was hospitalized for heart trouble a while ago. The old man is a real ball buster. He always tells me, "Why don't you just do yourself in?" Never asks where my case is. He just doesn't care. If it wasn't for Mom, I would go crazy. He has turned my brother against me too. Even Arthur hates him. That's why I want you to talk to my brother and tell him where I sit.

I go up for Pre-Clemency Friday Sept 6. Then, Bob Graham takes my case, and then I get a warrant signed Paul. It looks like by the end of the year I will be sitting on Death Watch.

That's why I want to see my brother, and you and Don Jacobson before I go. It doesn't look good Paul. That is why I also want you to help Kat get her interviews with me before it's too late.

Plus, I want you to promise me, that you will go see my parents (especially mom) when that day comes. It is drawing close for me Paul, and we have been through a hell of a lot, and I would appreciate your help in getting my brother up here to see me and keep an eye on him for me too.

I am glad that Steve (Paul's son) is playing football. He will be a good player if he listens and works with his father on weights. You have the right attitude about spending all the time with him you can. That's where my father went wrong. Never devoted any time to his sons.

Well, guess I will close for now.

Please help Kat get the interview, and come up with her too. I am asking on bended knee Paul. Also, have a talk with my little brother about coming up to see me with mom. Don't mention anything about the old man. Just mom and Arthur. Also, keep him straight Paul. I would appreciate it very much too. I care what happens to him. If he were to land in jail, mom would surely land in the hospital, and who knows what would happen then.

Hope to see you soon. Also, write me when you get a chance Paul. But please, help Kathy get her interviews with me.

Yours truly,
Jerry (aka Hammer)

P.S. I have a G.E. Stereo am/fm mom got me for Christmas last year with a pair of Pro-60's Stereo Headphones. Now, I can hear my music in Stereo and also listen to Bob (I-100) the way I used to. Tell Bob "Hello" for me and keep up the good work.

I have a new theme song, "Just a Gigolo" by David Lee Roth. Fits me to a tee.

Thanks,
Jerry

* * *

January 28, 1986
Tuesday p.m.

Dear Paul,

*Well, I have to admit you don't look any older. You look
real good Paul.*

*You really surprised me when you asked if I wanted
my family, or you, or Kathy there when I go. Like I said,
I would appreciate it if you were at my parents' house
just in case something happens to my mother. I can't
see my family having to see me die. Besides, they would
be asked plenty about me, by the "news media." As for
Kathy, I wouldn't want to put her through it. She means
too much, and I don't want her to see it. It's bad enough
she has to see some of that with work.*

*Paul, you have your hands full of stuff every day. I
couldn't put you through it either. Besides, we have been
through quite a lot together these past 5 years.*

*By the way—do you still have that box of tapes
of mine? Has Kathy listened to them? I know they are not
C & W.*

*Paul, I want you to put all clowning aside when you
do this for me:*

*Tell Kathy I like her very much, and I think she's
beautiful too. She is the "old fashion type." That is what
I like in a girl Paul. I would be very honored to have her
as my girlfriend if I was out.*

By the way, tell Bob Mitchell (1-100) to write me.

I have given up on my brother ever coming up again.

You might be right Paul. He may be jealous of me in here. Someone has to make him see where he is headed. Paul, if need be, have him arrested if he keeps following these girls. *Maybe that will help. That will put my mother in the hospital again. She can't take anymore Paul. You know what I'm saying. One in prison is bad enough. Am I right???*

Paul, when I get my warrant signed, call here and find out the procedure for visiting and phone calls.

Write soon Paul.

Yours always,
Jerry

*   *   *

March 6, 1986

Dear Paul,

Just thought I would write you a letter. I am feeling pretty low these days. Also, I have found myself daydreaming about the beach, my car and Pennsylvania. It's not going to be easy on March 20. You know what day that is. Maybe it's best I go out that way. I have been contemplating several ways to take myself out too.

I can't stand to see my parents suffer any longer. They have their hands full with my brother now. It might be a little easier on them if I leave Paul.

It seems Kathy has a steady boyfriend. So, I struck out all the way around, Paul. No girl wants anything to do with me. I am just a born loser, and always will be till I die.

---

* There is nothing to suggest that Stano's brother ever followed, much less stalked, any women.

My relatives won't even write to me anymore. Where have I gone wrong? It was September 12, 1951. That's when it happened, Paul. Here, my parents thought they could raise me their way, not knowing what was to happen in the future.

What is my problem, Paul??

I'll tell you what it is: I was born, and rejected from the start. My parents tried to correct it, but didn't see what was happening.

Well, what's the latest at the beach front? Bet you're busy with motorcycle week, and the college students there. Would be nice to see the old place once more. But I'll be watching from the big playground, and skating rink in the sky Paul. Maybe I'll find somebody up there who wants me.

I have to say one thing: When I fuck up, I do it right Paul. Even when I was out Paul.

They say, everyone gets a free stay the first time down there. Paul, I will surely crack during my first trip down there for sure.

Paul, I had to talk to someone beside my mother, cause she will have a heart attack if I told her this, and, what I was planning to do if need be.

Yours truly,
Jerry
"Casanova"

Three years went by before Stano wrote to Crow again, in response to a letter that Crow had sent him. But his letter focused almost entirely on his "fears" that a "contract" had been put out on him, fears that Crow felt were all bogus: another one of Stano's mind games to get what he wanted (in this case, a transfer to Q-wing with all of his belongings and weekly access to the canteen).

August 11, 1989

Gerald E. Stano
079701- S-2-N-8
Florida State Prison
Starke, Florida 32091
P.O. Box 747
Starke, Florida 32091
P.B. Crow—Chief of Police D.B.P.D.
P.O. Box 2166
Daytona Beach, Florida 32115

Dear Paul,

I was glad to hear from you. Yes, it has been a very long time. I have been in the hospital 3 days for a slight stroke on my left side, but am doing much better now. They had to rush me there by rescue truck from here. This was towards the first of the year 1989. As for working out—I've had to cut way back—but still do my weights. The heaviest weight we have on the yard is 195 (my weight.) I used to pick it up like paper—but not anymore. Plus—I was up to 220 lbs—but have lost 25 in 3 months.

Paul, I am very worried about the contract out on me. It has gotten real rough here now—since the news clippings come out. They are calling me—"a fag—a punk—a bitch—a dick sucka—gay—lesbian, etc." Plus, they also say that I am a Dead man. *Where it is coming from I have no idea. Now follow me—I have written letters to everyone up to the Governor himself. All of my answers were the same* No *help needed. It is a proven fact that this place (F.S.P.) and the chain of command up to the Gov don't want to help me. So that is why I turned to you Paul.*

Remember the problem of safety in the Volusia County Jail in Deland? Well, it's 100 times worse here. I have stopped going to the yard because of this, plus I am very nervous if I have a call-out for anything. When my family visits—I am watching all of the inmates cause I don't trust them. Remember when we were in court—the Sheriff's Dept had everyone sign in—doors locked and the floor sealed.

Paul, if they put me on Q-wing for safety reasons and security reasons—I will not have my t.v.-radio/ headphones—and most of my property, plus no canteen every week.

Paul, all I want is the following:

1) To be placed on Q-wing permanently—(2 EAST ONLY)

2) To have all of my property (everything I have now)

3) To have all of my canteen rights (every week)

4) To have my visits behind glass for safety reasons

5) To have my radio/headphones (to be played with headphones only)

I have asked that to everyone up to the Governor— and they won't help me. They want physical contact *first—then they will take measures for my safety. If I get stabbed in the right places, I'll die before medical treatment can be done on me. Why wait for that to happen Paul. That is why you had me put in a single cell in the County Jail—plus all of the security when I went to court. It will take you—and other officials outside to move me to Q-wing with my 5 requests. For God's sake, and my parents—please help me now with this. My parents are aware of the contract—and what I want done. Please—*

don't *let me down. You are my last hope. If need be— please contact John Tanner. He might be of some help.*

I had a legal visit yesterday from my lawyer. Whatever you do—DON'T HELP HIM PLEASE. It will mean sure death for me Paul. This is the person who said, "this is an outstanding warrant in Volusia County for me." Tell Dave Hudson the same thing. This is trouble with a capital T.

When you write, please send it the same way you sent the last one. This is the best way to handle the mail.

Paul, I wouldn't be surprised if he* was behind the contract. Paul, please help me. I'm scared about my safety.

Who did you talk to in the Attorney General's Office— and who did you talk to in the local State Attorney's Office? When should I be hearing from them? Don't leave me hanging in mid-air.

If my lawyer finds out we are writing—he will have a Cow. Plus, I will get bawled out big time.

Write soon,

Yours truly,
Jerry

---

* Stano meant his lead attorney, Mark Olive, although he had already done as much as was humanly possible under the law to defend Gerald Stano and save him from the electric chair.

TIMELINE

Here are the key dates in the story of the serial killer arrested in 1980 after murdering women throughout Florida. Investigators documented forty cases, although he claimed to have been even more prolific.

—September 12, 1951: Born in Schenectady, New York.

—February 1952: Adopted by Eugene and Norma Stano.

—1966: Came to Florida to stay with his grandparents briefly, then returned to Pennsylvania until 1973, when the entire family moved to Ormond Beach, Florida, permanently.

—March 21, 1973: Janine Ligotino and Ann Arceneau found stabbed to death in Gainesville, Florida.

—January 19, 1974: Remains of Cathy Lee Scharf found in Brevard County, Florida.

—April 10, 1974: Remains of Barbara Bauer found in Bradford County, Florida.

—November 7, 1974: Stano arrested on forgery charge, sentenced to three months in jail in Volusia County for stealing a check from his employer at a motel in Ormond Beach, Florida, then cashing it.

—November, 24, 1974: An unidentified body is found in a wooded area by police in Altamonte Springs, Florida. In the case of "Madame X," Stano claimed to have picked up the woman for sex, then stabbed her with a hunting knife when she refused.

—January 3, 1975: Body of Nancy Heard found near Ormond Beach, Florida.

—June 10, 1975: Disappearance of Susan Basile in Port Orange, Florida. Her body was never found.

—June 21, 1975: Stano marries Teresa Esposito at Prince of Peace Catholic Church, Ormond Beach, Florida.

—July 22, 1975: Linda Hamilton found asphyxiated and drowned in New Smyrna Beach, Florida.

—December 20, 1975: Susan Bickrest found strangled to death near Spruce Creek, Volusia County, Florida.

—February 11, 1976: Bonnie Hughes, 34, a Dundee, Florida, housewife, had been beaten in the face with a blunt instrument and was found slain in an orange grove February 11, 1976, in Polk County, Florida.

—June 15, 1976: Remains of Ramona Neal, who had been strangled and shot, found near Ormond Beach, Florida.

—September 23, 1976: Stano's wife granted a divorce on grounds of physical abuse.

—November 11, 1977, to March 21, 1978: Stano worked in the mailroom of the *Daytona Beach News-Journal* as a newspaper inserter.

—November 12, 1977: Body of Mary Kathleen "Katie" Muldoon found shot to death in a ditch near New Smyrna Beach, Florida.

—April 9, 1979, to August 7, 1979: Stano employed as an apprentice mechanic at Zeno Marine, described as a "perfect gentleman" by the owner.

—January 27, 1980: Mary Carol Maher disappears from a bar frequented by Stano. She is found stabbed to death three weeks later—February 17.

—January 31, 1980: Stano started to work as a prep cook at Hamp-